A77o18

Comrade Baron

translated by
LIZ WATERS

JAAP SCHOLTEN

Comrade
Baron

a journey through the vanishing world
of the Transylvanian aristocracy

*Happy Birthday
Dominic.

Love. Mother.
xxx*

HELENA HISTORY PRESS

Published in the United States by:

HHP

Helena History Press LLC
A division of KKL Publications LLC, Reno, Nevada, USA
www.helenahistorypress.com

ISBN: 978-1-943596-02-7

Order from:
Central European University Press
11 Nádor utca
Budapest, Hungary H-1051
Email: *ceupress@ceu.hu*
Website: *www.ceupress.com*

Support provided to the author by:
Fonds Bijzondere Journalistieke Projecten – Amsterdam

First Published as *Kameraad Baron – Een reis door de verdwijnende wereld
van de Transsylvaanse aristocratie* by Atlas Contact, Amsterdam 2010.

Translator: Liz Waters
Graphic Design: Sebastian Stachowski and Jaap Scholten

Printed in Hungary by Prime Rate Kft. Budapest
First Worldwide English Edition

For my sons
Zeeger, Jozsi and Otto

'Memory must be a road not only to the past
but also to the future.'
– Ana Blandiana

Sarola 1910

Contents

Part 2
They were divided *119*

Part 3

They were found wanting *271*

Appendix

Note to the English edition

It's a year before her death and I'm driving in Transylvania, through the hills midway between Sighișoara and Brașov. I'm going to see an English writer who lives in a remote Saxon village with a very beautiful gypsy girl. I stop at a parking spot on a bend. In the verge lies a mountain of garbage such as you come upon only in countries with an abundance of nature. I walk down the hill along a cart track that leads into the forest and arrive at a gurgling mountain stream. I step among the pebbles and scoop silt with my hands into a plastic bag. I've come to this spot deliberately, for some Transylvanian soil to put on her grave. I know she'll appreciate it.

The next day I fly back from Marosvásárhely to Budapest with the bag of soil in my hand-luggage and at the airport I receive a text telling me that Erzsébet has been admitted to hospital. I hurry home and drive the Land Rover out of Budapest towards the Pilis Mountains. There is something unreal about this. I need to hurry. It's Friday afternoon.

I've bought a bunch of yellow roses, from the flower stall next to the Szamos patisserie. I hesitated; were roses too frivolous for a critically ill 92-year-old? But I chose them all the same, an uneven number, otherwise they would bring bad luck. When the flower seller asked whether I wanted a ribbon around them I glanced at the black ribbon for a second, but no, that would be going too far. I had a feeling that her transfer to a remote hospital might be Erzsébet's last dance, so I opted for yellow roses. She once told me of a love affair when she was twenty-three. The love of her life, I suspect.

'In 1944 Kolozsvár was half depopulated. In the distance you could hear the guns of the advancing Russians and Roma-

nians. But we danced. Csak egy nap a világ. Just one day in the
world. Every day it was played and sung. Maybe we would die
tomorrow. My dance partner was a man of forty-four, a baron.
He was in the Casino in Kolozsvár night after night, the club
of the aristocracy. Only the high nobility could become members of the Casino in Kolozsvár. He had the head of a Roman
and the body of an athlete, and he danced like a butterfly.

"'Do you want to marry him?" asked one of my friends. "No,
I don't think so. He's a phantom. He's not of this world." He
was a mirage. You can't live with a man like that. He was elegant in everything. All the other men had black tailcoats; his
was of green velvet. He walked over to me, gave a four-centi-
metre bow and said, "Your highness." "I think you've mistaken
me for someone else," I said. Your highness is how you address a
princess. "No, I haven't mistaken you for anyone else." Then we
danced. From that moment on we danced only with each other.

'The front came closer. The last ball was that Saturday and
when it was over the Casino would close. He asked whether I wanted to go to the ball with him. I went straight to the
shop. I pointed to yellow silk: "Five metres of that." And black
silk: "Three metres of that." At Dornafalva I made a dress.
I wrapped myself in the yellow silk from the top down and
fastened it, as far as the knee. From knee to heel I wrapped
the black silk. I showed my father. His only comment was,
"I imagine your cousins will be less than pleased." In Kolozsvár much was said about that dress, mainly that it was too co-
quettish. I danced with him until dawn, until the gypsies went
home. He said, "Don't look at me, I have tears in my eyes. This
is our last dance. Farewell."

When I woke there was a bunch of yellow roses outside the
door to my room in Kolozsvár, tied with a black ribbon.'

In the midst of nature, a number of old buildings are set
against a hill, concrete barracks in an arcadian landscape. The

terrain is surrounded by a high fence. The gatekeeper lets me in. It's unclear whether this is a mental asylum, an old folks' home or a hospital. I can see no staff, only the man at the gate. The tall grass is flowering. A concrete ping-pong table, crumbling with age, is the only form of distraction in the middle of the barracks. The people walking in the overgrown garden are noticeably disturbed. Between the spruce trees I spot a white coat and go after it in the hope that the doctor or nurse can tell me in which building I will find Erzsébet. With an outstretched arm and a fixed stare he walks towards me, pyjama trousers sticking out from under the white coat, and asks if I have forty forint. After a brief search I find the right building, a four-storey concrete colossus.

Inside, a mild smell of faeces hangs in the air, more penetrating at certain rooms with little old ladies in them. The building looks as if the staff have fled an advancing army. The rooms are unlit, the corridors deserted apart from the occasional body parked in a chair or on a trolley. I find one nurse in a dark office, who tells me I need the first floor.

Erzsébet is lying in a room with three very elderly women. She looks dreadful. I barely recognize her. Violet eyes, the colour of a newborn bird. Thin white hair. In the bedside cabinet is a stack of nappies – an indispensable resource in understaffed hospitals.

This is the woman I have interviewed at least fifteen times, the lady who became the central character of this book, a countess born in 'the most beautiful castle in Transylvania' who earned a living as a charlady, painter and editor. She has become very dear to me. She's been extremely generous. The more I saw of her the more she told me, eventually revealing the humiliations and the pain, how in the 1950s she was taken by the secret police to the detached houses of Rózsadomb in Budapest's 2nd district, where she was interrogated and tortured.

'The AVO harassed me for four years. Every night. They threatened to take my child away from me. Occasionally they fetched me for a night-time interrogation. They would drive me to a villa in the 2nd district. They put me under pressure. They wanted me to hide gold coins in the chairs or under the carpets at the homes of other aristocrats, so that they could be arrested. They demanded I tell them who still had money or jewellery. I never said a word.' On one occasion the AVO broke her fingers, another time her toes. In the early morning she was thrown out of a car in a suburb of Budapest and had to make her own way home. 'Everything you experience in life is interesting. How the body deals with it is interesting.'

She told me how a few years ago she happened upon her tormentor. 'I was walking down the road, here in Budapest. It was daytime and I'd been shopping. I was carrying two plastic bags. An old man stepped out of a doorway. I looked at him. I recognized him. He was my torturer from the 1950s. He recognized me. He turned round and shot back into the doorway.

'The bad memories have steadily become darker, gloomy and drab, dim. The good memories have grown increasingly bright. Of childhood I have only good memories. We lived in a paradise, my brother and I, at Dornafalva.'

Now the woman who so generously shared her life with me is lying in a rumpled heap in a stinking hospital. I start talking to her, in German, as always. At first she doesn't seem to recognize me. I don't know whether she can hear or see anything; her eyes are glazed. The woman next to her has turned onto her side so that she won't miss a single word, a single detail. I give Erzsébet the yellow roses. I push them right under her nose in the hope that she can smell them. One of the scarce staff will probably make off with the bunch as soon as I'm out of the door. The neighbouring woman lies there calmly watching everything. I have found a chair and I'm sitting next to the bed, Erzsébet's hand in mine. After a while she recognizes me. She has great difficulty speaking. The words come out in fits and starts, as if speaking might choke her. She whispers. 'I can't say any more. I can't write any more.'

Then she is silent. I nod to let her know that I've heard. It's something she always did with great enthusiasm, telling stories of the past, about her fabulous girlhood. It's the reason I wrote this book, the reason I've travelled through Transylvania and Hungary and interviewed dozens of people: to give a voice to this group, the aristocracy that was persecuted and almost wiped out under communism, a generation the last of whom are dying now. Their story is virtually unknown and they themselves have too great a sense of noblesse oblige to publicize it. I did not want to compile a comprehensive survey of the Hungarian aristocracy in Transylvania, but simply to write down the recent history of those nobles who were still able to recount it.

I promised Erzsébet T. (a pseudonym) that for as long as she lived this book would not be published in Hungarian or Romanian, nor worldwide in English. Consequently this worldwide English edition is coming out only now. In 2014 Erzsébet died, at the age of ninety-three.

Not long ago I went to her grave at the Farkasrét cemetery in Budapest and scattered over it the Transylvanian soil I had scraped out of a stream before her death. A wooden cross marks her resting place. The grave is planted with evergreens from the grounds of the house in which she was born and where she spent her fairytale childhood.

Comrade Baron

Introduction

It's after the rain. In the valley thousands of frogs are croaking. We're sitting on a raised veranda, surrounded by the smell of wet grass. Our third bottle of rosé is empty. My wife Ilona's younger sister Zita is half turned towards me. I can make out her face intermittently in the light of a guttering candle. The villages I drove through this afternoon were holding street parties and funfairs, their lamp posts decorated with the Hungarian tricolour. The May Day celebrations are a legacy of Communism. There was always maypole dancing in the villages on International Workers' Day, while in Budapest crowds of workers were delivered to Heroes Square to walk singing, waving red flags and banners, past the party leadership gathered on a high platform, and until 1956 past a large statue of Stalin.

Ilona and I, with our three sons, have lived in Hungary for seven years now, and I've just spent almost a year and a half paying regular visits to Transylvania, travelling all over, on dirt tracks and crumbling asphalt roads. I've sought out the descendants of the once mighty aristocratic families in their apartment blocks, slums and ruined mansions to note down their stories, including what I suspect may be lies and distortions, fables or attempts at mythmaking. Elderly ladies have shown me the cellars they lived in for sixteen years. Former prisoners have told me about life in the Romanian gulag. In Bucharest nightclubs I've watched the new, post-communist elite at play. I've walked into vast forests with the latest generation of the old Transylvanian families to look for truffles, and discussed how they see the future.

'But what is it that interests you?' Zita asks. She looks at me as if she's found herself in the company of a craven courtier. 'What are you doing all this for?'

'The stories. I want to write down the stories of a disappearing world.'

Not entirely satisfied, Zita is grimly silent. I don't tell her I'm fascinated by the decline of an elite to the lowest ranks of society. The truth is, I've become captivated (for personal reasons) by the downfall of dynasties and their frantic efforts to hold on to their values, to the barely perceptible codes and rituals that are signs of survival in a group doomed to vanish.

'What I want to know,' Zita says, 'is what *really* fascinates you about all that.'

Flying from Budapest to Bucharest on a clear day, you look down on the endless forests, mountains and valleys of a broad expanse of land called Transylvania that harbours a third of all Europe's large carnivores – lynxes, bears and wolves. It's a magical realm, enclosed by the Carpathians, and it has served as a refuge for many over the centuries: Armenians fleeing genocide; gypsies from India escaping repression under Islam; Jews fleeing pogroms; Hungarian Protestants fleeing the Counter-Reformation; Bulgarians, Serbs and Romanians escaping the wrath of the Ottoman sultans; Saxons, Swabians and even Flemings escaping poverty. In that sense it has something in common with what the Netherlands used to be, a beacon of tolerance in a world populated by zealots.

In the 1980s Nicolae Ceauşescu tried to destroy the region's multi-ethnic diversity by allowing the Transylvanian Germans and Jews to emigrate for a fee, making life impossible for Hungarians and encouraging Romanians to move in. Up to a point he succeeded. Practically all the Saxons and Swabians have left Transylvania, but a vestige of the rural-cosmopolitan atmosphere lingers on.

Transylvania is now simply the geographical name for the part of Romania that lies to the west of the Carpathians, including the mountains of Máramaros* to the north and a low plain in the west called the Bánát. In total the region covers 103,000 square kilometres, an area two and a half times the size of the Netherlands that is home to around seven million people, most of whom live in the towns of the plains. Seventy-five per cent are Romanian, twenty per cent Hungarian, 3.3 per cent gypsies and fewer than one per cent German. There are small minorities of Serbs and Armenians too. The Transylvanian plateau is 300 to 500 metres above sea level, transected by four rivers. The mountains are rich in raw materials; for centuries they have been a source of lead, iron, copper, gold, sulphur and salt.

Across more than nine hundred years, beginning in 1003 when Saint Stephen I, king of Hungary (Szent István to Hun-

---

* Almost all geographical names in Transylvania have Hungarian, Romanian and German variants. I have chosen which to use based on the context, so names mentioned to me in Hungarian are in Hungarian, while names in a Romanian context are in Romanian. On page 397 you will find a list of geographical names in each of the three languages.

garians), brought Transylvania under Hungarian rule, Hungarian nobles held sway. Until 1526 the region was ruled in the name of the Hungarian king by a governor, a *voivode*. In the period when the Ottomans occupied Central Hungary, from 1540 to 1687, they allowed Transylvania to rule itself as an independent principality. The prince was chosen by the Hungarians, Széklers and Saxons, but the local Hungarian nobles had the greatest say, both in the election of the prince and in how he ran his domain. The Romanians who lived in Transylvania were generally poor peasants with no voice in government.

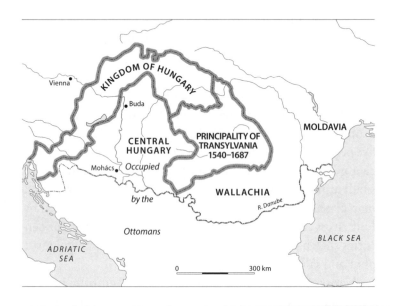

From the mid-sixteenth century onwards, Protestants had an increasing influence in the autonomous principality, since most of the princes, Prince Gábor Bethlen in particular, were staunch Calvinists. In the seventeenth and eighteenth centuries, hundreds of young people from Transylvania attended universities in the Netherlands. The influence of the Dutch churches and Dutch culture can be felt to this day. With the

Edict of Turda in 1568, Transylvania became one of the first regions in Europe where Catholics, Calvinists, Lutherans and Unitarians could all worship freely. Judaism was tolerated, as was the Romanian population's Eastern Orthodox faith.

After the Ottomans were driven out of Central Hungary in 1687, Transylvania was reabsorbed into the Hungarian Empire until the end of the First World War, when the Romanian army occupied the region. As part of the Austro-Hungarian Dual Monarchy, Hungary was on the losing side, and under the Treaty of Trianon in 1920 the occupied territory was officially assigned to Romania. So Transylvania became Romanian, as did the 1.6 million Hungarians who lived there.

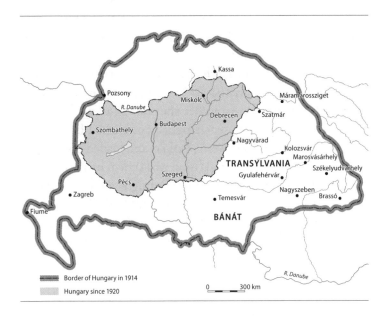

For centuries Romanians and Hungarians had coexisted relatively peacefully in Transylvania, but Trianon generated fierce animosity between them. During the Second World War the craving to be reunited with its lost lands drove Hungary to become a reluctant ally of Nazi Germany. The Second Treaty of Vienna, signed on 30 August 1940, returned Northern Transylvania to Hungary. Then, in the final months of the war, the Soviet Union occupied both Hungary and Romania (including Transylvania), and in 1955 both countries became part of the Warsaw Pact.

The aristocracy was officially outlawed in Hungary and Romania in 1947. The use of coats of arms, titles and double-barrelled surnames was forbidden. All good communists were henceforth to address one another as 'comrade', but tradition proved resilient. The often used form of address Hungarians and Transylvanians settled upon for the downgraded aristocracy, combining the mandatory egalitarianism of communism with the prohibited desire for a class-based society, was *Báró elvtárs*: 'Comrade Baron'.

In the night of 2-3 March 1949, between two and three in the morning, all the aristocrats in Romania were roused from their beds by armed men under the command of the militia and the Securitate (the secret police established by the communist regime just a few weeks earlier) and loaded onto trucks. Depending how much compassion was shown by the leader of the armed gang, the victims might or might not be given time to pack a suitcase with a little clothing and food. They were not allowed to take jewellery, gold or anything else of value. The deportees were driven to military headquarters in five towns, where their identity papers were stamped with the letters 'DO' for *Domiciliu Obligatoriu*, or 'obligatory place of residence'.

Domiciliu Obligatoriu denoted the stigma of the class enemy. Those designated DO were in the process of being 're-educated' but had not been imprisoned, so the slightest misstep was enough to see them sent to jails or labour camps. DO meant you could not leave town and must report to the militia every week. The Securitate would keep you under particularly close surveillance, you were eligible only for manual work, you and your children were excluded from education and training beyond elementary school, and everything you owned was expropriated. Those detained in the early morning of 3 March 1949 were large landowners living on their country estates, most of them nobles of Hungarian origin. Across Romania, 2,972 families, 7,804 people in total, were taken from their palaces, country houses and agricultural properties.

I first heard about the nocturnal mass deportation of the Transylvanian nobility and other large landowners in the autumn of 2006, when I was travelling in the region to write about illegal logging. In a deserted café in Sepsiszentgyörgy a sixty-three-year-old man who described himself as 'a nobleman kicked off his land' told me how he was dragged from his bed as a small boy. A rifle butt was jabbed into his back and he was barely given a chance to relieve himself before being shoved into the back of a truck. 'We moved from a castle to a cellar.'

Shortly after that conversation I read an article in the *International Herald Tribune* about a French priest who was travelling from village to village in the Ukraine, writing down the stories of the Jews still living there in an attempt to record what remained of an all but eradicated culture. It seemed only an outsider was able to undertake something like that. If I wanted to talk to the older members of the former aristocracy of Transylvania, I couldn't afford to wait too long; the generation born in the twilight years of the empires was on the verge of dying out. I enrolled at the Department of Social Anthropology at the Central European University in Budapest and researched how the Hungarian aristocracy in Transylvania survived communist repression and maintained a group identity underground.

I decided to immerse myself in the Transylvanian aristocracy, a clearly defined group within the Hungarian nobility. The hilly terrain and poorer farmland of Transylvania meant that its aristocrats were less wealthy and ostentatious. They had more contact with the peasantry than the nobles further west, in present-day Hungary. It is a group that still sees itself as distinct. Transylvania's aristocrats keep in close touch, not least because practically all of them are related. Comparatively isolated over the centuries, they did not enter into international marriages to the same degree as their counterparts in Hungary. I now had a reason to travel extensively in Transylvania, one of the most beautiful regions of Europe. In the spring of 2009 I took recording equipment with me, interviewed twenty-five Transylvanian aristocrats and wrote a dissertation entitled *From Ballroom to Basement. The Internal Exile of the Hungarian Aristocracy in Transylvania*.

I later returned to Transylvania several times and heard more and more stories. At first I'd been told mainly about the brighter side, about courageous perseverance under communist repression, about the kissing of hands, French lessons and elegant piano playing. Now came tales of humiliation, night-time interrogation and labour camps. Family histories began to converge with the vast, systematic destruction that took place in this part of Europe over almost half a century, horrors that people preferred not to talk about.

Transylvania remained part of Romania after the Iron Curtain was finally torn down in 1989. This fact is a perennial obsession among Hungarians and a source of concern to the Romanian politicians in Bucharest, who treat the residual Hungarian minority harshly. All overtures from Hungary are rebuffed and all local demands for autonomy suppressed. Some 1.5 million Hungarians still live in Transylvania, including just twelve families of titled aristocrats.

They are the subject of this book.

My aim has been to collect their stories. Part One brings together what I was told about life before communism, interwoven with my first experiences of Hungary and Romania in the early 1990s. Part Two revolves around stories and testimony about what happened after the communists came to power. I was reluctant to omit any of the many voices, since they add up to a comprehensive account of the oppressive world in which the Transylvanian nobility found itself. Part Three tells of the post-communist period, after the fall of Ceaușescu, with aristocratic families leaving and a younger generation coming back. I also attempt to describe the new Romanian elite that has recently assumed the position held for centuries by the aristocracy.

This book is different from anything I have previously written: in part an oral history of a group we know little about, in part the account of a journey through one of the most beautiful and mysterious regions of Europe, and in part a record of a Dutchman's impressions on finding himself in an extraordinary milieu in the company of some exceptional families. The families themselves and their traditions are not all that was lost through the eradication of the nobles as a social stratum. The history of the aristocracy and its disappearance is inextricably bound up with the way things are now in Eastern Europe.

Although this book traces the history of the Transylvanian aristocracy, my concern does not lie with patents of nobility, titles, or property (whether stolen, ravaged, returned or otherwise). In essence it lies with the people who lived in Transylvania, who fled, came back or stayed, with people who survived amid the destruction under Gheorghe Gheorghiu-Dej and the psychological terror of Nicolae Ceaușescu. Some preferred to forget the past while a few had the courage to speak about it, but there was one characteristic they all shared.

'Their indomitability, Zita,' I reply. 'That's what it's about. That's what I admire.'

Dani 1917. 7.

Part 1

They were counted

Megszámláltattál

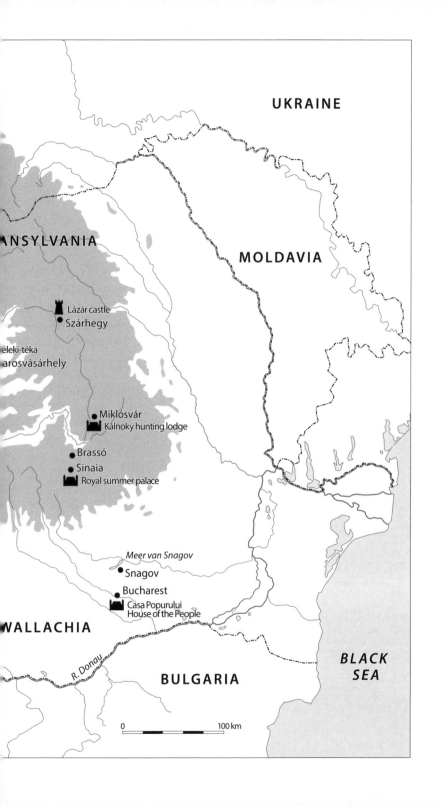

The song
of thorn birds

Vác, January 2010

She lives in a concrete flat in Vác, a town on the Danube twenty kilometres north of Budapest. On the outside of the door are two metal security gates. Erzsébet T., ninety-one, born in Transylvania in the family castle at Dornafalva, is wearing a finely woven pink shawl and bright-red lipstick. Her face is still handsome. I greet her and follow her into the narrow hallway. The apartment is a small museum, the walls decorated with copper engravings as well as photographs of the family castle and of her ancestors. In one corner two stuffed aquatic birds sit atop a bulging bookcase.

Keen to talk to someone from the older generation of Transylvanian nobility, I asked Botond, a friend who comes from Transylvania but now lives in Budapest, what the options might be. Botond told me that three grand old Transylvanian ladies were still alive. Two were in Leányfalu, a village to the north of Budapest where Ilona's grandmother lived for many years: Baroness Kemény and Countess Zichy, both a hundred and one. While I was touring Transylvania, one became ill and the other's mind became clouded. Suddenly she spoke only French, which no one had realized she knew. The third Transylvanian *grande dame* was Countess Erzsébet T., born in 1919, a mere girl compared to the others.

Our first meeting began as an interview about aristocratic life before the arrival of communism. Erzsébet was initially sceptical, but after she discovered that through my wife's grandmother we were related by marriage – and had accordingly dubbed me *Lieber Neffe* – I was promoted over a period of four months from rather suspect interviewer to prospective project manager for the restoration of Erzsébet's centuries-old family seat, Dornafalva Castle, recently returned to her by the Romanian state.

In the run-up to its accession to the European Union, Romania introduced restitution laws that were remarkably far-reaching. On paper the state is obliged to return to its rightful owners all property expropriated between 6 March 1945 and 25 December 1989, the day Nicolae and Elena Ceauşescu were executed. The claimant needs to produce documentation to prove entitlement to the property. It is then up to local officials to put the law into practice and comply with their obligations – nepotistic provincials who rule their domains like pashas of the Ottoman Empire. No business is done, no permit granted, unless a fixed sum or a percentage finds its way to the mayor.

In those early meetings Erzsébet told me the house of her youth was the oldest and most beautiful castle in Transylvania. I was shown photographs. It was stunning, a jumble of walls and towers set on a hill that made my romantically-inclined heart beat faster. Erzsébet's wish is for the part of the castle still standing to become a centre for artists, with space for all the ethnic groups in Transylvania: Hungarians, Romanians, Széklers, Saxons, Ruthenians, Serbs, Csángós, Swabians and

Armenians. In more recent photographs the castle looks as if it has been under protracted aerial bombardment.

'Erzsébet' is a pseudonym. She has asked me not to use either her given name or her surname. All the Transylvanian nobles I spoke to who were aged over sixty declined to be named in print. Only after long nagging from my side and some old-fashioned letters of supplication did a few of them relent. The omnipotence of the Securitate is the source of their reticence. The older generation in particular is still deeply fearful of the Securitate and to a lesser degree its Hungarian counterpart. In the late 1980s, in Hungary, Erzsébet was interviewed on radio about the old aristocratic life. The broadcast resulted in many nocturnal phone calls, volleys of abuse and death threats. The fear is no longer of violence or intimidation but rather of the prospect that property now returned could be taken away again. 'If I say anything bad about the Romanians and it appears in a book, they'll rescind everything.'

We will have to convince the local authorities in Dornafalva of the importance of our mission, both that the castle ought to be restored and that an artists' workplace is a good use for it. This afternoon I've come to discuss tactics with Erzsébet. She plans to travel to the castle in Transylvania with her son in the spring. She insists I go with them. The mayor must be persuaded to promise his cooperation. In Romania, as in Hungary come to that, it's crucial to get local government behind you, whatever it is you're planning to do.

'One day is enough.' She gives me a penetrating stare and goes on: 'Then we can take the next step. I need you to be there. The two houses built illegally in the castle garden can't possibly stay. I want to give those people a piece of land in the park to build a house on, but I can't say that. Every time I go there I'm given *pálinka* by the gypsy woman who lives in the house on the slope below the castle, as well as baskets of beans. There used to be many more gypsies at Dornafalva, but they were all killed in Auschwitz. One of our kitchen maids was half gypsy. Do you know anything about villagers? No? If they have two potatoes to eat, they don't give you one but two. That's what villagers are like. Come on, get your paper and write down the questions.

'Note that for the mayor you must take a Dutch cheese. He's called Constantin Dimitru. People call him Dinu, but you'll address him as Domnu Dimitru or Domnu Constantin Dimitru. I always use the polite form of address for the mayor. Then the deputy mayor. You must take a Dutch cheese for him too. Then you'll have made it quite clear; everyone in the surrounding villages will know once and for all that you're from Holland. The deputy mayor is Hungarian. He's a decent man. Gábor Gerevich. I want him to be on the board of the foundation.'

'Have you asked him?'

'No, you must never give a man time to think and come up with excuses, every woman knows that. You must confront him. In Dornafalva I'll ask him on the spot whether he'd like to be on the board.'

Erzsébet picks up a map of Dornafalva. The ruins of the castle are marked as black blocks. One part of the map is coloured yellow, another part red.

'We won't get back any of the red area. That was the park and it's full of houses now. The yellow is the land that's been returned to us. See? It's an oval. I don't know why, but parcels of land on which Transylvanian castles were built are always oval in shape.'

We stand up. Erzsébet walks slowly ahead of me. She has been talking continually for over three hours and I've scribbled eight closely-written pages. I now know how pet bear Nicolai met his end and that her mother died in 1922, at the age of twenty-seven.

'Why am I telling you all this? Three-quarters of what I've told you I've never told anyone else. One day I might even say what happened to father, in those final years between the arrival of the communists in the late 1940s and his death in 1955. It's a remarkable and terrible story. I say "might". Have you ever heard of the myth of the thorn birds? They can't sing, they're mute, they don't utter a note all their lives. Except when death approaches, just before they impale themselves on a long thorn. Then they sing beautifully. They sing just one inimitable song in all their lives and pay for it with their deaths.'

I kiss her on both cheeks. Stay alive for a while, I want to urge her, but that doesn't seem a terribly cultivated thing to say.

Nicolai
the pet bear

Vác, January 2010

Some family photographs were returned to Erzsébet by a villager she met in the street, black-and-white pictures with white edging, the first of them showing a large white pelican on a lawn. It was one of the creatures her father brought back alive from the Danube delta. He often went hunting there for several days at a time and he would personally stuff and mount the birds he shot. The second photograph is of a little girl with a roe deer: Erzsébet.

'The deer used to come indoors. We fed them chocolate and their hooves slipped on the parquet, making them do the splits.

'That's my father with Nicolai. He was still young then. Later he grew bigger than father. Nicolai was brought to us as a cub, just a few days old. He'd been found close to the Russian border, which is why he was called Nicolai with an 'i'. My father had an extraordinary relationship with animals. They

38

instantly felt at ease with him. People would bring him all the injured creatures or stray young from far and wide, found by villagers in the fields or by lumberjacks and gamekeepers in the woods. Any eggs would be given to the chickens to hatch. We had an entire zoo at the house, in the park. Whenever a young animal was brought to us, father immediately showed it to all the others one by one and let them calmly snuffle at it. That was the secret. That's why they didn't hurt one another. The deer, the cats and the birds all lived and slept in the same compound. Only the wolves had a stone house with straw. They were with us for twenty years.

'One day, when father was away hunting in the Danube delta, the foresters brought us a young wildcat from the mountains in a jute sack. He was tiny, curled up in a ball. We called him Picus. When I tried to pick him up he instantly lashed his claws at me and escaped. My brother and I searched all day for

Picus but we couldn't find him anywhere. The next morning, as soon as I heard from the servants that father was back from the delta, I ran to his study. He was bent over his desk, working, with Nicolai on the parquet next to his chair, lying there snoring with his front paws spread wide, as always. I told him excitedly that a little wildcat had been brought in, that it had escaped and it wouldn't survive if we didn't find it. Father said: "Shhh, you'll wake him up shouting like that." On his lap lay Picus, rolled up asleep on a cushion.

'He told me to take Picus through the zoo so that all the animals could smell him. The jay clattered its beak, that was all. Then I was sent to the attic to fetch a basket. Father put the basket down next to Nicolai, convinced he wouldn't harm Picus, and sure enough, after two days they started playing together. Picus clawed at Nicolai, who gave him a gentle tap. The little cat slid a meter across the parquet and ran straight back.

'When father was away, Nicolai would sit on the sofa on the covered terrace waiting for him. Father had a preference for small cars. They were good for the narrow mountain roads. He always chose the convertible version and always in white, so that if anything happened in the mountains, people would be able to find him. Occasionally he rolled one. We had a Diatto, an Italian car; I don't think they make them any longer. And an Essex. Nicolai would travel with him in those open-topped cars, in the front seat, resting his paw on the door. My brother and I sat in the back, without hats. We drove all over the country like that. Father raced along at 120 kilometres an hour. Everyone knew him.

'One time we stopped in a village where it was market day. Nicolai suddenly swung his paws over the door of the Essex and walked into the market. He started sweeping every-

thing laid out on the stalls onto the ground with single swipes of his paw. The market traders panicked. Father had to get out of the car and go after Nicolai as if he were a small child and lead him back to the car. Except that you don't lift a bear weighing 250 kilos into his seat. Nicolai was given a good talking-to and he climbed indignantly back into the passenger side.

'As a girl I used to lie on top of Nicolai for hours. Of all the animals, he was the only one that slept in the house. He had his own room, with a large square divan with pillows where he spent the night. He could open doors. When visitors arrived from Kolozsvár, we used to send Nicolai to answer the front door. Women especially jumped out of their skins when a two-metre bear swung the door open. He drank beer from the bottle and sat in the armchairs in the living room. He was a full member of the family, but then came the day when he hit the cook in the face.

'The cook had a bowl of raspberries. Nicolai wanted those raspberries and she didn't want him to have them, so she pulled the bowl away. That's when Nicolai hit her. He was angry. Her cheek bled. And as soon as there's blood, it's over. Nicolai had been with us for more than ten years by then. Father left for the mountains the next morning and was gone for four days. One of the gamekeepers came. Father had left his revolver at home and he'd explained to the gamekeeper what to do: play with Nicolai in the park. When he played he often lay on his back. The gamekeeper was to push the barrel of the revolver deep into his fur – father had explained which ribs to choose, here at the side – and then pull the trigger. Nicolai would hardly notice.

'He was buried under the oak tree, where a wild rose grew. No one ever spoke about Nicolai again, just as no one ever spoke about mother. Things that go too deep, that cause too much pain – those things you keep to yourself.'

Where the moon took us

Leányfalu, June 1991

On our first trip together, in an old Peugeot, Ilona and I drove right across Eastern Europe, where euphoria at the collapse of dictatorships still hung like morning mist in the streets of the little towns. We set course for East Germany, Czechoslovakia, Hungary and Romania, taking the hill roads whenever we could. We felt like fugitives, Bonnie and Clyde, sheltering in forests. We had two destinations in mind: Leányfalu and Bucharest. In Leányfalu lived *nagymami*, Ilona's Hungarian grandmother, and in Bucharest an uncle of mine, Coen Stork, who was the Dutch ambassador there. Other than that we went where the moon took us.

It was the start of summer and we drove with the roof down, even in the rain. We wore thick Russian army jackets. Of East Germany I mainly remember jolting over cobblestones. We slept in haystacks or on the ground in front of the Peugeot. One night our haystack was surrounded by police;

someone had mistaken us for cigarette smugglers. Taking the narrowest of forest tracks, we passed an abandoned red-and-white painted barrier in the middle of dense woodland and suddenly we were in Ilona's fatherland.

Leányfalu lies on the Danube at the foot of the Pilis range, where the slopes are covered in thick ancient forest, about thirty kilometres north of Budapest. The Hungarian grandmother after whom Ilona is named must have been a resilient woman. When the communists seized the extensive family estates in the 1940s she said: 'Well, now at least we no longer need to worry about the weather.'

The house was painted pale yellow, a shade with slightly less red pigment in it than the warm Habsburg yellow of all the government buildings in Austro-Hungary under the Dual Monarchy, as well as most of the Catholic churches, all the way from Slovenia to the far eastern border of Transylvania. It stood right at the edge of the forest. At the back was a narrow veranda with window boxes full of geraniums. The garden had an old apple tree in the middle and in one corner, as in practically every Hungarian village garden, a nut tree to keep away flies and mosquitoes. Ilona's grandmother welcomed us with open arms.

The interior was hung with family photographs and portraits. There were black-and-white pictures of proud men in *díszmagyar*, the ceremonial dress of the Hungarian nobleman – more ostentatious than the garb of a cancan dancer at the Moulin Rouge with a great fan of ostrich feathers in her piled-up hair. The grandmother's wedding photo showed her dressed in white with a long veil. The splendid *díszmagyar* worn by the bridegroom was reason alone to want to marry him. Between them stood a priest, a head shorter, in a habit. Ilona's grandfather's left hand rested on the family sword, a scimitar seized from an Ottoman by her ancestor Miklós I at the liberation of Buda in 1686. It was in that period that her family received its patent of nobility. In the early eighteenth century one descendant, József, became treasurer to the last Polish king, Stanislaus Lescinsky, who was later exiled to France and lived in Chambord Castle on the Loire. Another relative moved to France and founded the French branch of the family.

My first encounter with the rich history of this part of Europe was in that house, with Ilona's grandmother's stories and the photographs and paintings on the walls. They included a large print of a mounted hunting party, showing *nagymami*'s forebears, the Dőrys, who were raised to the peerage in the fourteenth century, making them part of the ancient Hungarian

nobility. The print dates from 1863 and it portrays the family's hegemony and power. Young and old radiate a sense that it's utterly natural for them to be on horseback, that theirs is the ruling class. That's simply how the world was. Elegant women sit side-saddle in long black skirts; children on ponies, dressed in dark jackets, look like little Lord Fauntleroys; the men have impressive beards. They all sit straight-backed on their mounts, the pride and discipline of generations in their genes. In the background, one of the Dőrys looks relaxed in the saddle, smoking a fat cigar. As a group they exude unshakable confidence.

One photograph on the wall of *nagymami*'s house showed the family seventy years later, in 1933. Standing on the grass, with a hedge for a backdrop, the men wear high boots with tassels, fur hats with plumes of white egret feathers, dolmans with gold buckles and fur-trimmed pelisses, and in their hands or hanging from their belts are curved swords inlaid with jewels and mother of pearl. They were tall men, but despite their superb attire, despite the understated joy of a father surrounded by his sons and the pride of the brothers standing shoulder to shoulder in invincible alliance, the photograph has a sense of futility about it, as if they're aware they inhabit a world that is on the point of vanishing.

Ilona and I drank gin with Ilona's grandmother from small crystal glasses. With cheerful self-mockery she described her childhood, her life, her family, but she said not a word about the period after the Second World War. She described how one of her ancestors once went to retrieve a runaway bride from his father-in-law's estate with his own hussars – every nobleman was obliged to provide a certain number of men in time of war, so practically every country estate had its own private army – and how one of her husband's brothers emigrated to America by ship with nothing more than a small suitcase containing a dinner jacket, for which he had little use since he was forced to make his living as a dockworker and gold digger.

There, 1,400 kilometres from the Dutch border, I found myself in a fairytale land, in a family with a grandmother who told me under the apple tree about her brother-in-law, brother to Ilona's grandfather, who had always said he did not want to be laid to rest in the clammy family crypt but in the ground next to the family chapel near the Danube, so that he 'could hear the geese flying over'. At the hour of his burial, just as his coffin was being lowered into the ground, a flight of geese passed honking over the family's place of worship.

After 30th of August 1940, *nagymami* lived for four years with her young family in Kolozsvár, Transylvania, in the old Mikes Palace. They frequented the Kaszinó, the club for Hungarian aristocrats. When company was scarce they would invite gypsies from a restaurant or a bar, drum up some friends and dance until deep in the night. Ilona's grandfather and his friends leased 40,000 hectares of hunting grounds in the Transylvanian highlands. In the autumn they hunted stags, in the winter bears and in spring capercaillies. *Nagymami* quietly told us that the years in Transylvania were the most beautiful and happiest of her life.

The wolves come up
to the monastery wall

Szárhegy, June 1991

As we travelled eastwards towards the Romanian border, hardly a single Hungarian neglected to warn us against the barbarous land we were about to enter. Some gently shook their heads, as if we were on our way to certain death. It sharpened us up, certainly. One of the first things we saw in Romania was a lake with a church tower sticking up out of it, a symbol of how the communists with their megalomaniac building projects attempted to destroy everything that had a human scale, everything that bound people together: rural life, traditional architecture, village communities, religious denominations, ancient customs. Ceauşescu's plan to systematize Romania by bulldozing more than 13,000 villages and replacing them with concrete highrise was one of the reasons Western governments, enthusiastic for so long, began to realize they might be dealing with a maniac.

Immediately on entering Romania we were struck by its poverty. As soon as we crossed the border near Oradea we

could see that the country was a quarter of a century behind Hungary. After fifty kilometres, when we arrived in Élesd, it seemed more like half a century and by the time we reached the first hills and left the main road, it was as if Ilona and I had driven into the Middle Ages. It was breathtakingly beautiful. Walled mediaeval churches; Saxon villages with pastel-coloured farmhouses, their wooden gates large enough for hay-laden carts to drive through; farmers' wives in local folk costume and headscarves; entire regions with no asphalt roads, and no petrol stations. Sometimes we drove for days on end, thick forests to our left and right, or mountain pastures speckled with shepherds and their flocks. We took russet-brown dirt tracks through the eastern Carpathians, dragging a dust cloud behind us, searching for somewhere to fill the tank. Only one in four petrol stations actually had any petrol. Usually someone was able to point on the map to a town that would probably have fuel supplies.

We slept in the fields and woods, in ugly communist state hotels with ballrooms for bedrooms that made you feel you were being both filmed and bugged, with Stalinist-baroque

interiors – all in dark oak – and lobbies that felt like mausoleums. We stayed at socialist camping sites in cabins that seemed built for anonymous sex, or in hotels whose porchways were crawling with whores dressed in brightly coloured leggings and tight sweaters, or in tiny guesthouses in mountain villages where you sensed that the inhabitants still expected the Securitate to descend on them after a visit from foreigners.

At the end of the sixth day, in Salamás, Transylvania, the sky turned a deep dark blue. The wind got up, flinging treetops back and forth to announce the storm. I put my foot down, as far as possible, trying to stay ahead of the clouds until they'd dumped their water. There was nowhere to bivouac. It was already getting dark; nature had turned against us. We searched for a refuge. We'd been driving through endless forests all day and now we were somewhere in the mountains, in the Harghita. Very occasionally there was a village, but none had a hotel. We asked a man walking along the road who spoke Hungarian where we could sleep. He said there was a monastery in the next village where we might be able to spend the night. The deluge began.

High on a hill, up against a pine forest, stood a large white
monastery. We knocked at the door. We were invited to dine
with the Franciscan monks and told we could stay the night.
Seated at long wooden tables, the men, with their ready laughter, told us you could hear the wolves howling at night and that
in winter they came searching for food right up to the monastery walls. Ilona and I had to sleep separately – which I was none
too happy about in a monastery full of young monks.

At six I was woken by all kinds of monastic activity. The
sky was clear blue. I made my way to the chapel and listened to
the singing and prayers. We were in Szárhegy, as it turned out.

The village had an ancient castle with battlements, built by
Count Lázár, a Hungarian. The boy who later became Transylvania's Prince Gábor Bethlen (1580-1629) had lived there with his
uncle András Lázár to be educated. Bethlen was the prince who
brought international renown to Transylvania, spending huge
sums on the theatre, grand balls, orchestras and dancers. After
his second marriage, to Catharina von Brandenburg, a German
princess from a Protestant family, Gábor Bethlen spent forty per
cent of the state budget on his court. He imported lace, masks
and jewels from Venice. Under his rule, prominent intellectuals

such as Simon Pécsi, who translated the Bible and the Talmud, were given top posts in government. In 1622 Bethlen, who also paid for young Transylvanians to attend the best universities in Europe, founded a university in Alba Iulia.

Gábor Bethlen was twice offered the Hungarian crown but refused. His branch of the Bethlen family, Bethlen de Iktár, has died out and only one descendant of the most famous of Transylvanian princes is still alive, a woman. She lives in Amsterdam, where she makes a living as an artist.

The Franciscan monks in Szárhegy – with three knots in the cords of their brown habits to symbolize the values of their order, poverty, chastity and obedience – whooped with pleasure as we treated them to short drives in the car. The whole order insisted on having a turn, down the mountainside to the village and back.

Each time mechanical failure struck, I managed to get the Peugeot 304 going again with pliers, wire, tape, water, oil and above all a good many affectionate thumps. On mountain ridges in the Carpathians, Ilona and I stopped at stalls where sausages were grilled on glowing charcoal.

In Sinaia we visited Peleş, a former royal summer palace at the foot of the Bucegi range. Commissioned in the late nineteenth century by the Hohenzollern prince Carol I (the longest serving king of Romania, who died in 1914) and built in neo-gothic style, the palace looks like something out of a children's picture book with its wooden turrets large and small. It has one hundred and sixty rooms. In the Ceauşescu era, Nixon, Arafat and Gaddafi stayed there, as did practically all the world's communist leaders. On the morning Ilona and I arrived it was cold and empty. The building was unheated, even though the brochure said it had been the first palace in Europe to have central heating. We were the only visitors and the bored guard didn't feel like showing us around; we got no further than the immense entrance hall.

There was no formal relationship between the Hungarian aristocracy in Transylvania and the Romanian royal family. Erzsébet T. told me that after the Treaty of Trianon was signed in 1920, the Hungarians regarded the Hohenzollerns as the royal house of an enemy state, with whom contact was to be avoided.

Like the Romanian state, the royal house is of fairly recent origin. Hohenzollern Carol I was crowned king of Romania in 1881. It was the period when, after the withdrawal of the Ottomans from the Balkans, the Western powers took to founding royal houses in all the Balkan states. There was usually a German prince who could be persuaded to become king of a country he'd never heard of before. The imported Hohenzollern prince Carol was given Romania to rule in 1866. He had the exuberantly romantic Peleş Castle built as a summer residence in Sinaia, where it fitted the landscape perfectly.

The Romanian royal family makes a passionate impression. Elisabeth of Romania married the crown prince of Greece in 1921, but the marriage was not a success. She had a series of affairs, about which she was far from discreet. She is supposed to have said: 'In my life I've committed every sin a person can commit apart from murder, and before I die I'd like to try that too.' She died in France, on the Côte d'Azur in 1956, the year of the Hungarian Uprising.

Elisabeth's mother was a Scot, born Princess Marie of Edinburgh, granddaughter of Queen Victoria, and later crowned Queen Marie of Romania. She too was notorious for her escapades. First she had a longstanding affair with Romanian aristocrat Barbu Ştirbey, then later with Zizi, Prince Cantacuzino. Of her six children, no one knows who fathered the last three. Marie spoke Romanian and took to wearing traditional Romanian costume, which made her look like a peasant woman. She was deeply loved by the Romanian people as a result.

Next to the great summer palace in Sinaia stands a smaller building, Pelişor, where Queen Marie lived. Local myth has it that in the early years of communism you could smell her perfume there, the scent of violets – an elusive enemy to the Securitate and the militia. With the death of dictator Gheorghe Gheorghiu-Dej, Nicolae Ceauşescu's predecessor, the scent vanished. The curse on Gheorghiu-Dej had been lifted.

When Ceauşescu became the new general secretary of the Romanian Communist Party in 1965, he appropriated the summer palace. In his quarter-century in power he slept there just once. He took possession of practically all the beautiful palaces and castles of Romania and regarded the Carpathians as his private hunting grounds, with the palaces as their accommodation, but he suffered from imperial overstretch. It was impossible for him to visit all the great houses he had seized.

You're an ambassador, I'm a minister

Bucharest, June 1991

I lona and I drove down out of the Carpathians onto the low plain of Wallachia. Passing the rusted petrochemicals plants of Ploieşti, we travelled to Bucharest to visit my uncle

Coen Stork at the ambassadorial residence in Bucharest. My cousin Daniël told us that the residents of Bucharest liked to visit the zoo to throw pebbles at Corbu, Ceauşescu's black labrador, who was kept in a cage there.

Ilona and I went to look at Ceauşescu's insane Casa Poporului, literally 'House of the People', the largest building in the world aside from the Pentagon. It was said to have tunnels beneath it, and an underground canal along which the dictator could escape by speedboat should any danger arise. There were even rumours that one of the ballrooms had a ceiling that would slide open so that a helicopter could land on the parquet. How much of this was true there was no way of telling. Other than a handful of insiders, only the workers who built the vast structure knew the full story in those days.

We were not allowed into the palace. Armed Romanian soldiers guarded the terrain. Coen thought it ought to be demolished – it was a fascistic monster that would bear fascistic children. Great swathes of old inner-city Bucharest, including Byzantine monuments and Orthodox churches, had been flattened on Ceaușescu's orders to make room for the People's Palace, while the surrounding boulevards were lined with neoclassical blocks of flats where Securitate agents and other loyal followers lived. It was hot in Bucharest and the air was so polluted that your eyes started watering after a few hours spent walking around town. The broad boulevards were practically empty. The only cars on the roads were Dacias. Outside the doors to the international hotels, nervous men offered to change lei. Bucharest still felt like a city suffering under a repressive regime.

In a dark-blue Mercedes with a Dutch flag, Coen drove us to receptions and exhibitions. Outside the car he told me the driver was a former Securitate officer. An unfamiliar world of bugging and spying revealed itself to me. The British representative in Bucharest, Hugh Arbuthnott, was one of the few ambassadors to have spoken out openly against Ceaușescu before the revolution. He was an example to Coen. He demonstrated that if you were creative enough you could organize meetings that reached out to dissidents, such as the Shakespeare workshops to which Romanian actors, dramatists, translators, writers and directors were invited. The Securitate controlled everything, so there was no way of knowing whether the invitations issued were ever delivered, but the main point was that the Securitate and the Communist Party would realize that a Western legation knew of the existence of certain people. That in itself provided them with some degree of protection. Both men invited dissidents to their homes and reported to their own ministries on the reality of daily life in Romania, whereas some of their fellow ambassadors stuck to protocol and others kept themselves occupied with receptions and parties. The Portuguese ambassador concentrated on trying to pick up shop girls, while the Danes, Norwegians and Mexicans closed their embassies in Bucharest.

Coen had met Ceauşescu several times. Their meetings were usually so rigidly stage-managed as to be pointless; the foreign ambassadors were always surrounded by an army of Securitate intent on safeguarding protocol. Their most enjoyable meeting, at a distance, was on 1 May 1988 in the Sala Palutului during a party congress to which the ambassadors were invited, an event punctuated by protocol and by song and dance in national costume. The Politburo sat at a table strategically placed so that they could see everyone, Ceauşescu in the middle, his chums next to him. Ceauşescu was holding binoculars, intending to spy on the party members and the diplomatic corps. Coen knew about this intimidatory habit and had tak-

en his birdwatching binoculars along. The protocol man next to Coen grew redder and redder, asking nervously: 'You are only using them for the stage, aren't you?' The diplomats were sitting with the party bigwigs and the Securitate on a steeply sloping balcony, peering down. Coen watched the folk dancing, but he focused mainly on the Politburo and on Nicolae and Elena Ceaușescu. At one point the two pairs of binoculars met and were trained on each other for long seconds.

Coen took us to a diplomats' lunch in what had been Ceaușescu's house on Lake Snagov. It was fourteen kilometres outside Bucharest, just enough to allow a dictator to sleep in peace, since it was too far for an enraged crowd to walk. Whenever Ceaușescu moved around Bucharest, three different routes were sealed off. No one knew which one he would take. The head of Securitate made the choice at the last moment.

The house at Snagov was a real gem, the product of a marriage between a xenophobic peasant and a hysterical woman. The sombre chalet was filled to the roof with kitschy porcelain and there was an underground cinema with fake sunking chairs, a vast collection of shoes, and a small library of leather-bound scientific volumes practically all written by Elena herself, mainly about polymer chemistry. How she found time to write in between watching every episode of *Dynasty* and *Dallas* is a mystery. In their daughter Zoia's room, furnished like a teenager's bedroom even though she was forty, I poked about among the LPs. She liked Western pop music, with a corny preference for bands like ABBA and Mud. The housekeeper, who had worked for the Ceaușescus, stood next to me throughout to ensure I didn't pinch anything, but she left the room for a moment and I was able to slip the brass key to Zoia's heavy wooden desk into the pocket of my jeans. I still have it.

When Ceaușescu visited Britain in 1978 as a guest of Queen Elizabeth II, he took his own sheets and pillow cases with him for fear of being poisoned. His clothes were kept in special cabinets and his food was tasted for him. He was given a black labrador puppy on that visit, Corbu. He'd been invited mainly because the British wanted to sell him aircraft and he was treated as an important head of state, with a reception at Buckingham Palace and a procession in an open carriage with the queen. On YouTube I watched a film of the ride across London. Ceaușescu waves deliriously to the

crowds, like a child, while the queen sits across from him completely motionless. She later called them the most wretched three days of her life. She'd had all the silverware and valuables removed from the Ceaușescus' rooms on the advice of the French president with whom the couple had stayed a few months earlier. In Paris the Romanian delegation had ransacked the rooms and dismantled everything – electrical sockets, ventilators, curtain rails – looking for bugging devices.

Coen, along with Bernard Kouchner, was the first foreign diplomat to speak to the Romanian people live on television and congratulate them in the revolutionary days of December 1989. Coen told me it had been an extremely emotional moment. The television building was a mess, unlit, with checkpoints manned by exhausted soldiers. French minister Kouchner arrived with a pack of journalists and tried to push his way

to the front of the studio where Coen had been waiting inter-
minably in the dark, saying: 'Is it alright if I go first? You're an
ambassador, I'm a minister.' Coen didn't think so. They appeared before the camera together. It was in the days when Iliescu wore a sweater all the time, to make himself look like
a revolutionary intellectual. Once he'd been appointed the
new president of Romania no one ever saw him in anything
other than a suit and tie. To this day he has an office in Bucharest where his staff beaver away at an accurate account of the
revolution – accurate from Iliescu's point of view, that is.

After three days in Bucharest, Ilona and I set off back towards Hungary. We raced over the Carpathian peaks into
Transylvania and then took a southerly route via Déva. We
drove along winding asphalt roads lined with nut trees, their
trunks whitewashed to a metre and a half above the ground,
past rolling meadows under a silver sky, to our right a railway
with tarred electricity poles beside it, like telegraph poles in
the Wild West. On the track ran a shabby pale-blue train, angular like the toy trains of my childhood. I accelerated and
we gradually caught up with the train and drew alongside, the
roof down, our hair coarse from weeks of sun and wind. The
road wound through the hills. We kept up with the train, veer-
ing in parallel with it across the fields. We waved and tooted at
the driver. The train tooted back at us, long and loud.

Back to her father's
country

Bucharest, October 1991

In the autumn of 1991, a few months after our journey
through Transylvania to Bucharest, Ilona moved to Hungary for a year and a half, driven to return to her father's
country by an instinct greater than herself. Her father was
twenty-one when the revolt broke out in Budapest in 1956
(a full seven years before he became her father). Because of
his origins he was excluded from further education, so he had
a job at a chemicals factory, but at the time of the uprising he
was in hospital in Budapest with hepatitis. He crept away and
joined the revolution. That November, after the Soviet Union
had quashed the revolt, he crossed the border into Austria
with his pregnant sister and her husband, on foot through the
woods, evading patrols of Russian soldiers. They had made
the decision to leave only the previous evening, so they were
unable to inform anyone or say goodbye to their parents. One
sister stayed. All Ilona's father had with him when he left his

fatherland and family behind was a lard sandwich in his trouser pocket.

They travelled the first leg by train, getting out eighty kilometres from the border and continuing on foot. Close to Austria, they had to cross a large empty field. Ilona's father said: 'I'm the youngest; let me go first. If it's safe, I'll wave to you from the other side.' His sister was carrying a child and his brother-in-law would need to look after her, was his reasoning. After plodding a long way over the clods he spotted a Russian soldier sitting at the next field boundary, training a weapon on him. Ilona's father considered his options: he could break into a run, turn around, or lie down. He decided to stay calm, look straight ahead and continue walking. He reached the far side of the field. The Russian soldier did not pull the trigger. 'Look ahead and just keep on walking' became Ilona's father's motto in life.

Dispossessed, a poor Hungarian immigrant with the social status of a guest worker, he managed to make a life for himself in the Netherlands and in the end he succeeded more than most. Thirty-five years after he crossed the border as a fugitive, his daughter Ilona was asked by a major English law firm whether she would be prepared to go to Budapest to set up an office there. Ilona immediately said yes.

In Budapest the streets had two names, old and new. Under the sign reading LENIN KÖRÚT was a new one saying TERÉZ KÖRÚT. MARX TÉR had NYUGATI TÉR underneath it and below ENGELS TÉR it said ERZSÉBET TÉR. There were even streets named after Transylvanian aristocrats once again: APOR VILMOS ÚT, UGRON GÁBOR ÚT, BETHLEN TÉR and TELEKI ÚT. The classical and eclectic buildings lining the avenues were peppered with bullet holes, façades were black from decades of coal fumes and the smell of brown coal hung in the streets. You saw hardly any cars other than grey and light-blue Trabants – it seems those were the only two colours available. Everyone chain-smoked, the taxi drivers especially.

I fell in love with that whole great mess beyond the former Iron Curtain. I find it impossible to say whether it was simply because of Ilona, a kind of Pavlovian reaction that led me to embrace the entire Eastern Bloc along with her, or whether I would have developed the same affection for the region even without our love. I do know that I've always been drawn to the unpredictable.

Budapest was ecstatic, as if seized with gold fever, wild and free. It was a new beginning. The Democratic Forum was in power and everything was going to get better. Hungary was filled with hope. After two months with her grandmother in Leányfalu, Ilona found an apartment on the slopes in front of the citadel in Buda, on a steep cobbled street, the Szalag utca, in a four-storey 1960s block where the stairwell always smelled of gas. In the adjoining courtyard belonging to the centuries-old baroque houses to which the flats had been abruptly attached, a madman was taken out for exercise every morning between seven and eight. He screamed the whole place down, a kind of urban variation on the cock that announces at the top of its lungs that a new day has begun.

At the bottom of the Szalag utca a small shop was open twenty-four hours a day. Half its range of products consisted of bottles of wine and strong drink. There Ilona and I bought white rolls, tomatoes and Hungaria Extra Dry champagne with an ice-blue label. That was our daily diet and there wasn't much else we needed, except each other's company. Stuck to the rolls was (and still is) a scrap of white paper with numbers and codes. The sticker is almost impossible to remove from the bread without tearing off the crust as well. In my imagination this was one of the subtler methods used by the former dictatorship to give citizens the impression that it controlled absolutely everything.

New cafés opened, glorying in freedom and the new affiliation with the West: Picasso, Maxim and Titanic, and underground bars like Nana, Bolshevita and Blue Box Cinema. Or Thalia, the bar next to the artists' entrance at the opera, where tenors and prima donnas came after performances to be served red wine from twenty-litre jerry cans. We ate at Tabáni Kakas, where the dishes cost 400 to 500 forints (less than two euro), or at Okay Italia, run by two Italian gigolos who'd kidnapped a toothless chef from Palermo. The action was confined to a fairly tight radius; everything happened within half a kilometre of the Budapest Opera House.

I was attending the art academy in Rotterdam and I visited Ilona as often as I could. Ten or more times I took the night train from Amsterdam to Budapest. We joined the company to be found at around midnight in the Piaf Bar, a David Lynch-style night club with thick upholstery, red velvet curtains and yellow spotlights trained on a small stage with a piano. Sometimes a third-rate pianist played there, or someone else who felt called upon to steal the show; otherwise the voice of Edith Piaf or Charles Aznavour would resound from the speakers. An almost hidden staircase led to the vaulted cellar. In that dark L-shaped space below ground, a deejay, usually György, or George as we called him, played jazz, Latin and soul.

Many adventurers, or simply drifters, came to Hungary by car, train or plane. To a great degree the wild Piaf crowd was made up of painters, writers and journalists. The thrill and romance of the old fatherland had drawn them to Budapest like a magnet. In the Piaf Bar we stood crammed together in the half-dark, shouting to be heard over George's Latin and jazz. In the cellar, lit by candles and a couple of spotlights from behind the bar, there was tireless dancing, joking and drinking. For 500 forints you could buy a bottle of Hungarian champagne and imagine yourself a millionaire. Those who smoked, smoked Gitanes, with or without a holder. Time ceased to exist.

György Kégl de Csala is Ilona's lively, dandyish second cousin, a close friend of the owner of the Piaf and the unrivalled spider in the web of aristocrats, artists and spongers that made up Budapest nightlife. He combined a string of indeterminate jobs – graphic designer for an advertising agency, deejay at the Piaf, exporter of secondhand computers to Transylvania and importer of Transylvanian timber to Hungary – with a hyperactive social life. In 1990, George was among the first to come to Budapest after the fall of communism, arriving straight from Florence. Under communism, Hungarian society, like that of all Eastern Bloc countries, had been deliberately 'atomized' into small, manageable sectors to make it easy for the state to control, but George got to know people in Budapest from five or six different social strata. They ranged from

aristocrats who had stayed in Hungary, usually living lives of unassuming decency, to recalcitrant artists and alcoholics with an alibi, who did nothing all day but talk and drink.

George was the breakneck locomotive to the joyful train of returned exiles. He took us all in tow. He knew a limitless succession of women, including a regiment of German dental students that he generously introduced to his friends. Of conquests by others I recall only their evaluations, particularly those concerning silicone breasts, a novelty in the early 1990s that drove the boys wild, as did the heated seats in a company car driven by Mihály, a more distant cousin of Ilona's.

Mihály has the same surname as Ilona, but he comes from the count's side of the family. Although regarded as a full cousin, he is actually Ilona's seventh cousin, if not even more remote. Mihály was the patriarch of the group – partly because he was three years older than us but mainly because of that astonishing novelty of a car with heated seats. His family fled Hungary in 1946, when the great expropriation took place, and settled in Germany, where Mihály was sent to a Hungarian school attended exclusively by the children of exiles. In 1991, having finished his studies, he moved to Hungary to work for a large insurance company.

As well as George and Mihály there was Pál Festetics. He completed the quartet. Ilona went around with the three of them, and unlike the other women she was one of the boys, expected to drink as hard as the rest and to pay for as many rounds. Apart from Ilona and Mihály, who both had proper jobs, everybody was broke. George, Mihály and Pál became good friends. I don't think I've ever found myself in a group of people with whom I felt more welcome than I did among those returned exiles.

Pál Festetics had wanted to be a professional skier, but his parents talked him out of it. He dutifully spent some time studying law, then fled Vienna and landed in Budapest without any obvious occupation. I suspect Pál experienced the closed circle of distinguished families in Austria, with their regular balls, receptions, cocktail parties, wedding feasts, christenings – and the expectations that accompanied all of that – as horribly oppressive. He derived great pleasure from dubious contacts, such as Russian icon smugglers and Hungarian rock stars. In 1993, after a year and a half in Budapest, he began a course at the art academy in Vienna and developed into a promising painter.

In the Piaf we met Felix Schilling de Canstatt, who looked like Errol Flynn. He'd returned from Germany and along with George he chased women day and night: the Bajza sisters, the beautiful Eszter and Réka Kund, the exulted, silky French transvestite Yves Bortolini, madcap Valéria Garai, and Ági Major, who was Pál's girlfriend for a long time. In truth the whole group was made up of people born in the wrong century. The Spanish ambassador liked to join them, finding more gaiety there than anywhere else in Budapest. He felt younger than he was, tried to dance cheek to cheek with all the women, and by three in the morning you would find him dancing blissfully in circles on the dance floor, alone, in his dinner jacket. At weekends horses were ridden, wine cellars visited, chest-hair burning competitions held and the *csárdás* danced to music performed by gypsies.

After one such evening of champagne and *pálinka* in the Piaf, Ilona and I were thrown out of a taxi on the Roosevelt tér for being drunk. It was three or four in the morning. Snowflakes drifted down, muffling all sound. The city was enchantingly silent. The Chain Bridge was covered with ten centimetres of untrodden snow. We walked across the Danube, watching the water flow beneath us, the snow crunching at every step. The magnificence of Budapest unfolded in its astonishing grandeur. There could be no doubting it: the world belonged to us and would never be more beautiful.

The honeymoon is over

Budapest, June 1995

It was a while before I realized that the core of the group
around George and the Piaf Bar belonged to the old aristocratic Hungarian families. Ilona never spoke about that
kind of thing. I found out when I went to the post office to
post letters and spotted a series of Hungarian postage stamps
showing the former family palaces of the guys and gals with
whom we danced on the tables almost every night: Festetics
kastély, Széchenyi kastély, Dőry kastély, Esterházy kastély. The
grandparents of those twenty-somethings lived thousands
of kilometres apart, in different cultures and on different
continents, but sixty years earlier they'd known each other,
intermarried, partied as wildly as we did – only on a different
scale; not in smoky cellars with cheap wine and vodka but
in city palaces and hunting lodges, in ballrooms or in parks
among fountains and box hedging, with French champagne
and liveried butlers.

During the day, while Ilona was at the office, I worked in a coffee house on the Andrássy út, writing my first novel. The place was deserted. I usually sat alone beneath the chandeliers. At about twelve o'clock the lunchtime lovers would show up, sometimes even visiting the toilets together. In the afternoons a few women might happen by for a cup of tea. Later I heard from a cousin of Ilona's that the coffee house was tainted. It had been the favourite haunt of members of the ÁVH, the hated Hungarian secret service. Their head office and torture chambers were just a hundred metres away, at Andrássy út 60. Hungarians avoided the place like the plague.

I wandered through the city for hours, stepping into cafés and courtyards. A lackadaisical fatalism emanated from the residents and their buildings. The courtyards behind the classical palaces and eclectic residential blocks were suffering, without exception, from half a century of neglect: peeling paint on walls and pillars, acacias growing through the courtyard paving, rusting Secessionist wrought ironwork, lopsided cast-iron lifts, crumbling Zsolnay tiles.

There were many transients like me at the Piaf: László and Gábor Teleki, descendants of a Transylvanian family, Miklós Almásy, and two brothers who wanted to fight the Serbs in Croatia because they were firing shells at their family castle, or the other way round, in Serbia against the Croats – at the Piaf I couldn't always follow everything in detail. There were always new people and ebullient visitors. Ilona guaranteed an endless supply of friends from the Netherlands, while Yves Bortolini brought hysterical Southern Europeans, and George and Mihály provided a constant stream of distinguished Germans, Austrians and Italians. One night I'd be sitting with a screeching group of French transvestites eating raw ground steak, the next night arm-wrestling in hazy after-hours bars with German princes blind drunk on *pálinka* and Unicum. At the Piaf people talked and dreamed about the estates and houses that had belonged to their families. George's owned a small palace to the north of Lake Balaton that had recently fallen into the hands of a Hungarian entrepreneur who wanted to start a casino there. The castle that was once the property of Mihály's family, in the province of Somogy to the east of Lake Balaton, had become a children's home. It was in an abominable state. As for the centuries-old palace of an aunt of his, Countess Lónyay, all the roof tiles had been stripped off in communist times to build a local house of culture. Trees were now growing inside. Sixty kilometres south of Budapest, on the Danube, stood Ilona's family's baroque country seat. After the expropriation it was given over to goose-breeding.

The only one of our number I never really heard talk about property was Pál Festetics. Having fled Hungary with his family, Pál's father became a pupil of Konrad Lorenz, the Nobel Prize-winning naturalist best known for his research on geese, and he in turn became a famous biologist and professor. He believed you shouldn't go on looking back but must achieve something yourself. Pál despised those émigré aristocrats in Austria and Germany who seemed to regard their titles as their greatest virtue.

Pál was the only male descendant of his branch of the family. Like Széchenyi, Batthyány, Esterházy, Károlyi, Pallavicini, Pálffy and several others, his was among the magnate families that had once held absolute power in Hungary. Pál told us that the famous Festetics Palace with its huge library at the southern tip of Lake Balaton had been surreptitiously rented out by the staff to producers of porn films – a nice example of the new democracy and the growth of the entrepreneurial spirit. The tourist groups that arrived wearing shorts, cameras slung round their necks, were guided straight past certain rooms by a cordon of attendants. In the ducal four-poster beds, cum shots were composed, while against the baroque tiled stoves, bodybuilders copulated wearing white wigs.

In Hungary Pál struggled with the fact that he was judged mainly by his name. For Miki Széchenyi, a painter our age who had also returned to Hungary and frequented the Piaf Bar, the experience of positive discrimination was reason enough to go back to America. He wanted to be judged on his own achievements, not on his family's former standing. István Széchenyi (1791-1860), an ancestor of Miki's, was a liberal-minded count who did a great deal to expedite the modernization of Hungary and was generally regarded as 'the greatest Hungarian'.

Every few months, all the recently arrived aristocrats were invited to tea by the former Princess Schwarzenberg. In her salon the returned nobles mingled with those who had never left the Eastern Bloc. After the communists took power in 1947 and her property was confiscated, the princess could do nothing but muck out her own stables, where she watched her horses grow thin and die. She'd survived it all, and now, as a grand old lady in a baroque house on the Citadel, she gave receptions as she had decades before. George, always in a fine tweed jacket with a breast-pocket handkerchief, relied on public transport, but he had the panache to get off the bus a stop early and arrive at the princess' house on foot, energetic and dashing.

The gulf between those who had returned and those who had stayed was barely visible in those first few months and years, concealed by the general euphoria, but as time went by and everyone in Hungary was gradually confronted with harsh reality – petrol prices rose, gas bills went up, there were taxi strikes, the Hungarian Democratic Forum was not re-elected and the socialists (largely the former communists) came to power again in 1994 – it became clear that there was a huge difference between people who had grown up in freedom and those who had survived dictatorship, even if they had the same background and culture and came from the same families. Those who lived through years of repression lacked a certain brash self-confidence and any conviction that rules enshrined in law guarantee justice.

Meanwhile the country was born again. Ilona, a twenty-eight-year-old lawyer for an English law firm, was put in charge of setting up a branch of a Dutch bank in Hungary and she brought in a large oil company as a client. She was perhaps the first of the Piaf crowd to discover what kind of banana republic we'd landed in. She had to negotiate with, and write out contracts for, secretaries of state who had once been professional circus clowns, or real estate magnates who were full-time taxi drivers only three years earlier. Hungary, it seemed, was truly a land of unprecedented opportunity.

In June 1995 one of the young returned nobles, Tibor Kálnoky, was married in Transylvania. The guests stayed with peasants in the nearby village. In dinner jackets and evening dresses, they walked along the dirt roads of Miklósvár behind cows on the way to be milked. I knew Tibor only by name. Ilona had travelled to Slovakia with him for a few days, along with Pál, George and several others, to ski in the Carpathians. Tibor was trying to get his ancestral castle in Transylvania back and renovate it. A delegation of guests travelled to Miklósvár from Budapest by bus. Pál Festetics got on that bus. As it was leaving Budapest, Pál suddenly stood up, walked along the aisle and asked the driver to stop and open the door. The busload of joyful partygoers watched in astonishment as Pál strode away along the pavement. Apart from his Hungarian girlfriend of the time, none of the Piaf friends ever saw him again after that. This was the period when the young generation of returnees, along with the new Hungary, lost its innocence.

Puss in Boots

Marosvásárhely, March 2009

Not until 2003 did circumstances permit us to take the definitive step. With our three sons, Ilona and I moved to Hungary. The desire for space and countryside was one important motivation and the travel book *Between the Woods and the Water* by Patrick Leigh Fermor undoubtedly influenced our decision as well. In the interwar years, in the twilight of the Transylvanian aristocracy, the book's author, then aged nineteen, walked from the Hook of Holland to Istanbul. He has been called one of the world's best travel writers. The British regard Patrick Leigh Fermor as a cross between Graham Greene and James Bond. His Bond image is based on a dashing exploit on Nazi-occupied Crete, when he captured the German commander of the island and managed to get him on board a British submarine.

During his journey through Transylvania on foot and on horseback in 1934, Fermor stayed with the old Hungarian families. He became a close friend of István (who in real life went by the name Elemér Klobusicky, Globus to his friends) and met the alluring, secretive Angéla. She was several years older and unhappily married. István proved himself a good friend by borrowing a car from the Lázár family so that

the three of them could take a trip to Kolozsvár. They crept through the streets like brigands; Angéla did not want to be spotted by anyone she knew.

Fermor also visited the Lázárs' country estate: '[László] Lázár, the owner of the house and the motor car, [...] had been a cowboy in America and a gaucho in Argentina, ridden in a circus rodeo when short of cash, and his side-whiskers, piercing eyes and handsome, leathery face perfectly fitted the role. His house was only a dozen miles south of István's.'

In 2009, seventy-five years after the escapade for which Patrick Leigh Fermor borrowed a car from a man he didn't know, I met the son of the car's owner, Pál Lázár. He told me that his father slept with a gun in the drawer of his bedside table and a lasso under his pillow. When a bull refused to be loaded for the drive to the abattoir one day, Pál's father took out the lasso, threw it around the bull's neck and pulled the animal to the ground.

Pál Lázár was an energetic, wiry man, seventy years old. He had the look of a lumberjack or a gamekeeper, someone who spends all his days in the mountain air and the forests, the kind of man who, despite being a quarter of a century older, walks off ahead of you as you scramble up a mountain track. His skin had the deep tan of an outdoorsman; his clothes and mannerisms were utterly unpretentious. In communist times he worked as a carpenter.

As a child Pál lived on the Laposnyak estate, but we met in Marosvásárhely, in the house of his niece Kati Ugron. We sat at the dining table near big sliding French windows that looked out on a stretch of wasteland where no doubt another forty houses will have been built by now. Kati translated his energetic Hungarian sentences into beautiful, musical English, although she had to divide her time between her uncle and a puppy kept in the kitchen behind a gate, trying to join us, jumping up and down with the inexhaustible fanaticism of a Jack Russell.

Pál Lázár: 'When I was young we lived in a very class-conscious time and society; even as children we knew that. We realized from our earliest days that we were different, although we didn't let it show. I played with the coachman's son, but when we visited Déva, which wasn't far, our clothing marked us out from the other children. I had big leather boots. The children called me Puss in Boots. We looked the way people look in old films: knee breeches, boots, long woollen socks. But we didn't pose. The nobles in Transylvania have always been different from the Hungarian nobility. We didn't build those gigantic palaces. The older generation found such things repellent. We managed the landed estates differently too, far more in consultation with the peasants and our staff. Hungary was more feudal. Here in Transylvania there was solidarity between the people and the aristocracy.

'With the Golden Bull of 1222, Hungary became the first country in continental Europe to set down the nobles' rights and duties: aristocratic privileges, such as exemption from taxation and military service; the right to intervene, by force if necessary, if the king ruled the country badly; the duty to mobilize an army in time of war.

'In the eleventh and twelfth centuries, two-thirds of the land in Hungary belonged to the king. If the king chose to reward you for achievements or loyalty, you'd be given a village or some bits of land, but scattered, never contiguous, to prevent concentrations of power. In the thirteenth century, by exchange and by marriage, the nobles acquired larger, joined-up stretches of territory. In 1351 a law was passed that said you could give country estates only to your own descendants.'

Pál's explanation made sense, for the first time, of the many adoptions that took place in the past, Ilona's family included.

Sons would be removed from their families and sent to a distant uncle to be adopted. This was not just to prevent the line from dying out but to ensure no property was lost; in the absence of descendants, everything would revert to the crown. Until 1848 estates could not be sold, and until that time there was serfdom in Hungary and Transylvania. A serf was bound to his lord and his lands, but the lord also had obligations, such as to care for all his serfs in times of famine. Bondedness to a specific location has a long history, both for the peasants and for the nobility. It's astonishing how reluctant even now the Hungarians are to move house.

Pál Lázár belongs to the untitled nobility. 'In Hungary and Transylvania the nobility goes way back, to the seventeenth century. It was a *una eademque nobilitas*, meaning all nobles belonged to the same category and had the same rights; there were no titles. A limited number of capable men received patents of nobility from the king; the rest of the population was made up of bonded peasants. Only with the arrival of the Habsburgs were titles introduced. In Transylvania that was in the late seventeenth century. Some families weren't at all interested in re-

ceiving titles from them. They said: Who are these Habsburgs?
We've been in Transylvania far longer. Titles were given not to
the oldest families but to those that were powerful and wealthy
at that particular time, and who showed no hostility towards
the Habsburgs. The last Habsburg emperor, Charles IV, was still
handing out titles between 1916 and 1918. There was a kind of
caste system; you married within your own caste. That changed
after the Treaty of Trianon. It became more important for the
Hungarians in Transylvania to marry Hungarians than to find
someone from precisely the same social level.'

In a sense, aside from the honour and status it brought to
the family, a title could be seen as a leash held by the emper-
or. Transylvanian families that regarded themselves as older
than the Habsburgs, such as Ugron and Bárczay, refused titles.
Pál Lázár told me that his forefather Kemény had thrown the
Habsburg offer of a peerage out of the window. His wife went
out and fetched the document in from the garden – the Keménys had her presence of mind to thank for their baronetcy.

I'd heard the same story in Hungary. The old families who
were ennobled by the Hungarian kings are proud not to have

Habsburg titles. Seniority has greater weight than rank. Ilona's family was said to have refused a title once, but according to family tradition the reasons were different. It was on the principle 'better a rich squire than a poor count'. The old Hungarian families are identifiable by their long names. Under communism double-barrelled surnames were forbidden, and even in present-day Hungary their use is seen as arrogant.

From the late seventeenth century onwards the grand tour was in vogue among the nobility. They travelled all over Europe. Latin was their lingua franca, but they all spoke several languages. Familiarity with foreign tongues, with the literature of other countries and with ideas from Western Europe is a mark of the aristocracy in all eras. They had international contacts, often through marriage. The aristocrats kept their eyes on developments elsewhere. In Hungary wealthy nobles with the title of baron or above had seats in the upper house.

The distinction between titled and untitled nobility was largely theoretical – status, as is always and everywhere the case, was determined partly by wealth, partly by the positions family members held and partly by the specific families to which they were related. The existence of an untitled nobility was important, however. There were families that had been ennobled by the king but did not have titles, and alongside them families of titled aristocrats (baron, count, duke, grand duke). In Transylvania the two were strictly separate until the Treaty of Trianon. The untitled nobility did not generally marry the titled nobility – or only in exceptional cases, as the result of an *amour fou*.

Pál Lázár: 'The isolated location of Hungary and Transylvania contributed to the retention of large-scale landownership. The fact that this region was sparsely populated with no easy access to the sea worked in favour of the large landowners. It delayed the arrival of trade and industry, which took off in Western Europe in the second half of the nineteenth century. But after Trianon and the land reforms of the 1920s, the Transylvanian aristocrats with the biggest estates had their land confiscated. Around 1900 there were a total of about two thousand large estates in Hungary and Transylvania, in the hands of eight hundred aristocrats. By 1930 there were only 745, owned by 350 aristocrats.'

A carefully considered policy, from the point of view of the House of Habsburg, lay behind the distribution of titles and patents of nobility. It was aimed at creating stability. Each elevation in status was recorded in the *Libri Regii Transylvaniae*. The families given titles and thereby raised to the peerage were generally the existing Hungarian noble families. In Transylvania, newly appointed untitled nobles fulfilled the role performed in the West by the wealthy bourgeoisie. Soldiers, conscientious civil servants, assiduous agriculturalists, clergy, lawyers and spa managers were ennobled by the Habsburgs. The reason most often given in the *Libri Regii Transsylvaniae* for a title or elevation ran: *'Der unserer Majestät und der Heiligen Krone des Landes geleisteten Dienste wegen.'* (On account of services to our majesty and to the country's Holy Crown.)

After his death,
wagonloads of books
kept arriving

Marosvásárhely, March 2009

I step through a large door into the Teleki-téka. Count Sámuel Teleki (1739-1822) founded this library and donated it to the town of Marosvásárhely. A white, U-shaped building, it has an arched gallery on the first floor reminiscent of a cloister. I climb a flight of stone steps and knock on a door. Beyond lies a long room with tables covered in papers and books. There are three women and one man. The man seems disturbed by my arrival. A young woman with black curly hair hurries towards me when I tell her I've come for the Teleki-téka. She has a giant key in her hand, as if for a mediaeval town gate. She's a specialist in the mediaeval Transylvanian nobility.

In the 1950s several of Count Sámuel Teleki's direct descendants lived somewhere in this building. I suppose it ought to be seen as evidence of the charitableness of the communist system that they were permitted a bolt hole. The space was so small that one of the Telekis slept on top of a cupboard.

I ask the woman whether she's heard of Gemma Teleki. Perhaps she knows where she lived? Certainly. She turns round and points to a side door, which opens onto a dark, dead-end corridor about five metres long and a metre and a half wide. It's the kind of space in which you would store cardboard boxes that might come in handy one day, empty bottles for the deposit, or a bicycle with a flat tyre. Here Gemma Teleki lived with two other Telekis. People who knew her well have told me that Gemma was an exceptional person, very intelligent, perhaps too intelligent for her own good.

My guide opens a tall door. After crossing a hallway we find ourselves in a large room. She turns on the lights. Since 1802, the year the library opened, nothing here has changed, except that there is electricity now. An inner sanctum. The windows have shutters. The bookcases are painted white and their doors have chicken wire instead of glass. The space is two storeys high; the upper-level walkway is lined with bookcases on all four walls. At the far end of the room hangs a large portrait of Sámuel Teleki as chancellor of Transylvania, an ermine robe over his shoulders and a sceptre in his hand. He is flanked by portraits of the two other noblemen who founded large libraries in Transylvania: Sámuel Brukenthal and Ignatius Batthyány.

On the wall is a map of Europe showing the twenty-five cities from which Teleki assembled his collection. They include Amsterdam, Leiden, Utrecht and Rotterdam, as well as Zurich, Padua, Rome, Leipzig, Ulm, Budapest and Pécs. He had contacts in all those cities, dealers and buyers searching on his behalf. Over his lifetime Teleki compiled a collection of 40,000 books. After his death in 1822, wagonloads of books kept arriving in Marosvásárhely.

Ninety-one-year-old Erzsébet T. has told me that many Transylvanian nobles attended universities in the Netherlands.

One of her ancestors studied at Utrecht and some of his letters have survived. From Transylvania and Hungary they usually travelled by boat along the Polish and German rivers to the Baltic, and from there they walked to the Netherlands. In the sixteenth and seventeenth centuries, around three thousand Transylvanians and Hungarians studied in the Netherlands, including 1,233 in Franeker, 740 in Utrecht and 655 in Leiden. Among them were sons of the powerful Transylvanian families. Erzsébet says that the son of an aristocrat was usually accompanied by two capable but penniless students from the village or surrounding district. The aristocrat's family would pay the two villagers' tuition fees and living expenses. In 1692 Mihály Bethlen went to Franeker, as did Pál Teleki in 1696. Wolfgangus Bánffy (known in Hungary as Farkas Bánffy) arrived in Leiden in 1747 to study theology and Joseph Teleki followed in 1760. Until the late eighteenth century, Protestants were not allowed to attend universities in the Habsburg Empire. If they studied there nevertheless, they would not be awarded a degree.

A few years ago I gave a series of lectures at the Dutch faculty of the Eötvös Loránd University in Budapest. At the first lecture I asked my students why they had decided to study Dutch. One of them, who was from Transylvania, said she'd chosen the course because she'd inherited her Transylvanian grandfather's Dutch library.

The aristocracy was essential to the dissemination of culture in Transylvania, and indeed in Hungary, founding academies, opera houses, theatres, libraries, spas, museums and arboreta. Sámuel Teleki was the prototype of this kind of patron. He studied at Utrecht, Leiden, Basel and Paris, and for the rest of his life he was influenced by the ideas of the Enlightenment. He developed an overwhelming desire to found a large library in Transylvania. The collection is still almost entirely intact, with fifty-two incunabula as well as rare works that include prints by Rubens, Dürer, Cranach and Holbein, and tomes featuring signed engravings by Giovanni Battista and Francesco Piranesi. He attempted to build up a broad collection in which both the humanities – theology, philosophy, jurisprudence – and the natural sciences were represented. The works range across time from Aristotle to Rousseau, including books by Luther and Calvin (as with most of Transylvania's aristocrats, nine out of ten Telekis were Protestants), and by Thomasius, Kepler and Newton.

The aristocrats of Hungary and Transylvania were traditionally patrons to new poets and writers. In the seventeenth century the diaries and memoirs of the nobles themselves were the region's most important literary expression. They alone had the time and opportunity to read and write. Virtually everyone else worked on the land.

János Kemény (prince of Transylvania from 1660 to 1662) was seized by the Tartars and taken to the Crimea. During his imprisonment there he compiled the first memoir ever written in Hungarian, and in it he says a great deal about Transylvania. The tradition of writing memoirs continues to this day. Ilona's grandfather wrote an account of his life entitled *Hier bin ich geboren* (This is where I was born). The grandfather of one of the Transylvanians I spoke to had made three handwritten copies of his life story under communism, like a monk. He describes all the property confiscated from the family, with drawings of roads, railway lines, villages and family estates. Based on those drawings, his grandson was able to specify exactly which properties in Romania the state was legally bound to return to him.

For centuries foreign authors had a huge impact on Hungarian literature and philosophy, in part because Hungarian nobles living in exile produced so much literature, such as Ferenc Rákóczi II, whose autobiographical work was influenced by Fénelon and Rabelais. The aristocracy often took its lead from the French Enlightenment. Francophile Transylvanian Count László Haller translated Fénelon's *Télémaque* and Hungarian Count Fekete corresponded with Voltaire. Interest in French Enlightenment thought was even greater in Transylvania, where for centuries there had been a bond with France as an ally and financier in uprisings against the Habsburgs. The ideas of the French Revolution were adapted to local conditions. 'Liberty' meant the nobles' own freedom as defined by the constitution, 'equality' meant the equality of all nobles, and 'fraternity' meant being prepared to cooperate with nobles of a different religious persuasion. They had no intention of extending notions of fraternity and equality to include the non-aristocratic. *Liberté, fraternité, égalité* – but strictly for their own circle.

It was usual for the aristocrats of Transylvania and Hungary to attend Western European universities. They went on trips to France, England and the Netherlands, and since they were subjected to fewer controls at international borders they smuggled Western literature back with them into the Habsburg Empire. Samuel Teleki's wife, Zsuzsanna Bethlen, built up an extensive book collection of her own. Miklós Bánffy at Bonchida and László Toldalaghi in Koronka were the last owners of large private libraries in Transylvania.

Between the wars Baron János Kemény was the publisher of the literary magazine *Erdélyi Helikon*, with Miklós Bánffy as its editor-in-chief. Kemény made his castle in Marosvécs available for an annual gathering of Transylvanian writers. The beautiful Baroness Carola Bornemissza was a muse to them all, and indeed to the Zsigmond Kemény Society in Marosvásárhely, named after a writer, thinker and relative of János Kemény. Carola cooked for the writers and noted down her Transylvanian dishes in an exercise book (published as a cookery book in 1998). She was immortalized by both János

Kemény and Miklós Bánffy in their written works. Bánffy had a barely concealed relationship with her for decades – before, during and after her marriage to Elemér Bornemissza.

In front of the bookcases in the Teleki-téka are low display cases with special editions from the collection. I walk past with my hands clasped at my back and look serious, as if I know all about them. At each glass case I lean forward for a moment. The oldest exhibit in the library is Galeottus Martius' *Liber de homine*, printed in Bologna in about 1475. Samuel Teleki's bookplate is on show too, with the family coat of arms stamped in gold and his motto DEUS PROVIDEBIT. One display case contains several volumes of Blaeu's *Atlas Maior*, brought from Amsterdam in 1689 by typographer Nicolaus Kis (known in Hungary as Miklós Tótfalusi Kis).

After I've been round, my guide tells me they also have rare prints from Plantijn in Antwerp and Elsevier in Leiden. On my way out I cast another glance at the dark arched corridor where three Teleki descendants lived in the 1950s like mice in a bottle.

Purdeys, plus fours
and whist

Marosvásárhely, March 2009

Stefánia Betegh, a woman of blue blood, shows me around the house where she lives with her sister. This kind of elongated, low white house can be found in all the villages of the former Dual Monarchy. It lies in the centre of Marosvásárhely, close to the citadel, a modestly furnished place with several beautiful cupboards and tables. This is where they took in Gemma Teleki after she'd slept on top of a cupboard in the Teleki-téka and then lived in a cellar longer than any of the other aristocrats.

Stefánia: 'I'm very attached to the old things. When I was six, irregular troops from Bessarabia, arriving in the wake of the Soviet Army, looted our house in Fugad. They loaded everything they could carry onto horse-drawn carts and they were planning to murder us. We were alone, just the women and children, and we hid behind the wine vats in the cellar while the pack marauded above us. I heard the heavy tread of boots.

Mother put my youngest sister to her breast to keep her quiet, while the governess held her hands over the mouths of the other little ones. Father was taken away by the Russians. We hoped for years that we'd suddenly see him standing on the front steps, but he never came back. We don't know how or where he died.

'These two glasses come from our house in Fugad. We have two or three things from there. Our governess, Erzsébet Biró, worked for us without pay for another twenty years. She hid the case of silverware under a mound of potatoes in the cellar. That's why we still have a set of table silver, although incomplete. It's ridiculous, but my sister and I always use that cutlery, just the two of us. We eat with it every day, even if it's only a sandwich. We even use it to cook with. I cherish those few things from my childhood.'

Stefánia stands straight as a rod and smiles modestly. 'Ah, now you'll understand why possessions can lead to discord within families.'

 The older Transylvanians were strictly brought up. Seventy-one-year-old Stefánia Betegh told me that as a child she had to stand at the table during meals and open her mouth only when spoken to. After the communists took power, Stefánia worked in a factory from the age of fifteen, making tin cups, knives, forks and spoons. There were a lot of other children at home and they all had to live from what they could grow in the garden, which meant there was little to eat. As a result Stefánia became a fanatical sportswoman, so that she could go to canoeing camps where there was plenty of food.

Stefánia looks energetic and extremely fit. I've visited her a number of times in Marosvásárhely and I can't avoid the impression that the discipline she learnt at an early age helped her to endure deprivation later. Decadence and spoilt behaviour were not tolerated. Practically all the aristocrats I spoke to in Transylvania had had the benefit of such an upbringing, with its patriarchal simplicity.

Pista Pálffy, a friend in Budapest whose family is from Upper Hungary, told me he'd once heard his mother say that she didn't particularly care how he got on at school as long as he behaved like a true gentleman. 'That was the idea behind the way I was raised; you were to behave correctly and to be a good person. My mother had a strict, principled upbringing. Her father was Count Albert Apponyi, the man who refused to sign the Treaty of Trianon and thereby became a Hungarian hero on a par with Winston Churchill. One time she took the train to Fót. She was too late to buy a ticket and no conductor came along, so she paid neither the fare nor a fine. When her father heard that, he made her go to the post office and buy stamps to the value of a train ticket to Fót, then bring them home and burn them. 'My grandfather was a government minister at the time and he believed it was wrong to take money from the state. Can you imagine a minister in present-day Hungary or Romania doing a thing like that?'

Pista's mother told him there hadn't really been any writers who succeeded in properly describing their circle, by which she meant the titled nobility. The one exception was Tolstoy. He was born into it. The same goes for Miklós Bánffy, the Tolstoy of Transylvania. As well as being an aristocrat and the largest landowner in Transylvania, Bánffy was the author of a remarkable trilogy that focuses on the Transylvanian aristocracy. It was published in Hungarian before the Second World War.

His godchild (also called Miklós Bánffy) told me how the trilogy came to be written. A young author, Áron Tamási, had written a novel set in aristocratic circles and he gave it to Bánffy to read. Bánffy read the manuscript and handed it back with the words: 'You're an ass, my son! You know nothing about us at all! I'll show you people.'

In the second volume of Bánffy's trilogy the central character, Count Bálint Abady, relates what his grandfather told him about the family: 'There is nothing at all marvellous or wonderful about it, my boy, and especially there is nothing to boast about. What has happened has been entirely natural. Long ago, when the country folk were all serfs, everything belonged to the landowner, the so-called noble who himself held

it from the king. It was therefore nothing less than his bounden duty to take care of everything, to build what was needed and to repair what needed repairing. That our family have done this only shows that they have always done their duty, nothing else. Let this be a lesson to you!'

Grandfather Abády goes on: 'That members of our family often obtained great positions in the state was no accident and no particular merit to them. Such places were naturally offered to people of high rank, nobles whose fortunes and family connections were necessary if they were to do a useful job. We can be proud that our forebears honestly carried out what was expected of them, that is all. Family conceit because of such things is not only ridiculous but also dangerous to the character of those who come to believe in it.'

A few years ago I read a report in the Dutch daily newspaper *de Volkskrant* about Eton, the English boarding school for descendants of long-established families. I'm convinced it's because of its school system that Britain has so many eccentrics. When I was thirteen I spent a summer at a similar sort of school (Stowe) and I can still remember the dark corridors, the halls, the wide staircases, the grey stone, the follies on islands in the lake, the enormous playing fields, the private golf course, the draughty dormitories, the canteen with sausages and greasy eggs for breakfast, and I can imagine the influence all of that must have on a child's constitution. Sometimes I think the brain is little more than a camera obscura, with an image of the surrounding architecture on its projection screen.

Taking young children away from their parents and putting them in huge Victorian buildings surrounded by parkland and misty meadows, usually with other children of the same sex, and the stress on sports, that strange combination of competitiveness and intimacy – it must all make for a special kind of upbringing. A more distant, more formal relationship with the parents and the development of a phlegmatic character are almost inevitable.

The article about Eton included a list of former pupils and their current occupations. The school continues to produce ministers, explorers, writers, artists, directors, mountaineers, balloonists, ambassadors and the sort of men who walk across Afghanistan with a dog for company. I asked Pista Pálffy in his capacity as expert on the English upper classes – he spends half the year in England and the other half in Hungary – how such a school could calmly go on producing adventurers and eccentrics in this egalitarian age.

'It's very simple,' he said. 'At the average school you don't learn manners. You're put into a mould and taught how to think. At public schools like Eton you learn how to behave, you learn to feel at ease in a dinner suit and tails, you learn how to greet someone and how to get along with all kinds of different people, those formalities that seem so pointless. In short, although you learn manners you're left completely free in your thinking. That's why those schools produce students with true freedom of mind, whereas the state schools turn out people who think in the obligatory clichés: perfect bureaucrats.'

In Hungary and Transylvania I have friends of my parents' or grandparents' age. Theirs is a witty, original, forthright way of speaking, with an elegance and spirit that belong to a different era. You can speak freely about anything. The older generation seems to have a preference for the eccentric, just as the English commonly do. Their childhood, with distant parents, an army of strict governesses and tutors, and castles and palaces with long corridors and extensive grounds, had something of the atmosphere of an English public school.

Erzsébet T. pointed me to John Paget's *Hungary and Transylvania; with Remarks on Their Condition, Social, Political and Economical.* Paget, an Englishman, travelled through Transylvania in 1835-1836 and was received as a guest by the aristocrats. He was introduced to one of them and from there consistently referred on from one castle to the next. Roughly the same happened to me, except that only a few of the mansions and palaces were still inhabited. The grandeur that revealed itself to Paget 175 years earlier seemed consigned to the past, yet the hospitality and the sense of finding yourself in one big family remains. I too was referred on from one to the next and received with tea, wine and dinners.

Paget fell in love with the writer Polixénia Wesselényi, widow of László Bánffy. He married her, absorbed himself in agriculture and viticulture, brought innovations with him from England and was admitted into the Transylvanian nobility in 1847. In the 1848 revolt he fought with the Hungarians against the Habsburgs. After the uprising was put down by the Habsburgs with the aid of the Tsar of Russia, John Paget fled to

England with Polixénia and wrote, in exile, his *Hungary and Transylvania*. In 1855 he returned to the mansion in Aranyosgyéres, where he died in 1892.

John Paget describes the daily life of Transylvanian noblemen in the nineteenth century. Most landowners had large stables with ten or twenty horses. They hunted everything from partridges to wolves. If an aristocrat harboured an ambition to hold public office he could simply have himself appointed deputy governor of the province; if he chose to devote himself to agriculture, thousands of hectares of land were waiting for him, Paget says, and if he wanted to work for a good cause, then there was the peasantry, which depended on him for practically everything and looked up to him.

Paget describes the sense of isolation and how long it took to reach the nearest town, partly because of the poor state of the roads. In the past century and a half this has changed somewhat, but not a great deal. The distances are still considerable. One major difference is that the majority of the remaining aristocrats now live in cities, usually in Marosvásárhely or Kolozsvár. Generally speaking, only the young descendants live in the Transylvanian countryside, in old-fashioned isolation, having taken it upon themselves to renovate family properties recently returned to them, to get those places up and running again.

In the first half of the twentieth century the Transylvanian aristocracy felt strongly attracted by English culture. Aristocrats used English hunting rifles, bred English thoroughbreds, organized fox hunts, went about in plus fours and tweed, had their suits made on Savile Row, played whist and later bridge, even in a few cases studied in Cambridge or London, or married Englishwomen. When Hitler came to power in the 1930s, most Transylvanian nobles sided with the British, partly because they were repelled by the proletarian cast of Hitler and his cohorts. Weren't most Nazis sweaty boors in tight uniforms? Many aristocrats favoured the Allies and opposed any alliance with the Germans; some, including Prime Minister Bethlen, repeatedly expressed this view in the Hungarian parliament.

In his memoirs Miklós Bánffy explains how in Hungary between the wars the influence of the aristocracy, which was generally in favour of reinstating the monarchy, declined under the Horthy regime while the Hungarian gentry, by which he means lesser nobles, gained in influence: 'It must be said that the gentry as a class were far more reactionary and opposed to any form of modernization than the aristocrats had ever been. One can say many things detrimental to the Hungarian aristocracy, but it was certain that they never lost their international outlook.'

Patrick Leigh Fermor crossed Transylvania on foot in 1933-1934 on his way to Istanbul, and in the neighbouring region of Moldavia he fell in love with a Wallachian princess. In his introduction to Miklós Bánffy's Transylvania trilogy he writes: 'The grand world [Bánffy] describes was Edwardian *Mitteleuropa*. The men, however myopic, threw away their spectacles and fixed in monocles. They were the fashionable swells of Spy and late Du Maurier cartoons, and the wives and favourites must have sat for Boldini and Helleu. Life in the capital was a sequence of parties, balls and race-meetings, and, in the country, of *grandes battues*, where the guns were all Purdeys. Gossip, cigar-smoke and Anglophilia floated in the air; there were cliques where Monet, d'Annunzio and Rilke were appraised; hundreds of acres of forest were nightly lost at *chemin de fer*; at daybreak lovers stole away from tousled four-posters through secret doors, and duels were fought, as they still were when I was there. The part played by politics suggests Trollope or Disraeli. The plains beyond flicker with mirages and wild horses, ragged processions of storks migrate across the sky; and even if the woods are full of bears, wolves, caverns, waterfalls, buffalos and wild lilac – the country scenes in Transylvania, oddly enough, remind me of Hardy.'

Forbidden love

Marosvásárhely, 2009

Erzsébet T. admired Carola Bornemissza, Miklós Bánffy's lover, for being such a proud and forthright woman. She tells me that Carola's mother was a Transylvanian countess, but her grandmother came from Hochstadt, where the wine-growers lived, so she was partly of peasant stock. To Erzsébet this explains why Carola was such a strong, brave woman who made other women jealous. She was no hypocrite, never making a secret of her lovers. According to Erzsébet there were

two: Miklós Bánffy, the former Hungarian foreign minister, and István Bethlen, the former Hungarian prime minister. In her salon she had large portraits of both of them in oils, Bethlen on one wall, Bánffy on another.

In Marosvásárhely I meet Emma P., who knew both Miklós Bánffy and

Carola Bornemissza. Emma welcomes me in the corner flat of a residential block of unmistakably communist vintage. The place is full of boxes and reams of paper. Threadbare shawls and tablecloths lie everywhere. Emma is descended from the old Transylvanian nobility. She studied chemistry and at eighty-four she still has an extremely sharp mind, but as soon as I walk into her apartment it's clear to me that she has to get by on very little money.

Emma was born in 1925 in Kolozsvár. She knew Miklós Bánffy in the 1940s, when he was approaching seventy. Baroness Carola Bornemissza was younger than Bánffy. The friendship between Emma and Carola néni ('aunt Carola') was intense, despite their great difference in age. Carola was a great beauty, and she liked to surround herself with eccentrics and artists. For a long time she had a maid whose former lover was a murderer who had been executed. The maid lived in Carola's house, along with her child by the hanged man. A century ago, Carola travelled across South Africa by train, boat and donkey, to erect a gravestone for a cousin who had fought in the Boer War and died in battle. Carola's marriage to Baron Elemér Bornemissza was not a success. They had a child who died young and from then on they lived apart.

Emma: 'On 30 August 1940, the day the northern part of Transylvania was awarded to Hungary under the Treaty of Vienna, when practically all the Hungarians in Kolozsvár paraded through the streets in celebration, Carola néni came into the room crying and said: "Transylvania is being split in two." The rest of the Hungarian population in Transylvania was hysterical with joy, but Carola understood it meant disaster. She was extremely sensitive and intelligent, a really strong woman with a powerful personality that permeated the entire house. In the afternoons I often went to visit her. She would always be lying on the sofa with a violet rug and cushions that had a pattern of white lilies.'

Emma produces a photograph album, oblong with a fabric cover. The pages are of faded black card, and the wafer-thin transparent sheets in between have a spider-web pattern. Emma slowly turns the album towards me. I carefully pick it up.

'That's her; that's Carola néni.'

I'm a ladies' man. I may have seen a woman more beautiful than Carola néni, Baroness Bornemissza, but I couldn't say where or when. On her head is a white nurse's cap. Her face is both powerful and melancholy, radiating a robust pride. The picture was taken during the First World War. 'Carola néni was a volunteer at the front,' says Emma. Of course. How could it be otherwise? A lady with a noble streak, who cares for wounded men, the sort of woman who knows no fear and makes you, as a man, instantly forget your own fear. I hold the album and look at Carola. She must be in her thirties. What a superb face, the dark eyes filled with a mixture of astonishment and wisdom.

Emma: 'In the summer of 1940 we often went to Szamosfalva. Carola néni used to swim in the nude. The young women had reason to envy her; she still had a wonderful body. At that time she had a rule that one day a week she would eat only fruit, nothing else; she was modern in that. She was on the women's committee of the Protestant church and she often went to help János Kemény at his castle in Marosvécs, where all the writers came together in those days. She was the centrepoint of Transylvanian literary life. Her clothes were always elegant, always black and white. Since her son died she'd never worn any other colours. He died very young. She never had any more children after that  and she lived apart from her husband. Carola néni died with the nuns in Kolozsvár. She didn't want to see anyone any longer, not even me.'

Carola Bornemissza passed away in 1948, a year before the entire Transylvanian aristocracy was deported in a single night. She was buried at the Házsongárd cemetery in Kolozsvár. Miklós Bánffy covered her grave in red roses. In 1939 he married an actress from Budapest called Aranka Váradi-Weber; some of the older Hungarian ladies in Transylvania ask themselves to this day what he saw in Aranka.

'I was a child,' Emma says, 'but Miklós Bánffy always spoke to me as if I were an adult. He was the only person who did that. After my grandmother died he was the only one I could

go to. He helped me. It was a difficult time. War brings tragedy. He was a good person, extremely clever and certainly not arrogant. He returned from Budapest to find that the Germans had looted his property. He came to Kolozsvár at the risk of his life to try to save his palace in the city and his country mansion, Bonchida. His actress wife refused to come with him.'

Miklós Bánffy was a discreet man; in his memoirs he writes not a word about Carola Bornemissza.

For four years
we did nothing but dance

'One day a Frenchwoman arrived to be our governess. Jeanne. She was very pretty. All father's friends came to lunch and dinner, leaving their wives at home. One time Jeanne danced for them by the light of flaming torches at the edge of the fountain, scantily clad. That caused quite a fuss. She was sent back to Paris.' Erzsébet goes on: 'The other staff were from the village here or the surrounding district. They often belonged to families that had worked for us generation after generation. Village children would come to us when they were young to be trained as cooks, gardeners or grooms, depending where their aptitudes lay. We had a chapel at the house. The staff attended the morning services there on Sundays. The most faithful servants were buried at Dornafalva.'

I'm hoping the sun will come out. The awful weather has lasted too long. At ninety-one Erzsébet still wants to go to her country cottage in Márianosztra as she does every year, in the hills not far from Vác. She's shaky. Her voice is thin and unsteady, and the skin is stretched tight on her scalp. Two weeks ago she had a heart attack. There's a woman doctor living in the apartment block who helps her. In the two months since I first visited her I've watched her grow more fragile. Erzsébet was not just a relative but a friend of Ilona's grandparents, although they were more than ten years older. Their friendship went back to the 1940s, when Ilona's grandparents lived in Kolozsvár for several years. They once stayed at Dornafalva, Erzsébet's family castle, for three or four days.

'Father was on first name terms with Ilona, your wife's grandmother,' Erzsébet tells me. 'In those days you only used the familiar form of 'you' if you were related; people were absolutely strict about that. Men could be on familiar terms with men, or women with women, but members of the opposite sex always addressed each other formally. Ilona was a beauty, tall, slender and blonde. And half of Kolozsvár was in love with your wife's grandfather.

'I visited your wife's grandmother later, too, in Leányfalu, over on the other side of the Danube. You can get there from here in no time by ferry and bus. But I saw them mainly in Kolozsvár in the 1940s, when Northern Transylvania was made part of Hungary. For the Hungarians it was a gift. There was a cheerful mood, every night a ball. For four years we did nothing but dance. The Hungarian word *mulatni* is derived from "to pass the time". If you say *mulatság*, you immediately think of gypsies, drink, and that's what it was like: wine, beautiful women and music. I was still young then.'

The conversations I have with Erzsébet gradually go further back into the past, to her childhood in the interwar years, at the family castle in Transylvania. A happy childhood is a solid foundation. It's as if the self-confidence that comes from happiness in early years is impossible for any tyrant to knock out of you.

'I was born just before the Treaty of Trianon. According to the first land reform after Transylvania was made part of Romania, which became law in 1921, the Hungarians in Transylvania were allowed to own no more than 200 hectares of arable land. My mother was Countess Bethlen. She died very young, in 1922. When she married my father and came to live at Dornafalva she went to all the houses in the village with a thick notebook and knocked on all the doors, sat round the table with every family and interviewed them: How many peo-

ple live here? How many children? How old are they? Which of them are doing well at school? Is anyone sick? How many chickens do you have? How much land? She noted everything down. Father didn't know what she was doing. She compiled an inventory that identified everyone who needed help, every child who should be encouraged to continue studying, where to find the seriously ill – all without saying a word. Weeks later, when she'd finished, she simply laid the notebook on father's desk, confident that he'd take action where necessary. And he did.

'As a child I wrote a lot. In the winters we were often snowed in for ages and I couldn't go out. My father managed the estate. He got up at six each morning to inspect everything and discuss it all. At harvest time and in the sowing season he'd be up at three. He was an ornithologist, too. We had the largest private collection of stuffed birds in Europe, around 10,000 of them. My father had learnt taxidermy. As an ornithologist and hunter he knew exactly how the birds behaved and how they moved, unlike many other taxidermists. The medal hanging on the wall over there was won by my father in 1937 with a brown bear that he shot in Máramaros. It was the largest bear in the whole of Europe that year.'

I find it moving to hear a woman of ninety-one speak so lovingly and admiringly of her father, almost like a little girl showing off in the school playground. Her mother died when she was three. From then on, in a time when parents behaved formally towards their children, and when governesses, tutors and battalions of servants further increased the distance between parent and child, her father must have been affectionate and caring towards Erzsébet and her brother, who was a year older.

'We always wore old things. Only when there was a ball did everyone dress up. The ermine, the tiaras, diamonds and satin were brought out then, and all the ladies looked like princesses. But normally the aristocrats went around in their old clothes. The Transylvanian aristocracy has never liked to show off. Whenever my father had a new suit made, he would get one of the servants to wear it, to take the newness out of it, before he put it on.'

'When the staff or the children were around, the adults never talked about money, debts, divorce or any juicy matters like that. A man, an aristocrat, never mentioned his mistresses, not even to his best friend. Not a word. At table they talked about books, travel, nature and what would best serve the children's development. We had a fixed daily rhythm: schoolwork from six or seven, breakfast at eight, more studies until twelve, lunch with the nanny. From the age of fourteen you were allowed to take lunch with the adults and from eighteen to dine with them, but you were to speak only when spoken to. Those were the rules with us, and I think with most aristocrats in Transylvania.'

The children were forbidden to complain, whine, snitch, stare, or eavesdrop on other people's conversations – actually everything the Securitate would later specialize in.

Erzsébet: 'We had governesses from Britain, Germany and France, and my brother and I had a tutor. He lived with us. He was a good teacher. You have to teach by showing children things, not just by talking to a class, that's dreadfully boring. Our tutor accompanied us on our trips abroad. We went skiing with him and horse riding, and along the way, as children of eight or nine, we heard all about the ancient Greeks. We lay on our stomachs in bathing suits on the banks of the Szamos while he drew the countries of Europe in front of us in the sand with a stick. He repeated it in the snow with his ski pole in the winter. We did four years of elementary school and four years of grammar school at home. Then I went to Budapest to study for my exams and my brother was sent to the Piarists in Kolozsvár.'

Erzsébet tells me that in Transylvania the eldest son would inherit the castle with its contents and estate, while the daughters and younger sons were given a house in town or a smaller estate, as well as jewellery and investments. All the children received the same amount, in theory. An old lady I knew in Budapest said that in Hungary there was a system of primogeniture. Her father's eldest brother inherited the castle and the estates, whereas the youngest of the brothers received an allowance that was barely enough to buy drink and cigarettes. The sisters were expected to make a good catch. The second and third sons were able to build careers for themselves with the Hussars or in the Church, where they would become bishops. As a result, in Hungary the properties were not divided up, so they were larger.

Immediately before the Second World War there were still thirty-four aristocratic families in Transylvania. They were all interrelated, from a long way back. In *Between the Woods and the Water* Patrick Leigh Fermor quotes a Transylvanian aristocrat as saying that they intermarried more than the Ptolemaians and actually all ought to be insane. One countess, Claudia Rhédey, is the great-great-grandmother of the English queen, so practically all the present-day Transylvanian aristocracy, whichever way you turn, is related to the British royal family. Erzsébet is a seventh cousin of Queen Elizabeth II. According to Erzsébet the rule in Transylvania was that you must not marry a first cousin, but marriage to a second cousin was fine. Mihály Teleki is credited with saying that in Transylvania everyone is related to everyone else, and if you're not related then you have an affair.

Erzsébet says that children born out of wedlock were sent to other castles, where the family would make sure the child was given a good upbringing and perhaps a chance to study abroad. A girl grew up at Dornafalva who was the illegitimate daughter of one of the other aristocrats.

Erzsébet: 'From the age of eighteen, girls were allowed to powder their noses and wear silk stockings and low-cut dresses. They were introduced into society accompanied by their mother or another relative. The boys were allowed to smoke from the age of eighteen, to run up debts and to wear the family's signet ring. Before 1920 it was out of the question for boys and girls to be seen together in public. There were secret rendezvous, usually in the church or at a museum. If children wanted to marry, they consulted their parents, who would settle the issue between themselves. The intended's ancestors were looked up in the *Almanach de Gotha* and their family's property in the land register.' It was a stable world in which everyone knew his or her place. Erzsébet is sitting in her armchair. As darkness falls her eyesight fades. She still has one good eye. I have to go. When I stand up, Erzsébet asks whether I know how to kiss someone's hand. She'll demonstrate.

The hand-kiss

Vienna, February 2010

Every year more than two hundred balls are held in Vienna and fifteen in Budapest. In all the years we've lived in Hungary, Ilona and I have attended Budapest's Opera Ball just once. In the foyer of the Opera House stood gleaming new Audis and Maseratis with the purchase price on a piece of card under the windscreen wiper. The organizers had managed to endow the imposing staircase of the neo-Renaissance building with all the elegance of a car showroom. Every year an internationally renowned sex bomb is flown in as guest of honour. Since 1996 it has been the social event of the year for the Hungarian nouveaux riches. Women parade in highly flammable purple dresses and the former communist nomenklatura ape the aristocracy.

Anyone in today's Hungary who has power, or aspires to it, puts in an appearance at the Opera Ball. The political and business elites show how interconnected they are while the common people watch, gaping at the black Mercedes and stretched Hummers from behind tape barriers near the steps to the Opera House. The ladies imagine themselves archduchesses for the night, their candy-floss hairdos stiff with hairspray. The men in black suits silently shovel one course after another into their mouths, elbows on the table. At Budapest's Opera Ball, like it or not, I was a gentleman among the parvenus, but at the St. Stephen's Ball in Vienna, which Ilona and I will shortly attend, the roles might well be reversed.

The St. Stephen's Ball is also known as the Hungarian Ball or the Szent István *bál*. Dress code: Ladies, long evening dress; Gentlemen, tails with decorations, dinner jacket, or uniform. I don't have any medals, apart from one heavy one for completing the New York marathon. I've never fought in anyone's war, never won myself a hero's reputation.

Keen to avoid looking like a conjurer on a cruise ship, I've had tails made for me by an old Viennese firm. It was a chilly Saturday afternoon. The master tailor mumbled – a row of pins clamped between his lips as he pulled the fabric tight and secured it around my buttocks – that they used to have a regular client from the Netherlands: Prince Bernhard. Perhaps I had indeed come to the right place. I had reached the first floor by climbing a cherry wood spiral staircase. The interior was intimidatingly beautiful: leather chairs, wood panelling and glass cabinets designed by Adolf Loos, the architect of rhythmic simplicity. According to Loos' manifesto *Ornament und Verbrechen*, an ignominious architect can be recognized by his superfluous ornamentation as surely as tattoos are the mark of a criminal.

The official ball season lasts until Ash Wednesday, the first day of Lent. Any professional group in Austrian society that takes itself seriously organizes a ball, so they range from the bonbon ball, the coffee house owners' ball and the shoemakers' ball to the media-besieged Vienna Opera Ball, which takes everything a step further (and has a larger budget) than the Budapest Opera Ball, where they'll invite someone like Paris Hilton or Carmen Electra to be guest of honour. For centuries balls were a court affair, until one of the Habsburg emperors opened the doors of his palace to the bourgeoisie and the democratized Viennese ball tradition was born.

The Szent István *bál* takes place at the Hungarian embassy – a great pile of a building constructed in 1747 as the Hungarian court chancellery (*Hofkanzlei*) – stripped of its desks, computers and filing cabinets. The ceiling is edged with gold-painted ornamentation that would have made Adolf Loos reach for his double-barrelled shotgun.

Only gentlemen with privy-councillor locks and chests heavy with medals actually wear tails. Practically all the men under seventy walk about airily in dinner jackets. In a narrow corridor we come upon a lady in a glacier-blue dress who looks vaguely familiar. Ilona enters into an animated conversation with her, while I stand off to one side smiling politely. Ambrose Bierce called politeness the most enjoyable form of hypocrisy, and almost any polite person will understand what he meant.

It's the perfect evening to practice the hand-kiss. To me this rather archaic greeting, which I'd never seen until I came to Budapest, symbolizes a nostalgia for a time that has gone, the elegant residue of a major imperial power preserved in a minuscule subculture. In 1991 I noticed to my amazement that in Budapest apartments men of my age would kiss the hands of older women and sometimes even greeted their own female contemporaries that way. I couldn't decide what to do. Should I adapt to my new surroundings?

Erzsébet recently demonstrated the correct way to perform the ritual. 'You're the woman now. Stay sitting down,' Erzsébet ordered as she got up. She came to stand in front of me, took my right hand in the palm of hers, lifted it up while turning it so that the back of my hand was uppermost, then bent towards me. 'Four centimetres, never more! You can lean forwards as much as four centimetres – with your shoulders only; never bend your head. Stay standing nice and erect with a straight back. Don't bend from the lower back. That's what the peasants do. The peasants actually used to kiss their lord's hand.' She stuck up an index finger as a warning. 'But you don't kiss the hand, just the air. If a man looked into the woman's eyes as he did it: ohlalala! And even more frivolous was this.' I was being given a lesson in old-fashioned flirting. Erzsébet took my hand again, turned it over carefully so that the inside of my wrist faced upwards. 'If you kissed there...' She rolled her eyes. 'The old saying was that if a lady said "no" she might mean "maybe", if she said "maybe" she meant "yes" and if she said "yes" she wasn't a lady.'

The eighteen-year-old debutants will open the ball in a few minutes from now. They're standing at the top of the stairs, 'ladies' and 'gentlemen', their cheeks aglow with excitement – boys and girls, really, with puppy fat on their chins and jaws. For centuries this was an introduction to court, a rite of passage, an entrance into society. The boys are in tails and have very straight backs, chests thrust out, their right elbows proffered to their partners. The girls are wearing the *párta*, a white cap with embroidery, pearls and silver stitching, tied at the back of the head with a ribbon, and tightly tailored long white dresses with embroidered lace aprons. The long white silk gloves, which reach up beyond the elbow, succeed in making the look as a whole more palace attire than folk costume. Thirteen pairs stand arranged in rows in front of the door to the main ballroom, like a line of racehorses waiting for the gates to open, nostrils trembling with excitement.

We find ourselves in a flood of people politely pushing towards the ballroom. An older woman turns to me, looks me up and down and tells me this entrance is for guests of honour only. The invitation makes mention of a presidium of honour, consisting of a Countess Bethlen and three Archdukes of Austria, along with a ball committee and a forty-strong committee of honour. So that's who they are, the elderly people shuffling in through here. Despite my impeccable Knize suit, I've been rumbled. It's perfectly possible I'm the only unknown person here. There are seven hundred invited guests and I believe they are all related. It's said that in Viennese society everyone has a Hungarian grandmother.

Looking highly respectable, as if at a parade of the royal guards, the debutants enter the ballroom and arrange themselves in a long line. With an elegant bow, the boys focus their attention on the girls. Parents gleam with pride. Deathly silence reigns. Then the orchestra at the back strikes up, not with Strauss and a waltz but with a *palotás*, the palace version of the *csárdás*, the Hungarian national dance, best danced on a stamped-earth floor after five *pálinka*s and accompanied by drunken gypsies on the fiddle, musical saw and cymbals. It's great that they open with this dance, except that the Hungarian-Austrian debutants dance the *palotás* in Austrian style, with military precision and a clear devotion to duty. The Hungarian irrationality is lacking.

After the *Ausgleich* in 1867, Hungary went through a period of intense Magyarization. Hungarian rather than Latin became the language of parliament, while Hungarian literature flourished, Buda and Pest amalgamated, a building frenzy took possession of the Hungarians and Budapest grew into the metropolis it now is. Nationalism, repressed since the 1848 revolt, was revived. Even the ball traditions changed after the *Ausgleich*. The women started wearing traditional Hungarian attire, and nobles who declined to arrive at a ball in *díszmagyar*, Hungarian national dress, were regarded almost as traitors. The *palotás* and later in the evening the *csárdás* became the dances of Hungarian balls. The Viennese waltz was banished to the city from whence it came.

In the twenty-first-century the St. Stephen's Ball in Vienna opens with the Hungarian *palotás*, whereas the Opera Ball in Budapest opens with a Viennese waltz. Why is that? Dramatizing just a little you could say that the Budapest Opera Ball represents the future and the Viennese St. Stephen's Ball the past. Despite the primitive and in some ways entrancing vitality that emanates from those women with bulging bosoms and those corpulent men with bull necks at the Budapest Opera Ball, that unrestrained urge to climb, I believe my preference inclines towards the past. Less visible breasts, less breadth to the shoes, less ruthless ambition and naivety; more elegance, more *weltschmerz*, more history, a more deeply ingrained culture, and more stories.

In *Il Gattopardo (The Leopard)* by Giuseppe Tomasi di Lampedusa, the love-hate relationship between Don Fabrizio, prince of Salina, and the enterprising nouveau riche Don Calogero Sedára gradually develops into a kind of admiration on Don Fabrizio's part. Calogero solves all sorts of problems in a trice: 'Free as he was from the shackles imposed on many other men by honesty, decency and plain good manners, he moved through the forest of life with the confidence of an elephant.'

At the Opera Ball I could tell I was surrounded by confident elephants; at the grand St. Stephen's Ball in Vienna it becomes clear how relative these things are and suddenly I feel I'm the elephant, moving through the forest of life unimpeded by any burden laid on me by the past.

After the opening, Ilona and I set off through the many rooms to find the table where we have been seated for dinner. We've joined up with Gergely and Zsolna Roy Chowdhury, who have put together a table. We wanted to be certain we wouldn't end up surrounded by elderly people. We know

Gergely from Budapest. He's the son of a Transylvanian countess who managed to flee Romania as a young woman in 1960. Gergely is thirty-three and grew up in Austria, but he's been living in Transylvania for the past eight years, attempting to renovate the centuries-old property that belonged to his mother's family, the Mikes counts. He's married to Zsolna Ugron, a journalist born in Transylvania and brought up in Budapest.

It's a table for twelve. To my left sits Zsolna, to my right a young American opera singer who spouts nothing but platitudes. She's enraptured by Europe and is trying to find work in Vienna while getting by on singing lessons and intermittent jobs. The young man next to Zsolna is in forestry. I turn my attention to him. He manages the family forests in Austria. A good bit younger than me, he's a pleasant, enthusiastic chap, without the stiffness that attaches to some in the room. I ask whether he's going to clear-fell whole parcels of land.

'We try to fell patches here and there and leave plenty standing, but because it's a mountainous region you can't always do a terribly precise job of it. The most difficult part is getting the trees out.'

'Yes, everything depends on the roads.'

I picked up this bit of wisdom a few months ago in Transylvania. A former Securitate agent explained to me that the economic value of a forest depends on its accessibility. The roads determine how easily, or not, you can harvest the timber.

'We're in a suitable location, a place where forestry is long established. We have a lot of good roads, made of hardcore, 400 kilometres in all. They're passable with heavy equipment and semitrailers all year round.'

'And how many hectares of forest do you manage?'

'Eight thousand.'

Eight thousand hectares is more than sixteen thousand football pitches. On flat terrain that's already a good amount, but in a mountainous area it's vast. I wasn't fully paying attention when I went round shaking hands with everyone at the table, but later I understand that his name is Liechtenstein.

The food is abominable, but we're surrounded by a racket to rival a cormorant colony. The festivities go on until four in the morning. People loosen up with every hour that passes. Outside the night is raw and dark, but in here the crystal chandeliers throw light in all directions. I imagine that the downfall of the Dual Monarchy must have taken place in roughly the same atmosphere of *gaieté* and *laisser faire*, in a glow of intoxication. People drank, smoked, dined, conversed, gambled, flirted and danced until morning. Then they drew back the curtains and the old empire was gone.

Part 2

They were divided

Darabokra szaggattatol

SLOVAKIA

Budapest

Szatmár

Sighet

Baia Ma

R. Szamos

Gherla/Armenierstadt

Bánffy palace

Oradea

Bonchida

Kolozsvár

Pusztakar

Bánffy mansion

Aranyosgerend

Aiud

Kükűllőv

R. Maros

TRANSYLVAN

Timișoara

Laposnyak

Lázár mansion

Déva

ROMANIA

BÁNÁT

SERBIA

🏰 Castle

🏛 Mansion

🏛 Palace

🏛 Prison

💂 Labour camp

Above 1000 m

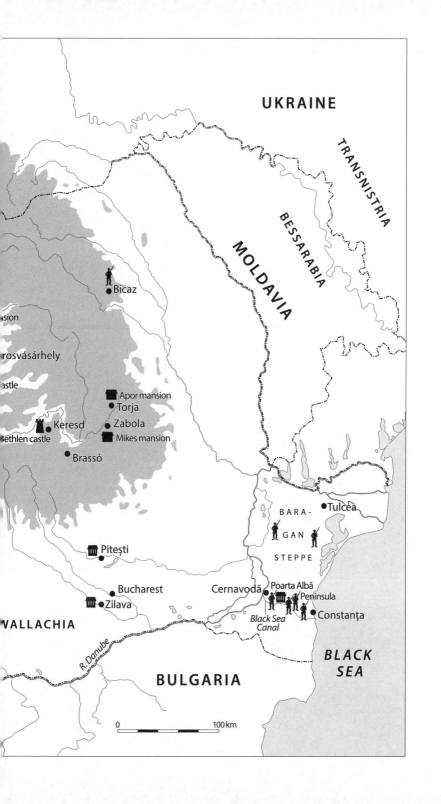

I heard the dogs barking

Marosvásárhely, March 2009

A fter the deportation of 3 March 1949, the government was able to tell the plenary meeting of the Central Committee of the Romanian Workers Party in Bucharest that all large landowners had been demoted overnight. Sixty years later, almost to the day, I'm travelling through Transylvania to speak to the victims.

As in all the new satellite states of the Soviet Union, the Kremlin exerted great pressure, demanding fast and ruthless land reform. For the Romanian Workers Party it was essential to strike the right balance. Suffering a shortage of horses and cattle, and a series of bad harvests, the Romanian people were on the verge of starvation in the immediate post-war years. The peasants were needed, so care would have to be taken that twelve million rural Romanians did not turn against the regime. The expropriation of land from large landowners was a prelude to expropriations from more modest farmers and eventually small farmers too. To that end a body called the Agrarian Commission was established, chaired by Ana Pauker, who enjoyed Stalin's personal protection, although she was later forced out of the party leadership nonetheless. The Commission was composed of the inevitable Soviet advisor, the Romanian agriculture minister and three others, one of whom, Nicolae Ceaușescu, was starting to make a career for himself.

Anikó Bethlen is seventy-one. She lives in Marosvásárhely, the capital of the Széklerland (Székelyföld) in eastern Transylvania, where a majority of the population is ethnically Hungarian and where quite a few descendants of Hungarian aristocrats still live. Most of the meetings I'm to have in Marosvásárhely over the coming months will take place as a result of Anikó's help as an intermediary; she is the city's social focal point. She's lying on a sofa bed in a room crammed with books, boxes of newspapers and magazines, and collections of pots, pans and earthenware dishes. At the foot end are two fat *vizslas*, usually lightning-fast Hungarian hunting dogs. Anikó is partially paralysed.

'I was visiting my grandmother in Marosvásárhely with my sister, because we were at school there. On 3 March my parents suddenly appeared at the door with some luggage. The previous night a group of armed men had come and roused them from bed, along with my youngest sister, but they weren't brought into town until the afternoon. The authorities in the village had tried until midday to stop the deportation, because my parents did so much for the villagers. As a doctor my mother treated the sick free of charge. My father had distributed wheat on loan after a terrible drought. But the Securitate and militia refused to relent and they were brought to Marosvásárhely later that same day, by horse and cart.'

The Apor family had lived in the house on their estate in Torja since the fifteenth century. Kati Apor's grandfather is now eighty-eight. He gave up riding after being thrown by a horse last year. A giant of a man, he radiates rustic angularity and infectious energy. Grandfather Apor was twenty-eight on the night of the deportation. He tells me about it in German.

'I heard the dogs barking and a lot of people approaching. Then a knock on the front door and there stood a man with a small army behind him. He said he was the mayor and he was looking for my father. I replied that my father was asleep and asked them to come back in the morning. I was ordered to open the door immediately. They came inside, armed with rifles and hand guns, some fifteen of them. Aunt Tima from Zabola was staying with us and she asked them who they were. They told her they were a committee, to which Tima exclaimed: "Oh, thank goodness! I thought for a moment you were a gang of bandits." They woke father and mother and told us that everything had been expropriated. We were to get dressed. They gave us half an hour, saying we couldn't take anything with us, and led us out to a truck. There was already one family in it. Kulaks they were, affluent farmers. Four families were deported from Torja and the surrounding district. When they'd got us all out of bed and out of the house we left. The truck stopped among the fields and we thought: now they're going to shoot us.'

Katalin Mikes is sixty-four, refined and unassuming. Katalin's mother was staying with the Apors on the night of 2-3 March. The two estates are twenty-three kilometres apart as the crow flies. The Mikes family, which was composed of three generations of women at the time, no longer lived in the main house in Zabola but in a small outbuilding in the park, the same house that Katalin is living in again now, sixty years later. She speaks beautiful English, searching for the right words. Katalin was alone with her grandmother that night. She was four.

'There was a group of them, one woman and four or five men. They hammered on the door. My grandmother was frightened and refused to open up, so they smashed the glass, forced the lock and came in. Grandmother said they could take everything, but please, they must leave us in peace. They said it was us they were after, not our things. We were given half an hour to get dressed. Grandmother wasn't allowed to go up to fetch extra clothing for us, only to put some food and the clothes we had with us in a bag. Then we were loaded onto a truck. The shards of glass from the smashed door were lying on the steps. That image is engrained on my memory.'

Emma P. is eighty-four. She doesn't want me to use her surname. She describes it all with clarity and precision. Her stepfather and brother were held in Romanian labour camps and prisons; her stepfather also spent time in Russia as a prisoner of war. All her relatives survived the camps but refused ever to speak about them. On her father's death in 1938 she had become the owner of the family estate along with her brother and sister. At the time of the mass deportation Emma wasn't living on the estate but in Marosvásárhely, so she evaded capture, for a while at least. She speaks in German. She was twenty-four at the time.

'Everyone was taken to the nearest village hall. A truck was waiting there. No one knew what they were planning. They made my husband get dressed quickly. He had only unmatched shoes, but he wasn't allowed to go and get any others. He was permitted to take only one shirt. The authorities made a list of the possessions they found. A year later you had to sign an incomplete list of things they'd taken. You had no choice. In the meantime the house was looted, completely stripped. My sister was taken away on 3 March. She's a writer, but she wasn't allowed to take a single book with her, no notebook, no notes, nothing. She had to leave years' worth of work behind. She never saw any of it again.'

Béla Bánffy is seventy-three, a large man, descended from one of the most powerful Transylvanian families. For more than forty years he was a factory worker, a gatekeeper and a truck driver. He tells me his story in Hungarian.

'We lived in Hungary from 1944 to 1947, having fled the war and reprisals by the Romanians and Russians against the Hungarian Transylvanians. When we got back to our estate near Hadad in Romania in 1947, the house and land had been expropriated. So the communists didn't need to do that on 3 March 1949. By then we were living in Kolozsvár, where my father owned a wine business. They took it from him in 1949. My younger brother and I were excluded from school. There was a new law that said the children of barons and factory owners no longer had a right to an education. I started work in a factory at the age of thirteen.'

Stefánia Betegh, seventy-one, is not large in stature but she has a powerful face. She wears shoes with bouncy soles and looks as if she'd have no difficulty running a half-marathon. Her father was taken away by the Russians in October 1944. She and her mother, younger brother and sisters were living on the family estate in Fugad, close to Aiud. She was ten. She speaks English.

'It was a life full of uncertainty. We kept hoping father would come back. The estate in Fugad was from my mother's side of the family. Apart from us, a Bánffy family and some servants, the villagers were all Romanian peasants. When the armed militia arrived in a truck to take us away, the villagers came to our house and stopped them from deporting us. The peasant population wasn't going to allow a mother with children to be loaded onto a truck in the middle of the night. Mother lived on the Fugad estate for another seven years after that. The house fell into a terrible state of disrepair because it had been comprehensively looted by irregulars from Bessarabia during the war. She had no money to do it up and she was forced to leave in 1956 because it was on the point of collapsing.'

Pál Lázár is seventy, a wiry, lively man. In 1949 his father was in prison for 'acts of sabotage' against the regime. Along with his mother and younger brother, he was living on the Lázárs' family estate, Laposnyak, in southern Transylvania. He tells me, in Hungarian, about his experiences.

'They arrived everywhere the same night and said the land and all our property had been nationalized. My mother refused to sign the expropriation papers because my father was in prison. There was a Jewish man who said she'd better sign, that it wouldn't change anything about her current situation and refusing would only make things worse. He was right about that, because if you didn't sign you were persecuted. My mother was really frightened; she thought she was the only one being targeted. When the truck arrived in Déva, the provincial capital, and she saw all the other aristocrats being held by the militia she was relieved.'

Kati Ugron is forty-three. She was born a Lázár, a niece of Pál Lázár. She has a sonorous voice and speaks English with a lilting accent, which makes her instantly likeable. Her father died recently and she is still in mourning for him. It was he who told her the stories of the deportation.

'My mother was in Marosvásárhely looking after my grandmother. Father was running the estate in Fiatfalva. In the middle of the night the Securitate came. They waited for him to get dressed and ordered him to empty his pockets. Then they grabbed him by the arm to take him away, but he wanted to fetch a handkerchief. The Securitate said that if they didn't have handkerchiefs, he didn't need one either. They tried to make him leave his wedding ring behind. Father told them that wasn't customary. His friends teased him about that for years: How come you know what is or isn't customary when you're dragged from your bed by the Securitate in the middle of the night?'

György Ugron is sixty-seven. He's a distant relative of Ádám Ugron, Kati's husband. His suit and shoes are of a cut and quality that is unmistakably Eastern European. On 3 March he was living in Pusztakamarás, forty kilometres to the east of Kolozsvár. He was seven years old. He tells me about it in Hungarian.

'In a single night, all the rich and aristocratic families were deported, but our story is a bit different from the others. They knocked at the door in the middle of the night and checked our identity papers. We were all at home, my parents and my two brothers. My grandparents were in the other house we owned in Pusztakamarás. My grandfather had just come back from Siberia, where he'd been a prisoner of war of the Russians. Everyone was allowed to pack a bag with clothes and enough food for one day. On the edge of the village a truck was waiting for us. There was one other family in Pusztakamarás, the Keménys. They were also deported. My father was a lawyer and he wanted to know under what law we were being held. It turned out that every family still in possession of fifty or more hectares of land was to be taken away. My father protested that the land had never been transferred to his name. The militia men rang their boss in Kolozsvár. Sure enough, the land registry didn't have my father recorded as the owner. In the end we weren't loaded onto the waiting truck.

'When morning came we each had to pack a suitcase. Among other things, they made us take a knife, fork and spoon – not silver, of course. We were transferred to a small farmhouse in Pusztakamarás. Later that morning we quickly took some of our furniture to peasants in the village for safe keeping. The men who had come in the night to fetch us were supposed to compile a list of everything they found, but instead their wives arrived the next day by bus from Kolozsvár. Walking back to the bus stop at the end of the afternoon, every one of them was followed by two peasants carrying suitcases with the things they had collected in our house. Depending how intelligent they were, they'd packed either oil paintings or *pálinka, kolbász* and bacon, but of course they all realized they should take gold and silver.'

Charlady offers
her services

Vác, September 2009

'While half of Kolozsvár was in flames, and Romanian and Russian troops were fighting the Hungarians and Germans at the edge of the city, we were married in the Mátyás Church. I only just managed to get a message to father, to let him know. He sent a telegram back: "Every happiness!"'

I'm sitting in the flat in Vác with Erzsébet T. She tells me how in the final year of the Second World War she served as a volunteer nurse for sixteen hours a day at the hospital in Kolozsvár and married a surgeon. She'd received two previous offers of marriage but declined. She'd grown up in Dornafalva, the most beautiful castle in Transylvania, and she wasn't going to exchange it for a lesser castle. Those earlier suitors didn't particularly thrill her anyhow. She speaks affectionately about everything to do with the castle and her youth. The castle was the great love of her life.

'Not very long before that, I'd managed to travel to Dorna-falva again. Father had all the valuables in the house bricked up in a room in a tower, invisible to casual looters: paintings, jewels, carpets, including the d'Anjou tapestry presented to my forefathers in the fourteenth century by a Hungarian queen.'

Kolozsvár station was under continual enemy fire. The Russians were trying to stop trains from leaving the city. The railway staff, Hungarian soldiers, passengers and the wounded were all crammed together in the station's small air-raid shelter. Erzsébet had the good fortune to be able to leave Kolozsvár with her new husband in a train with seventy carriages packed full of the wounded, the dying and as much hospital equipment as possible. They headed westwards, across ruined Europe, ahead of the advancing front line, finally ending up with their casualty transport at Zellerfeld in Germany. There Erzsébet worked as a nurse until 1947. She then moved to Hungary, but it was no longer possible to return to Transylvania. The border was closed. In Hungary the regime treated the class enemy almost as harshly as in Romania. As a countess, Erzsébet was eligible only for manual labour.

'For many years I worked as a cleaner. I found a job with an engineer who was married to a peasant woman. I spent seven years working for Mrs. Szabó. I arranged everything in the house. First of all I told her she should take down the portrait of Lenin that was hanging on the wall. A thing like that belonged in an office or a chancellery, I explained to her; you don't hang a politician on the wall at home – a writer or a painter at the outside. So that worked out fine. I taught her everything. If I gave her a list of a hundred French words to learn, the following day she'd know them all off by heart. And a day later she could still remember them. Her head had simply never been used until then. I had to teach her how to lay the table, how to cook, how to give a dinner party, how to dress, how to go to the Opera, how to hold a conversation.

'When she held a dinner she would hire silverware and porcelain crockery. I laid and served, because no one else knew how to serve from the left. I wore a black skirt, a white apron, one of those white caps in my hair, and of course white gloves. After the meal I washed up the porcelain, so it was ready for returning, and the cutlery too, which had to go back in the silverware case. I didn't mind doing that at all. I've always liked order. It was fine, clearing up, making people happy that way. It's good to come back to a tidy room after a day at work. One time the hostess came into the kitchen and told me the guests would like me to go and sit with them. I explained why, unfortunately, that wouldn't do at all: "Mrs. Szabó, you want everything to be the way it used to be at the count's home. Well, that never happened there; the maid never came to sit with the guests."

'Mrs. Szabó's husband was a technocrat who was making a career for himself in communist Hungary. The woman of the house, this peasant, spent ten years leading the kind of life that meant she had to rely on me to teach her all the niceties. Then she returned to the village she came from, to her adobe farmhouse, leaving her engineer behind. Her true happiness lay in nature, with the cows. She'd lived a great life, travelled abroad, seen all the operas in Budapest, but it wasn't her life. Her heart was always with the meadows, the cornflowers and daisies in her village. I went to visit her there once. A thoroughly good person.

'After seven years working for Mrs. Szabó, I had to look for a job again, so I pinned up notices in shops: "Charlady offers her services." Later I painted ceramics. The wages were low but I learnt a good deal. I found these chairs thrown out with the rubbish. It's fairly easy to use fabric from furniture to make little tablecloths. I made some two hundred and sold them. The cloth on the table here comes from a blouse my grandmother was given by the dalai lama when she travelled through Tibet.

'In 1971, with the money I earned in all those years as a cleaner, I bought a bit of land at the foot of the hills, in Márianosztra. I was able to buy one hectare, for a price of 70,000 forint. One hectare of forest. I spent the first two years clearing it, the whole stretch. It was a mess. All that grew there were scrawny acacia trees and weeds, man-high. Nothing else. I refused to accept any help from anyone. It was a test; I wanted to see whether I could do it on my own, whether I could make something out of nothing. I worked at it for forty years. There's a small house. I live there all summer.

'I can't say that my life has been hard; that's just a point of view. It could have been considerably harder. My husband and I separated because my aristocratic background was a threat to his career. We obtained an official divorce. After the divorce came through I was harassed for four years by the ÁVH, the Hungarian security service. They wouldn't leave me alone. I was picked up and interrogated for hours at night. But I didn't give anything away.'

Erzsébet tells me that under oppression people acquired a flowery way of speaking that was hard for others to follow. For example, if someone said on the telephone 'Do you perhaps have the time to call round?' it meant you must go to them immediately. Erzsébet: 'We relied on each other for survival. We knew everything about one another, but we never spoke about any of it explicitly. Everything was veiled.

'My brother managed to flee to Western Europe and create a good life for himself. I was in Hungary, my father in Romania. Immediately after the war, father sent postcards that made it clear my brother shouldn't go back. He wrote: "I've bought new livestock. What a shame my son doesn't want to return to help me with the cows."'

Erzsébet still hasn't told me what happened to her father between 1945 and 1955, nor what befell the castle. She's offered me just a few glimpses: how the Russians split the large conifer

 in the courtyard with a bayonet; how the villagers used the castle doors, which dated from the Renaissance, to build a latrine in the grounds; how the sixteenth-century ceiling paintings were destroyed, the castle plundered and later largely demolished so that the stone could be used elsewhere. The Russians didn't discover the hidden treasure-chamber, but it was ransacked later, probably by the men who bricked it up. I conclude that Erzsébet's father was no longer at Dornafalva to prevent that from happening. 'It was the time of *sjetskonesko*; everything belonged to everyone. Father became known as *Tovarăş Conte*, comrade count.'

On top of the bookcase in Erzsébet's apartment are two birds, a red-crested pochard and a common sandpiper. They've been carefully stuffed. The sandpiper looks alert, with its right foot raised. The duck has turned its rust-brown head to one side, lifted high, as if it can hear something in the distance. The birds were returned to Erzsébet recently by a villager in Dornafalva. Her father worked on them with his own hands for hours. Erzsébet looks at them affectionately. These are the only survivors. She describes how the entire collection was hurled out of the windows at Dornafalva after her father left the house. I imagine thousands of stuffed birds flying. Down in the valley, in a cloud of billowing feathers, they break their necks with a snap.

Bridal suites
and celibacy tax

Baia Mare, September 2009

The border crossing between Hungary and Romania at
Şimian is sensational. After leaving Hungary, where two
sleepy customs officials wave me through in surprise, I drive
200 metres across no man's land. The road is lined with tall,
closely planted spruce trees. The white line at the centre of
the road has almost worn away. At the end of the avenue of
spruce is the Romanian border post, a building of faded-green
corrugated metal, like a hanger someone has driven straight
through, front and back. Beneath it are two customs cubi-
cles. The terrain, covering a hectare if you include the green
hangar and the tree-lined avenue, ought to be transplanted
in its entirety to an open air Museum of Communism. It's all
here, everything intimidating, unnerving, lousy, cheap, tasteless. The urge to control.

At the Dana Hotel in Satu Mare only the bridal suite is
available. Room 208. They give it to me for the price of a nor-

mal room. It's nine in the evening – understandably perhaps, they're not expecting freshly married couples to turn up unannounced at this time on a Monday night. If the receptionist hadn't mentioned it was the bridal suite, I wouldn't have noticed. The room, with its square, light-brown laminated furniture looks more like a provincial assistant manager's office.

The next night, in Baia Mare, I again sleep in the bridal suite, this time in Casa Rusu. On stepping into the room you, or at least I, can think of only one thing: sex! There's a vast bed with a panther pattern on the cover, a large mirror across from the bed, gleaming gold fabric stretched tight against the walls and a red, deep-pile, synthetic carpet that runs forty centimetres up the walls. Above the bed hangs a length of material draped in a circle, as if someone has parachuted in through the ceiling, and on the wall is a device that sprays scent into the room every so many seconds. The doors are padded with fake leather and there's an adjoining en-suite room with another double bed, this time with a zebra-print cover. The point of the second-round bed is a mystery. Sometimes I think that the greater the terror in a given country – Romania, Albania – the more traumatized and unstable it still is twenty years later. The bridal suite at Casa Rusu has all the allure of a Belgian brothel, endearingly raunchy. Young couples will need to watch what they do with their post-coital cigarettes – the room would go up like a torch.

Ceauşescu intruded even into the intimacies of marriage. Romanians were ordered to have a bit of fun in bed once more. In 1966 he issued decree 770, forbidding abortion and contraception. Condoms and the pill were smuggled into the country, but there were also price reductions and tax benefits to encourage people to have large families. Single women paid a celibacy tax. Not getting pregnant was a form of treason and sex education was forbidden. Love life was to be industrialized. There was a phase when women were herded together at

work every three months in the presence of government functionaries – quickly dubbed the 'menstruation police' by ordinary Romanians – to be tested for pregnancy and interrogated about their sex lives. The most intimate things became
matters of state. Nicolae Ceauşescu announced: 'The foetus is
the property of society.' Sixty per cent of pregnancies ended in
a back room somewhere with a quack wielding knitting nee-
dles. A shortage of milk, food and medical care pushed child
mortality up to 83 per 1,000 births (more than eight times the
rate in the West in the same period).

Historical Atlas of Central Europe by Paul Robert Magocsi has
never been bettered. On page 24 is a large map from 1815 – not
so very long ago, really. It shows the borders as drawn by the
allied powers at the Congress of Vienna that year. The map is
in four colours: pink for the Russian Empire in the top right-
hand corner, purple for the Prussians at the top left, grey for
the Habsburg Empire in the middle and light green for the
Ottoman Empire at the bottom right.

To the Habsburg Empire and its sphere of influence belonged Hungary, Transylvania, Galicia, Moravia, Bohemia,
Austria, Tyrol, Lombardy, Venice, Tuscany, Dalmatia, Croatia, Slovenia and Slovakia. The Ottoman Empire included Bosnia, Serbia, Wallachia, Moldavia, Greece and present-day Turkey, while Albania, Montenegro, Macedonia and Kosovo bear
the name 'Rumeli' and Bulgaria is labelled 'Silistra' – all ruled
by the Ottomans.

The map makes it easy to understand why certain alliances
arose: Germans and Ottomans collaborated from time to time
against their neighbour Russia. Nothing does so much to encourage friendship as a common enemy. The French supported anyone eager to put a spoke in the wheel of the great power
at the centre, the Habsburg Empire, whether they were Serbs,
Transylvanians or Slovaks. The map explains to me the tradi-

tional alliance between Russia and France, aimed at keeping all those German-speaking people between them under control. But most striking of all is the way the eastern and southern borders of the Habsburg lands are formed by the crescent-shaped curve of the Carpathians. Several Transylvanians have said to me: 'Europe stops just beyond Transylvania.'

One of the people I spoke to said that the culture of chivalry and honour reached no further than the peaks of the Carpathian mountains. Beyond them, although they didn't say it in so many words, lay Barbaria. The influence of four hundred years of Ottoman rule on the eastern side of the Carpathian range should not be underestimated. Daily I see around me how four decades of communism have influenced Hungary and Transylvania, even though there are still people living who remember an earlier time.

Botond, a friend, a member of a breakfast club I belong to and a relative of Anikó Bethlen, told me about growing up in Marosvásárhely in the 1980s, under Ceauşescu. It was the period when households had electricity for just two hours in the morning and a few hours in the early evening. Practically everything was rationed and to buy meat you relied on the black market. You led a double life. At school you carefully concealed your origins – Botond's mother is Baroness Kemény, an offence serious enough to see a person excluded from everything for life – perhaps confiding in a best friend but no one else. They lived in a block of flats, but the interior breathed a vanished world: the old cupboards, the books, the carpets on the floor, the framed photographs. Occasionally they found minor family possessions at the market and bought them back; sometimes villagers returned things they'd managed to salvage from the family home.

Botond's grandmother lived with them, perpetually afraid of the black car that came to fetch you in the dead of night. She spoke Hungarian, German, French and Romanian. After

3 March 1949 she worked as a cleaner. Later she made leather gloves at home, on a metal last in the shape of a hand, while listening to Radio Free Europe at whisper-volume. Botond told me that he was still scouring every flea market and antiques shop in Transylvania for his grandmother's glove-making last. If Botond or his brother were ill, their grandmother would come and sit with them in that dark house and tell them about the past.

Botond: 'My grandmother was strong and quiet, but if she found us in bed with a fever she would start telling stories. She told us about her childhood, about holidays on Capri and in Lugano. We listened to her for hours. It was wonderful to be ill. We knew we were different, but we didn't really know how.'

Botond was the first of my contemporaries to tell me about communist Romania from his own direct experience. When he was a child, class was never spoken about. Botond's grandparents were among those removed from their homes on 3 March, and once again the family library was thrown outside and burned. It included a collection that had belonged to the nineteenth-century writer Zsigmond Kemény – an ancestor – and without anyone batting an eyelid that too was tossed onto the burning heap. The deported Kemény children, including Botond's mother, were each allowed to take one toy with them.

The destruction
of the elite

Sighet, September 2009

For Romania's Orthodox Christians, the feast of Dormition, commemorating the burial of the Holy Virgin Mary, is almost as important as 15 August, the feast of Assumption. In Negreşti, a provincial town between Satu Mare and Sighet, it seems as if the inhabitants of all the surrounding villages have laid their work aside and poured in by car, bus and horse-drawn cart. There's a market. The streets are filled with fat peasant women in cheerful skirts and floral headscarves. They're in excellent mood. With legs like hippos, they swirl their skirts frivolously with every step. Among them walk gypsy women in grass-green and fire-truck-red attire.

In Certeze, a village just outside Negreşti, whopping great houses have been built, three or four storeys high. They must be virtually impossible to heat in winter. They're almost as big as the megalomaniac blocks of flats Ceauşescu built along the broad avenues in Bucharest for his most faithful followers.

Some of the houses in Certeze compete with each other not just in size but in ornamentation, with decorative stucco friezes and concrete lions. One such palace is faced entirely with dark-grey veined marble: Caligula meets Ceaușescu.

The villagers are in France, earning the money to finance the building boom. Whole villages in this part of Máramaros moved to France en masse to make their fortunes with hard, filthy work. I see more stray dogs in the streets than people.

Sighet is another fifty kilometres further east, close to the Ukrainian border, a small town of 45,000 people in the far north of Transylvania. Its centre has the feel of a typical provincial town from the time of the Dual Monarchy: a long central square with stately, highly ornamented houses in pastel tints. There's a baroque Catholic church and right in the middle of the square an imposing Habsburg-yellow town hall, first rebuilt as a cinema and now divided into small bars and cafés of the worst kind. No one feels responsible for repairing the shared toilet, which is flooded, so that the dark interior of the building – no one feels called upon to replace the blown light bulbs either – is saturated with a smell so penetrating it makes your eyes water.

In Hungarian the town is called Máramarossziget. In 1910 eighty per cent of the residents were Hungarian, a figure that now stands at fifteen per cent. Sighet has two sad claims to fame. It's known as the birthplace of the writer, Auschwitz survivor and Nobel Prize-winner Elie Wiesel, one of 600,000 Jews who in 1944, after the German occupation began, were put on transports to Auschwitz from Hungary and Northern Transylvania. Hardly any of them survived. Then there's the prison. Under communism it was one of the five most notorious jails in Romania, along with Jilava, Aiud, Gherla and Pitești. Erzsébet T.'s brother was held here in 1944 before he was taken to Russia.

The prison building, in a narrow street, is fairly inconspicuous. It could be a school, a warehouse or a small clothing factory. The entrance is remarkably narrow. Prisoners were brought in through that door and in many cases never left again. Thanks to the efforts of a number of determined Romanian intellectuals, most famous among them the writer Ana Blandiana, the former prison is now Sighet Memorial Museum, part of the Memorial of the Victims of Communism. Hundreds of people visit the museum every day. It's the only project of its kind in Eastern Europe. The number of locations recognized as part of the Memorial is extremely limited. (According to figures produced by Marius Orpea of the Institutul de Investigare a Crimelor Comunismului şi Memoria Exilului Românesc, or IICCMER, an organization that investigates the crimes of communism, over 600,000 people were either held in prisons or labour camps or deported, 10,000 were officially sentenced to death, 7,000 were illegally executed and an estimated 200,000 died in prisons, labour camps or torture chambers.)

On the back of a folder showing a map of the prison is a text by Ana Blandiana: 'Memory must be a road not only to the past but also to the future. The Sighet Museum will be the museum of all Romanian post-war prisons, the museum of a country which, in the end, itself became a prison, even a prison of minds, in which the echo of terror still persists. With pain, reason and hope, by comparing ourselves in space with those around us, by comparing ourselves in time with our past and future, the Sighet memorial will gather, present and analyse the evidence of our collective memory, transforming it into history.'

Before setting out I told my Hungarian friends that I was going to try to spend a night in a Romanian cell. The response, demonstrating the distrust of Hungarians towards everything Romanian, was invariably: 'Just you be careful and make sure they let you out again!' I want to sleep in a cell in Sighet tonight not because I'm sick to death of bridal suites but because

I'm so naive as to think it will give me some idea – the cold, the hard bed, the sense of oppression – of what it's like to be held in a cell like that. I ask the friendly woman at the front desk.

'No, only groups from Bucharest can stay overnight,' she says firmly, not realizing how odd her answer sounds. That's exactly what the notorious prison was known for: receiving groups from Bucharest.

Mass deportation was one of the main means by which the Communist Party gradually acquired absolute power. Its victims were roused from bed at night by an overwhelming number of armed men – a method first used on the night of 20 March 1947, when 315 members of the opposition parties were arrested. Another six hundred were picked up on 4 May 1947. The aristocrats, the untitled nobles, the kulaks and other large landowners were next, with that single night-time operation in 1949. In the night of 5 April 1950 the Romanian political elite was dragged out of bed. Ninety people were arrested on that occasion: ministers and secretaries of state, liberals and con-

servatives as well as pro-communists, members of all the governments from 1919 to 1945, which included a number of fellow-travellers. Several of the distinguished gentlemen loaded onto trucks that night in Bucharest were over seventy years old.

In the course of 1950 and 1951, specific groups belonging to the Romanian elite were seized in meticulously prepared nocturnal raids and deported, each in turn, to Sighet. First Greek Catholic priests and bishops, then Roman Catholic prelates and after that the entire leadership of the Romanian Peasants Party. By August 1951 the number of prisoners in Sighet had grown to one hundred and eighty. Of all the mostly elderly gentlemen brought to Sighet in April 1950, fifty-three died there, mainly from the effects of the harsh conditions, the cold, hunger and disease. Several were taken out to a field on the edge of town and shot in the back of the neck.

Later all the prisoners in Sighet were moved to a prison in Râmnicu Sărat. Cosmin Budeancă, deputy director of the Institute for the Investigation of the Crimes of Communism in Romania, would explain to me later in his office in Bucharest why these two prisons were chosen. At both Sighet and Râmnicu Sărat there was a railway line with the same gauge as railways in the Soviet Union. Usually everyone and everything had to switch trains at the border, since the track was narrower in Romania. Should a revolt break out, in Bucharest or anywhere else, the former Romanian elite could be loaded into cattle trucks and transported, without stopping, deep into the Soviet Union.

The prison at Sighet remains almost entirely intact. I can't resist looking with the eyes of a prisoner to see whether there might be some way to escape: a wall you could climb, a window, a drainpipe. But I can see no opportunity anywhere. The small courtyard has an extremely high wall with barbed wire and two watchtowers. It's an old-fashioned prison with a ground floor lined with cells and a long central space as high as the roof. On both sides are galleries leading past the cell doors on the first and second floors. Several metres below the metal balustrade of each storey a net has been stretched across the central space, so that no one can commit suicide by throwing himself down.

There are eighty-seven cells, bare rooms an average of two metres by four, and nowadays each treats a different subject. Cell II: Destruction of the political parties. Cell 14: The Securitate from 1948 to 1989. Cell 18: Collectivization: revolt and repression. Cell 20: Monarchy versus communism. Cell 47: Deportation to Baragan. Cell 50: Piteşti, re-education by torture. Cell 76: Daily life under communism.

In a long corridor on the ground floor, photographs of people who died under communism have been stuck to the wall and labelled with their names. There are thousands of them and they all look directly at you. In silence I stare at the black-and-white photos. Many of the men have powerful faces. Handsome fellows. There are fewer women, but they are no different: characterful, strong faces. I look for a Hungarian name, ideally a Hungarian aristocrat, but I fail to find one. I'm slightly disappointed, but then I realize that compared to the total number of victims of communism in Romania, the contingent of Hungarian nobles is minuscule.

Now that I'm walking past a wall in Sighet that shows the extent of the destruction of people and talent by the communists, I start to have doubts. Isn't the project I'm working on idiotic? Why devote my time to a handful of aristocrats? They had a prominent and privileged position for centuries; under communism they were treated the same way as ordinary people for once, tyrannized just as terribly. Isn't it a bit embarrassing to talk about their destroyed property and their lost world in light of the hundreds of thousands of victims?

I find myself in a room with a map of Romania on the wall, several metres wide. At the top it says in bold lettering: 'Roma-

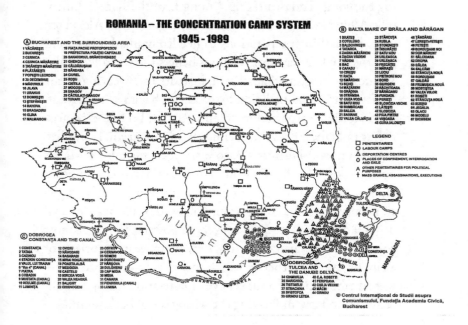

nia – The Concentration Camp System'. The legend explains that each little square represents a 'prison'. There are forty-four of them. A circle stands for a labour camp, seventy-two in total. A triangle represents a location where deportees were sent, sixty-three in all. An oval indicates a place of interrogation, sixty-one of those. The crosses, ninety-three of them, are places of execution and mass graves. Then there are ten psychiatric institutions of a political nature, and more than a hundred local and regional Securitate headquarters, equipped with interrogation rooms and cells. A total of almost four hundred and fifty places of detention, repression and murder. A complete industry of annihilation.

I step into another cell. The wall is covered in names, with the offences of which they were accused and the sentences that resulted. Here the hundreds of thousands crushed by the Romanian annihilation industry are reduced to their names. I note down a few: Stefan Bozsodi: five years for singing the song 'Traiasca regele' ('Long Live the King'). Gheorghe Albu: twelve years for cursing the regime. Dan Alexu: ten years for making preparations to flee Romania. Ludovic Fulop: twenty-five years for religious beliefs (he was a Jehovah's Witness). Gheorghe Sabadis: eight years for swearing at the Soviet army. Fruzsina Béldi: five years for having a negative attitude to the expropriation of land. (At last I'd found an aristocrat in Sighet; Fruzsina Béldi was a Hungarian Transylvanian countess.) Dumitru Bacon: six years for taking Marx's portrait down from a wall and dancing on it while singing an old song. A year earlier, in 1957, Gheorghe Profir had been given twenty years in a labour camp followed by ten years of civil degradation for pasting up subversive posters. The three most common criminal acts punished by many years in prison or a labour camp – either of which meant a descent into hell – were membership of a subversive organization, being a counterrevolutionary, and having the wrong social background.

I walk on into a pitch-dark cell, number 2. This was the punishment cell, insulated and painted black. No light entered; you were locked up in utter darkness. I pull the door shut behind me as far as it will go and sit on the floor. A strip of light still shines in past the door. Sentenced to five years in prison for singing a song. The severity of the sentences is dizzying. The communist regime's combination of arbitrariness, insanity and sadism makes me feel sick.

In an article entitled 'Teaching about Elites in the Era of Equality', historian Ellis Archer Wasson quotes Francis Bacon, who wrote three hundred years ago that a monarchy without an aristocracy renders up a tyranny just as brutal and absolute as that of the Turks several centuries earlier. The aristocracy has a moderating effect on the holder of power, standing between ruler and people. As early as 1222 the Golden Bull gave the Hungarian nobles the right to depose a king for misrule. The removal of that buffer had far-reaching consequences. The destruction of a cultivated elite and an increase in brutal terror went hand in hand. Archer Wesson writes that the horrors of the twentieth century have made us aware that flogging and whipping are trivial compared to sending people to gas chambers or the gulag. He suggests we have paid too little attention to the importance of honour and culture in moderating the cruelty of the powerful.

Romanian publisher and philosopher Gabriel Liiceanu said of communism: 'It creates a society founded on terror that hides behind the mask of a debate about a better society.'

Seventeen truckloads
of Bánffy treasures

Bonchida, September 2009

Between Baia Mare and Kolozsvár the landscape is ancient and magnificent. There are more horse-drawn carts on the road than cars, variously loaded with dung, maize, hay, families, weary men, and elderly couples on their way to the nearest village shop. Fields are ploughed by horses, fields mown with scythes. Haystacks are built around three long stakes. Farm labourers sit in groups in the fields to eat. Three gypsy boys climb in a cherry tree. Further south, between Dej and Kolozsvár, I see a lone, angular, apple-green Claas Senator combine harvester in a field of grain, clouds of golden dust rising from it.

I'm on my way to the former palace of the Bánffy family and I'm intrigued as to what I'll find. The surrounding estates and the castle came into the hands of the Bánffys in 1387. Over the course of the centuries the palace grew larger. In the seventeenth century a late-Renaissance extension was added, and in the eighteenth century a horse-shoe-shaped baroque building was constructed around it and a French garden laid out. In the nineteenth century the palace was extended in the Romantic style, with the addition of an English garden, an obelisk and a chapel. It was known as the Versailles of Transylvania.

The final stretch of road to Bonchida is made of loose hardcore. The building was blown up twice. To punish its last owner, Count Miklós Bánffy (1873-1950), the retreating Germans comprehensively looted the palace and undermined its walls with dynamite. Bánffy was a citizen of both Hungary and Romania and on 6 June 1943 he travelled to Bucharest in an attempt to persuade the Romanian government to side with the Allies. Hitler never forgave the Anglophile Bánffy. In 1944 Hungary contemplated abandoning the Axis powers and switching sides, which was reason enough for the Germans to invade the country on 19 March. On 24 August that year Romania joined the Allies.

The Germans filled seventeen trucks with art treasures and furniture from Bonchida before setting fire to the palace with

its library of thousands of books and its centuries-old archive. The column of trucks full of Bánffy treasures was bombed on its way westwards by the Allied air forces. Nothing was ever recovered. In the 1970s the Romanian government arranged for the Nazis' work to be replicated, and what remained of the palace was blown up for a feature film directed by Sergiu Nicolaescu. I'm not expecting to find much more than a heap of stones.

I park the car in front of the entrance to the Bánffy palace and walk through a large covered gatehouse towards a number of detached buildings. Practically all of them have new roofs, made of dark-red tiles. In every other respect they are ruins. The long main building lies to the right. It's immense. On the most distant outside corner are round stumpy towers that I suspect must be the oldest structures here. At the far end, on the park side, is an English-looking Romantic extension made of stone. Everything has been shot to pieces, bombed and burned, leaving blasted walls. Nowhere can I find the remains of plasterwork or refined detailing. I walk through the carcass. In room after room I see the same rubble, but the door open-

ings are still in line, so I can look deep inside as if through a tunnel with light at the end, a hundred metres away. You have to watch your step. There are large holes in the floor, with a long drop into the vaulted cellar.

To the left of the courtyard are the stables. The stone ornamentation around the entrance has been restored, including a group of sculptures at the edge of the roof. Inside, craftsmen are hard at work. The horses' drinking troughs are hewn out of Transylvanian marble. Large pillars support the brickwork ceiling. This isn't a stable, it's a cathedral. Across from the entrance are three niches in the wall. I suspect they once contained statues.

There are several other buildings. The chapel tower is supported by a decaying wooden structure. It has a more dramatic lean to it than Pisa. At the far end of the stables stands a big ungainly building, possibly once the servants' quarters. Students of art restoration from all over Europe are up on the scaffolding plastering, when they aren't flirting.

At a little stall I buy postcards, black-and-white photographs of the palace in better times. The dining room strikes

me as rather cheerless. It's as big as a tennis court and in the middle stands a square table with four chairs around it, laid for four people, with a damask tablecloth. Above the table is a colossal chandelier. Another photo shows the landscaped garden, which is also rather sparse. It's clear from the old photographs that the Bánffys were Protestants.

Miklós Bánffy died in the knowledge that the palace in Kolozsvár and the estates in rural Transylvania had been confiscated, Bonchida blown up and burned, all the art treasures, family documents, library and archives destroyed, his work was unavailable and forgotten, and he and his wife and daughter were cut off from the country he loved so much.

In Bánffy's trilogy the village of Bonchida and the palace are lovingly described. He calls the house Dénestornya. Bánffy understood even in the 1930s that the aristocracy was doomed and in the trilogy the Transylvanian nobleman László

Gyerőffy symbolizes its downfall, a man who gambles away his fortune and his estate at the gaming tables. This cousin of the protagonist is a man seemingly brought low by gambling, drink and apathy, but in fact he is eager to rectify the dishonour of having chalked up debts to a woman. Bánffy writes of him: 'And at that time he had felt that there was something noble and uplifting, cruel but at the same time triumphant, in choosing social death over private dishonour.' In retrospect the titles of Bánffy's trilogy – *They Were Counted, They Were Found Wanting, They Were Divided* – sound ominous. It's as if he's referring to the night of 3 March 1949.

After the Second World War, Bánffy stayed in Transylvania to try to protect what was left of Bonchida and the Bánffy mansion in Kolozsvár, and to recover ownership of the Bánffy forests. His wife had fled to Budapest with their daughter in 1944. The border between Hungary and Romania was closed, so he was unable to reunite his family. In 1949, the year the Transylvanian aristocracy was robbed of all its rights and possessions, the Romanian communists finally allowed Miklós Bánffy to leave for Budapest. He died there a year later.

You can dump us at the North Pole and we'll still survive

Kolozsvár, September 2009

On his walk from the Hook of Holland to Istanbul in 1934, Patrick Leigh Fermor passed through Kolozsvár. He wrote about it in his introduction to one of the volumes of Miklós Bánffy's trilogy: 'It was in the heart of Transylvania – in the old princely capital then called Kolozsvár (now Cluj-Napoca) that I first came across the name of Bánffy. It was impossible not to. Their palace was the most splendid palace in the city, just as Bonchida was the pride of the country and both of them triumphs of the baroque style. Ever since the arrival of the Magyars ten centuries ago, the family had been foremost among the magnates who conducted Hungarian and Transylvanian affairs, and their portraits, with their slung dolmans, brocade tunics, jewelled scimitars and fur kalpaks with plumes like escapes of steam – hung on many walls.'

Seventy-five years later, I'm about to visit Béla Bánffy in Kolozsvár. I've already met his son and after some urging the father is now willing to receive me. His son has told me about him and the strict upbringing he and his brothers and sisters were given: an appointment is an appointment and you must always stick to your agreements to the letter. If the son turned up a minute later than arranged, his father would give him a dressing down, since any form of misconduct was unacceptable. 'He taught us to keep our backs straight. We bore the

name Bánffy, which conferred obligations. Even without any possessions we had a duty to behave with dignity. We had to do our work well and be honest under all circumstances.' Every Sunday the family would gather for lunch in the modest little house where his grandparents lived. It provided continuity, as if the grandparents still lived in a castle.

I drive through a district of 1970s apartment blocks. In the car park are long lines of Trabants and Dacias, plus a few Mitsubishis. Now that I finally have an appointment I don't want to arrive late. I know what gentlemen of rank from the old times are like. Béla Bánffy senior is seventy-three, born in 1936, and he no doubt grew up with strict governesses and tutors. The Prussian and Hungarian school system is still evident in gentlemen over seventy. There's a military discipline to everything they do. It's as if they're trying to preserve all the honour, class and integrity cast aside by the rest of post-communist society. In short, I'm in a hurry, trying to avoid immediately acquiring a reputation for Dutch insolence.

I'm in a jumble of long blocks of flats four storeys high with a maze of streets between them. They all look the same. There's little to help you get your bearings. At last I find the street and the flat. I'm a quarter of an hour late. In Budapest I filled the boot of the car as a small grocer might, with bottles of Hungarian wine and chocolates from Szamos, the patisserie named after a river that winds through Transylvania. I put a bottle of red wine for Béla Bánffy into my shoulder bag, along with an audio recorder and notebooks.

It's a decrepit structure, like many residential buildings in the former Eastern Bloc, built decades ago with substandard materials by men judged on quantity rather than quality. The collapse of communism's planned economy, in which all anyone worried about was the production quota, was inevitable. The bankruptcy of that system can still be seen all over Eastern Europe. Tiles are missing from the shared stairwell; the metal entrance gate no longer shuts; the handrail has come loose.

Béla Bánffy is an extremely amiable man, it's just that I'd imagined him very differently. Dressed in tracksuit trousers with a lumberjack shirt and white pointed shoes, he has a hefty paunch and thick glasses. In the living room the television is turned up to high volume, showing Formula One with a Hungarian commentary. It's not clear to me whether the race is live or happened some time ago. Just as these countries are fobbed off with unmarketable batches of textiles and furniture from Western Europe, local television broadcasters are sold old football and boxing matches by the dozen. In the concert venues and football stadia you can watch entertainers who were put out to pasture in the West years ago and if there's a major tennis tournament, Lendl and Wilander will play each other once again.

I greet his wife, who is also wearing a tracksuit. On a long table between the television and a three-man settee of an indeterminate colour, an ashtray overflows with cigarette ends. There's a low veneer sideboard and little else in the room. I can't see anything that points to an aristocratic past. The family seems to have been successfully severed from its history. On the sideboard are cartons of Viceroy, filter cigarettes sold these days only in countries with heavy smokers: the Middle East, Chile, Turkey. Romania is the only place in Europe where you can buy them.

I sit down on the settee next to Béla Bánffy and switch on my audio recorder. The television with Formula One is making too much background noise. Béla Bánffy turns the sound off but leaves the set on. The interview takes place in Hungarian. Béla's wife brings black coffee in gleaming little fluted cups. He sits slumped relaxedly, using the stub of each cigarette to light the next. There are Bánffy counts and Bánffy barons. The baron branch was repeatedly offered the title of count by the Habsburg emperors but refused every time. The family is also divided between *Bánffy pipás* and *Bánffy kupás*: a branch of smokers and a branch of drinkers. The quantity of cigarettes on the sideboard, enough to get you through a short war, leads me to suspect that Béla senior belongs to the former.

Béla tells me his story. His father qualified in Vienna as a forestry engineer and managed the Bánffy forests near Hadad. Throughout the Second World War the family lived in Hungary and after the war they returned to their estate in Transylvania, but it was taken from them by the Romanians. Béla's father accepted the communist revolution as inescapable. He moved to Kolozsvár with his family and opened a wine warehouse. He had five children to keep. As far as the family was concerned, not much happened on 3 March 1949. The change came later, when the wine warehouse was nationalized and Béla's father was forced to work in a crate repair shop to keep his family fed. They moved to a small house in the Donát út, outside the city on the banks of the Szamos. Béla was barred from attending school. He became a gatekeeper at a factory, leaving at four every morning to get to work on time.

Béla Bánffy later worked for a while as a locksmith and then trained to be a truck driver. He drove trucks for twenty-five years, mostly ten-tonners. As a class enemy he wasn't allowed to do any runs abroad, but he could work all over Romania. He never had any trouble from his workmates, only from the bosses, all of whom were party members.

As a child Béla did not have Domiciliu Obligatoriu. His father did, though, and he was under constant political supervision. Béla's father had a problem with his eyes. Whenever he needed to make an appointment with an eye doctor in Marosvásárhely, he first had to go to the Securitate. If they were feeling well-disposed towards him, they would issue a document giving him permission to leave Kolozsvár for five days. Apart from that he always had to stay within the city limits. The Securitate kept an eye on him. His phones were bugged, letters opened.

'Everyone had to watch what he said and what he wrote; you couldn't say anything stupid in a letter. The aristocrats used to meet every week on Sundays in the Donát út and sometimes on a weekday evening as well. We played bridge until eleven or twelve o'clock, and before leaving we always agreed with our bridge partners what to say if we were interrogated by the Securitate, because after almost every meeting someone would be picked up and questioned. The men agreed to say they'd talked about women, whores and sport.'

'So the Securitate would be waiting for you after an evening of bridge?'

'Usually, yes. They liked to pick on people who'd been convicted of something, who could be blackmailed, which included anyone with Domiciliu Obligatoriu. Those detained

were often released after they'd signed a document saying they would cooperate with the Securitate the next time. But it was pointless, because nothing important was ever discussed. When we were with the family, we deliberately avoided talking about politics, so that no one would be in any difficulty if interrogated. There were people who said things on the street that they'd have done better not to say; they disappeared.'

When I ask how the traditions were upheld, Béla tells me that the older generation explained which country estates had been in the family and the ins and outs of each one. I ask him whether he still has any photographs. He stands up and searches in a cupboard, coming back a little later with a beautiful worn leather photograph album. It's an object from another world, right there amid the veneer and the cartons of Viceroy. The pages are of black card, with wafer-thin transparent paper between them. The album turns out to be a subtle record of decline.

It starts with black-and-white photos with scalloped borders: fathers and grandfathers with impressive faces and imposing grey moustaches; admiring locals in the background; babies in princely lace dresses; country estates with gardens full of blossoming peonies and lilac. The photographs from the interwar years are in tones of grey and have an aura of exclusivity: relaxed men in plus fours, hunting attire or riding gear standing beside their horses, with clematis- and ivy-covered walls as a backdrop. The country estates, the parks, the companionable dogs, the well-tended mounts and the long white dresses no longer feature.

Halfway through the book, simple square snapshots are suddenly in evidence, with a cheap gloss to them. The medium is the message. The decor shifts to nondescript houses and gardens. They show the family in the 1950s at the little house on the Donát út. The older generation is still elegantly clad in tweed jackets, the women in skirts and silk shawls, all radiating a kind of dauntlessness. In the later photographs that too is gone.

When the pictures switch to the polychrome of the 1970s, the colour slowly goes out of the older generation. They become frail, their jackets threadbare, but even so they preserve an air of distinction. Only the elderly who have left the country, photographed in front of Argentine museums and mediaeval French churches, still exude the natural ease with which life should be faced – a handkerchief sticking nonchalantly out of the breast pocket of a chequered jacket. The young lack such elegance. They wear shapeless Comintern clothes. They have grown up. They have turned inwards. They no longer have that air of distinction.

I ask Béla senior how he sees his family's future. Béla: 'The name Bánffy means something again now. When I go to the market to buy a string of onions they address me as "Baron". The man who sells me onions calls me that. The title of baron is honourable. Under communism the aristocrats worked hard to survive. The communists did nothing. They were the weak ones. Others had to work hard and keep their mouths shut, otherwise they'd be taken away to the Danube – Black Sea Canal.

'I'm trying to get as many family possessions back as I can, but it isn't easy. Property deeds have been stolen and lost; the judiciary is full of Securitate and former party members. But the Bánffys have preserved their honour. My children are doing better. They work hard. People who work hard will always manage. It's said of the Bánffys that you can dump us at the North Pole and we'll still survive.'

I thank Béla Bánffy for his time. The Grand Prix continues. I walk down the shabby stairwell and make my way off under the scrawny trees between the blocks of flats. The sunlight falls through the yellow-green foliage above me.

It is part of me

Aranyosgerend, September 2009

Travelling through Transylvania, what catches the eye most of all are the crazy colours daubed on the new houses. They are usually shoebox-shaped and as big as possible, quite often with pillar-box red or navy-blue tiles on the roof. The colours of the walls range from lurid purple, stick-of-rock-pink or mint-green to piss-orange, but you'll see McDonald's-yellow and Ikea-blue homes as well. Orange is the most common colour. Zsolna Roy Chowdhury-Ugron has explained to me that it's the most expensive paint, chosen above all to show the neighbours that you can afford to splash out. As an unsuspecting visitor, you occasionally feel as if you're in a provincial LSD trip.

I'm driving from Kolozsvár to Marosvásárhely, where I'll visit Anikó Bethlen again. I've driven this road many times before. You really do have to watch out, since it features a treacherous combination of BMWs racing along at 180 kilometres an hour – despite this being only a secondary road – and slow, plodding horse-drawn carts with their loads of timber and manure. The road winds through the hills. On the first stretch near Kolozsvár a public notice gives the number of fatal accidents over the past few years: thirty-three between 2004 and 2008. Everywhere along the road are signs reading TEREN DE VÂNZARE; the entire country seems to be up for sale. In the linear villages are hand-painted notices announcing VULCANIZARE. It's reminiscent of Africa, this emphasis on fixing punctures – as if that's the only economic activity around.

In the middle of a roundabout in Torda stands a large statue of a wolf with two infants sucking its teats. You see the same sculpture in nearly every small town. They're fairly new. I didn't see them anywhere in Transylvania in 1991. They're designed to emphasize the mythical connection with Rome and the Romans, and the ancient Romanian past in Transylvania, a land dominated by Hungary for so long. The wolf's teats are swollen, hanging down like fat ice-cream cornets. The infants have greedily turned their mouths upwards, like baby birds in a nest. In many villages all the lamp posts have the Romanian tricolour hanging from them, as if every day is a national holiday.

Twenty kilometres beyond Torda I reach Aranyosgerend. Here, outside the village, is the old Bánffy mansion. There's an unfinished Orthodox church surrounded by scaffolding and just beyond it the large ghost house. Close by is a twelfth-century chapel where many Keménys are buried. I drive up to the house along a bumpy dirt road across a patch of no man's land. Near here lived Englishman John Paget with his Transylvanian lover, the writer Polixénia Wesselényi. Béla Bánffy senior has shown me photographs of his own childhood, the house as white as the Romanian Orthodox churches today. The garden was an oasis bordered by potted yuccas and agaves. Anikó Bethlen's father and grandfather were both born here.

In this house, as a ten-year-old girl, Kinga was roused from her bed at two o'clock in the morning of 3 March and led away. She is one of the countesses who prefers not to be mentioned by name. Like so many, Kinga fled to Hungary when the Russians crossed the River Prut in Moldavia. After the war the family returned to Transylvania – her father had said it was safe there as long as Romania still had a king – and came to live here in Aranyosgerend. On the day before the deportations, someone from the nearby town came to warn them they would be taken away during the night. They quickly loaded some things into a van and sent it on to Kolozsvár. They too ended up in a small house on the Donát út. Kinga says life in poverty wasn't hard. Her mother returned to the house in Aranyosgerend not long after their deportation. It had been looted and laid waste. She picked trampled and torn family photographs out of the mud.

When restitution came, the house was returned to the Bánffys. Farkas Bánffy told me it was inherited through the female line, so quite a few of the Transylvanian aristocratic families had owned it at some point. Béla Bánffy junior, sad about the sale of that other family house near Hadad and eager to renovate family property, believes Aranyosgerend is an impossible project.

I park the car and walk the last hundred metres to the house. I want to take in the surroundings. Béla junior has told me the house is inhabited by gypsies and I don't want to invade their domain without warning. I light a cigar, which gives me something to do with my hands – and I can share out cigars among men with whom I can't communicate.

Béla junior: 'It's all about the family roots. I've never lived there. I never even visited Aranyosgerend until after Ceauşescu was executed. Still, it was the house of my father's childhood. I know it from his stories. I know exactly where he played, where the horses were kept, what life there was like. It's part of me. But what can you do with it? Restoration would cost an incredible amount of money. And then you'd still have to come up with a function for the place. Not a day goes by that I don't think about the family houses, but Aranyosgerend is simply too big and in too poor a state...'

The house stands abandoned on a high point at a bend in the River Aranyos. In the surrounding area I can see nothing but tall, drab-brown weeds. The yews planted in a circle out in front have grown tall. There's no longer any glass in the windows of the seventy-room country house. Plastic has been fixed across a number of them, along with some grubby cloths. That must be where people are living. The roof is full of holes, with crows flying in and out. Many of the window frames are missing. There are two stately flights of steps up to the first floor, minus their balustrades. I visited this house once before, in 2006, and on that occasion three gypsy boys came out of the front door, scampered down the steps, calmly pissed against the side wall and walked off through the long grass towards Aranyosgerend village.

In 2006 István Bánffy, who inherited the house along with several other members of his family, was still alive. He was eighty-seven and he died later that year. He was one of the aristocrats convicted in a big Romanian show trial in 1958, about which he said later: 'I admitted nothing, I even denied the starry sky!' Nevertheless he was sentenced to fifteen years' hard labour, several of which he spent at the Danube – Black Sea Canal, where prisoners often had to sleep two or three to a bed. István had lost his right leg during the Second World War. It made him a popular bedfellow. Before he went to sleep he would remove his artificial leg, which meant there was more space beside him.

Thursday afternoon,
five o'clock

Marosvásárhely, September 2009

'A person is never completely happy or utterly miserable. My parents were an example to me. They met right here in 1951, not long before my father was sent to a labour camp. There at the top of the stairs is where the militia had their offices. Every Thursday afternoon at five o'clock they had to report to this courtyard,' says Béla Haller.

We're on the Trandafirilor tér, the central square in Marosvásárhely, close to the Concordia Hotel where I'm staying. It's a designer hotel in a classical building. The porters, receptionists and waiters, Romanians included, all speak Hungarian. They know me here. I'm the Dutch writer who speaks a bit of Hungarian and walks around town for days on end. I've come with Béla Haller to see the militia headquarters. It's a pleasantly cool evening. We've walked into the courtyard under a tall Art Nouveau building. Two cooks from fish restaurant Posilano are sitting on the steps to a side door, smoking. The busi-

nesses around the courtyard are a reflection of the new Romania: Club Europe Internet Non-Stop, Hair Look Anka and Body Muscle. Internet, hair, muscles. Marosvásárhely is one of the five Transylvanian towns to which the deported landowners were brought. The other four were Sepsiszentgyörgy, Nagyenyed (Aiud), Gyulafehérvár and Balázsfalva.

'On Thursday afternoons about two hundred people used to gather here. Your name was called out and you had to go up. Everyone was in the same situation. They lived in cellars and were forced to do heavy labour to earn a living. Most knew each other; they were all former landowners, many of them aristocrats, who had become factory workers, chimney sweeps or coalmen.'

Two cats are sitting on top of a large metal dumpster, looking quizzically down into a stench of fish and rotting vegetables. They seem to know that although they could easily get in, it would be harder to get out again. The courtyard is closed off at the back by a tall two-storey building in Art Nouveau style with wavy lines and bulges à la Victor Horta. A central set of steps leads up to a double door. That must be where class enemies with the Domiciliu Obligatoriu stigma had to report every Thursday to prove they hadn't left town.

'It was thanks to the deportation that I found my husband,' Emma P., another 'class enemy', told me. 'The third of March 1949 brought me to him. We both had Domiciliu Obligatoriu. That was the great thing.' He was the love of her life. They met here on the square and on evenings in cellars with people who also had DO. All the years that Emma had to report here she felt ashamed. She always hurried through into the courtyard, fearful that one of her pupils might notice that she had to go to the militia. It would mean losing her job. As well as class enemies, the prostitutes of Marosvásárhely had to report here. The militia asked Emma: 'Which register are you here for? Whores or countesses?!'

On entering the square we first speak to an elderly Romanian woman. She used to work for the militia. The decisions were taken by the Securitate, but the militia did the administrative work and registration. One of her jobs was to search the women, all the places where you could hide money, gold or jewellery. 'It was awkward and embarrassing,' the woman told us. 'Both for them – they were ladies – and for me. I felt sorry for them. Some were sent to the Danube – Black Sea Canal, where they were made to do terrible, heavy work and died like rats. I knew they were innocent.'

I'm standing on the cracked concrete paving of the courtyard under a steel-blue sky, looking around me, trying to imagine what it must have been like here on those Thursday afternoons: the gentlemen who had hurried here from their work as rat-catchers or warehouse clerks, from jobs in pig-fattening units and chicken abattoirs, who greeted the slender ladies – factory workers, seamstresses and servants – with hand-kisses.

Emma's husband, who had a job as a cobbler, had to report here, as did her mother, who worked in a button factory, and her stepfather, who gave language lessons and was sentenced to hard labour at the Bicaz dam, and his brother, who worked in a jam factory. There were many who had to report every week: Anikó Bethlen's father, who worked on a kolkhoz; Károly Orbán, who taught English, played bridge and rummy along with Emma and the others, and was executed on 1 September 1958 in the Securitate prison in Timişoara; Gemma Teleki (who towards the end of her life lived with Stefánia Betegh), who tried to earn money selling dried flowers and had slept on top of a cupboard in the Teleki-téka; and Kati Ugron's future father-in-law, who worked as a gardener.

Béla told me that in those days the men usually saved one good suit for Sundays and for the days they were able to meet. They preserved the old rituals. Families received guests on specific days, they carried on kissing hands and using other formal gestures, their conversations were governed by long-established rules (for example that men and women used the polite form of 'you' even though among themselves each sex was on first-name terms), and people talked about particular subjects, using the idioms of their class. They met in their cellars to play bridge, rummy and canasta. They read poetry aloud and made music. The older aristocrats taught the children foreign languages and gave them music lessons.

There was a fox farm in Marosvásárhely. Mihály Teleki and Misi N. worked there. Misi was married to a Kemény widow and some said she was a bit of a snob. The foxes were fed on horsemeat. Misi managed to rescue a few horses from the food troughs and start a small riding school. For the Hungarians from noble families, horse riding came naturally, like learning languages. When I met Ilona, twenty years ago, I immediately began to learn to ride, somewhere on the edge of an industrial estate in a sand pit with a loud-voiced woman for a teacher, who bellowed at her horses and her pupils in the same commanding tone. I don't think the riding style I developed could be described as elegant, but if necessary I could trek across the Carpathians on horseback. Several of the elderly gentlemen I know in Hungary and Transylvania have an unmistakably aristocratic posture: heels together, ramrod back, chin up. Even in their eighties, they ride horses every day.

Béla Haller is a slim man with a refined, narrow face. He was born in 1955 and he teaches Italian at a secondary school in Marosvásárhely. He's vivacious and doesn't seem to have suffered any permanent harm from a difficult childhood. He stands very straight, has a modest manner and speaks beautiful French. In fact he has all the elegance of a French nobleman; I can just see him in morning dress with a top hat at the races in Neuilly a century ago. He lived in a kind of scullery with his parents, his sister and his father's sister. They stayed there for twenty-five years; his father called it 'permanent camping'. He took me there. It was a wooden extension at the back of a small house in Marosvásárhely. Between the two rooms was a glass door. It had no running water, no drains. Outside were a toilet and a tap where they filled buckets. Béla told me about his childhood with great affection. In the bushes behind the scullery, he and the girl next door explored their anatomical differences. His parents played music, and from everything Béla has told me about them they must have doted on each other. The aunt was important to Béla because she read a lot and talked about books, as well as teaching him languages. She slept in the part that served as a kitchen. She would lie there reading until late in the evening and the light fell through the glass door into the room where Béla slept. He was grateful to her for that, since he was afraid of the dark.

After we'd met several times, Béla Haller told me that his father had two children from his first marriage, two boys. They lived some of the time with the family and the aunt in two small rooms. One of his half-brothers was a schizophrenic. That was a great worry. At the age of twenty the half-brother was admitted to an institution. Béla's father went to see him every day. One afternoon in 1999, the father died suddenly of a heart attack. For Béla's half-brother the loss was unbearable. He stayed in the institution and died two months later.

Béla: 'I think my father suffered a great deal in his final moments because he hadn't written down how everything was to be arranged from then on. We never spoke about principles, about important family business, about the family. I had to reconstruct it all from old conversations, clues, odd phrases here and there. I had to create a way of thinking and an inheritance that was not yet available to me. I think about it a great deal. I try to organize everything and carry on with everything he said and did in a coherent manner. He'd decided we would need to let the castle in Küküllővár go. Now it belongs to an entrepreneur from Constanţa.'

A bat flits over the former gathering place for people with Domiciliu Obligatoriu. The only sound is from ventilator motors.

Béla: 'My father and mother met here in the courtyard. They'd both been married before and divorced. My mother had a daughter and my father had two sons. In 1939, as a boy of nineteen, he'd eloped with the daughter of an officer in the Hussars who was stationed close to the castle in Küküllővár. He left while my grandmother was away from home for a few days and married the girl before his mother could prevent him. It was heroic, but it wasn't appreciated. My grandmother was a widow. My grandfather had been murdered in the castle bathroom in the spring of 1927 by his chauffeur, a nationalistic Romanian who hated Hungarians. Three shots from a revolver.'

At our later meetings Béla wore a black tracksuit top and drank beer. Even that he managed to do elegantly. In his jog-

ging jacket, cutting thick slices of salami, Béla Haller exuded chivalry. At our very first meeting he told me how, in communist Romania, his father instilled certain values in him.

'My parents' marriage would have been unthinkable a few years earlier. My mother came from a long line of teachers. Her father was a professor at the agricultural university in Hungary who came to Transylvania after the Second World War with his wife and three daughters to work a piece of land owned by his father. He'd left everything behind and was intent on putting theory into practice. They'd been living in a village close to the Austrian border and they spoke German. A capable bourgeois family. The three daughters were musical and performed operettas and popular music. My father played the viola, but exclusively classical works.

'My father had been in the army; honour, truth and sincerity were crucial to him. Things were simple. He disapproved of using theories and long stories as a means of self-justification. He expected everyone, especially a boy, a future man, to make categorical choices and never vacillate. Communism didn't suit him and neither did the type of capitalism that came after it, the corruption in agriculture, the mafia that came to power across the board. He couldn't adjust to the new system. The old way worked according to laws and universally respected rules. That's what he was accustomed to.'

I've visited Béla a number of times in Marosvásárhely, and on each occasion he and his wife and son have invited me to dinner in their soberly furnished house and treated me to

 red wine, *pogácsa* and pasta. Béla has told me how friends and family used to call on each other uninvited at their castles and country houses, when no one had a telephone. People sat at the table to eat and stayed the night. Béla displays the same natural, casual hospitality. He always has time for me. That is one essential difference between Transylvania and Budapest or indeed other places I know – a fundamentally different concept of time. On every visit I had that same sensation. In Transylvania time seems to pass more slowly. I've made a number of trips and it always turns out that as soon as I cross the Hungarian-Romanian border at Oradea, all the aristocratic families in Marosvásárhely, Kolozsvár and the Széklerland are aware of my arrival.

'My mother was extremely serious. In the period when they met in this courtyard, my father was working in a furniture factory. The very first time he invited her out, it was to a musical performance there. In communist times every factory had its own orchestra and dance group. The standard was extremely low, but my father took part and he enjoyed it. My mother sat in the audience and in the row behind her two people were talking about my father. One said, "The viola player on the stage is a count who was deported from his castle. But he's an optimist; he loves life." My mother heard that. I think it was important. When you're just getting to know someone, overhearing something like that by chance can be hugely influential. *Consolider l'image*. My father had grown up in the family castle. That was a different world. Later our aunt told us about it, but she never called it the "castle", it was always "the big house".'

The Hallers' castle had come from the Bethlen family and was originally built, or so tradition would have it, for the brother of Prince Gábor Bethlen. It was known as the Chambord of Transylvania. One of Béla's ancestors won the castle at cards, which explains why they weren't hugely attached to it. After all, it hadn't belonged to the Hallers since time immemorial, only for a mere two centuries.

'Shortly after they met, my father was arrested and sent to Bicaz. It wasn't an extermination camp but a forced labour camp. They were building a dam in the mountains. My father was accused of making a comment about the monetary reforms, but that doesn't sound like him at all. Nothing of that sort interested him a scrap. All those prisons and labour camps were useless. No one changes their thinking because of camps and torture. He had to break rocks at Bicaz. He became very ill and got bad diarrhoea. My mother visited him as often as possible, in the labour camp in the mountains. That's the reason he survived. He had the prospect of a fresh start, a second chance. He wanted to live for that.

'After nine months my father was released from Bicaz. At Christmas 1952 he came home. He was extremely thin. On 22 December that year his mother died and on 27 December my father and mother were married. The death of his mother, the funeral and the wedding a few days later – that must have been a dramatic time for my father. He was accused of insensitivity, but I think he had a primal urge to start a new life. Eleven months after that I was born – 3,460 grams.'

Béla gives me a cautious smile. Every gram he weighed at birth feels like evidence of mankind's tenacity.

The horses were eaten

Marosvásárhely, September 2009

I visit Anikó Bethlen whenever I'm in Marosvásárhely and now I'm pulling back the net curtains in my hotel room to look down over the square. The sun is shining. To the right stands the Orthodox church, with the old fortress up on the hill behind it. In front of me lies the square, beautiful in its broad layout, although its detailing is typical of the aesthetics of the workers' paradise: cheap conifers in concrete planters, ghastly benches and wide, unimaginative asphalt paths full of cracks and potholes.

There they come, walking straight towards me, crossing the street now: two men and two women. Gábor gypsies. They're lighter skinned than most gypsies and they look fantastic. The men have enormous black hats, large moustaches and short black jackets over chequered woollen sweaters. One of the women is wearing a gleaming red dress and a pink headscarf, the other a wide, ankle-length purple dress with white spots, a mauve sweater, a black leather waistcoat and a dark-green headscarf with a refined design on it – a scarf that wouldn't look out of place on a lady at the Royal Haagsche Golf and Country Club.

Ninety per cent of the Gábors around Marosvásárhely are Seventh Day Adventists. The church and the market are the only places where they mix with *gadjo*s. Their mother tongue is Oláh, but they also speak fluent Hungarian and Romanian. They live in several of the villages around Marosvásárhely and earn a living as tinkers and merchants. They're extremely segregated and traditional; daughters are given in marriage from the age of twelve. If a daughter fails to satisfy – not a good cook, no good in bed, no longer a virgin – and is brought back by dissatisfied in-laws during the honeymoon period, her family has to pay several thousand euro in shame-money.

The first time I went to see Anikó Bethlen, in 2006, I was with my old friend Judit Hajós. It was Judit who brought me to Transylvania and introduced me to Anikó. One of Judit's

distant ancestors was diplomat and bishop George Martinuzzi, who called himself Brother György, the man who negotiated the 1541 treaty that made Transylvania a semi-autonomous principality. Two gypsy women were standing next to Anikó's bed, by way of a welcoming committee. They had bags full of embroidered tablecloths, which they were trying to sell. After we'd greeted Anikó, the two women laid out all their wares in the room. I bought two cloths.

Now I'm visiting Anikó alone and I meet her Russian teacher. There's also a kind of house servant and a delicate boy with glasses who looks ill. Not to mention the elderly woman who usually stays in the kitchen, asleep in her chair, occasionally bringing us something to eat, or sometimes sits in a chair in the living room, humming a little to herself. The Russian teacher, who has brought some textbooks, leaves after five minutes.

Anikó Bethlen seems to be keeping all the old Transylvanian handicrafts alive single-handed. She's surrounded by pottery, a collection of crystal glass, cardboard boxes and piles of books. On the wall hang rows of hand-painted plates, in the cupboards are hand-painted pots and carafes. Embroidered tablecloths, bedspreads and headscarves are scattered about. The content of the bookshelves reveals broad interests.

Anikó's bed is in the corner of the room. She's the conscience and archive of the Hungarian community in Marosvásárhely. At the foot of her bed is a landline telephone along with three mobiles, and during my visits they take it in turns to ring. A continual procession of visitors comes by to consult with bedridden Anikó: friends, gypsies trying to sell tablecloths or reed baskets, people bringing packets of coffee for the social care organization she runs, people fetching walking frames for that same care service, men offering antique plates, students coming to ask advice or simply to pay tribute to her. It puts me in mind of a friendly version of Marlon Brando in *The Godfather* – Anikó is the godmother of Marosvásárhely.

The housemaid, with her black eyeliner and bobbed ponytail, has a large swelling on her right cheek. She's wearing a skirt over her trousers and an apron on top. She places plates of unidentifiable food next to Anikó's throne and then sits down. The rest of the time, hands folded in her lap, she stares at an old television set showing grainy halftones, black-and-white stills of the front door and the three steps leading up to it. The two plump *vizslas*, those celebrated Hungarian hunting dogs, a triumphant reddish brown, rule the house and are allowed to lie on the sofa bed at Anikó's feet. When I lean forward to hear Anikó better, they let out a guttural growl. Anikó speaks softly, almost in a whisper, in Shakespearean English.

Her parental home and a country estate inherited from her mother's family lie in the hills near the village of Mezőmadaras, seven kilometres from the Second World War border between Northern and Southern Transylvania.

'Towards the end of the war they fetched us out of bed every night to flee into the woods by horse and cart with my mother, my three sisters and the servants, to hide from Romanian looters. We finally left for Hungary in late September 1944, I and my father, mother and sisters. Rózsa was still a baby. The road was full of people on foot and in horse-drawn carts like us, or pushing handcarts. An exodus. Everyone was fleeing the Russians. Once you were on the road it was impossible to stop. My godfather was somewhere in that endless procession and at one point he saw his wife come past in a car, but he couldn't reach her. The horses were unable to eat and we couldn't urinate. There were dead horses lying at the side of the road with swollen stomachs, their legs in the air.

'In Transylvania we were put up every night by friends or relatives, but we didn't have any family in Hungary any longer. The first evening we knocked at a Hungarian peasant's door to ask if we could spend the night in their yard – one of my sisters was ill – but they refused. We slept outdoors that time, but in September the nights were already cold. We went to Budapest, where a great uncle, Dániel Bánffy, had been minister of agriculture before the Fascists took power. He had a house on the Rózsadomb where we could stay. The uncle wasn't there; he'd been taken prisoner by the Germans. At Christmas the Russian bombardment began. The town was full of corpses.

'There was thick snow on the ground, but that was a bit of good fortune, because it meant everyone in Budapest had fresh water. My grandfather, Bálint Bethlen, was in a prisoner-of-war camp south of the Carpathians. He used to live at Keresd, the family castle in Southern Transylvania. When the Romanians changed sides in August 1944 he was arrested and taken to a camp. He was there for seven months. He was freed in April 1945, at the age of fifty-eight. In the chaos of the camp he'd realized what was going to happen to Hungarian culture in Transylvania and he came to us in Budapest. Only much later did I realize he'd come there to say goodbye. I was six years old. I remember him. He was very tall. He smoked cigars.

'After visiting us he went to Keresd to take the family archive to a place of safety. His second wife stayed in Budapest with their children. He was seriously ill. He took the archive by ox-drawn cart from Keresd to the station in Segesvár and from there by train to Kolozsvár, to the library of the Transylvanian-Hungarian Academy. The archive is there to this day. Grandfather died in Segesvár shortly after that.

'Just before he died, in January 1946, he made a new will declaring all his previous wills null and void. He'd divorced my grandmother, Marianna Bánffy, who'd returned to Fugad, to her family home. She was one of the best catches in all of Transylvania. A divorce is such a loss, in every sense: spiritual, financial. A tragedy for the family. Grandmother Bánffy told me a great deal about that house in Fugad. She loved the place so much.

'We survived the siege of Budapest and then we tried to come back. Father had already returned to Transylvania that April. He'd taken fruits and seeds with him, intending to make a start on agricultural work. Our horses in Budapest had been eaten, either by the Germans or by the Russians. It took two days to travel by donkey cart from the Rózsadomb to Budapest's Nyugati Station. All the bridges over the Danube had been blown. From there we travelled eastwards on a goods train. The journey took two weeks, the same length of time as it had taken to get to Budapest by horse and cart. The train sometimes stood still for hours or even days on end, to let long trains full of prisoners of war pass by on their way to Russia. They had priority. Between the rails were huge piles of excrement from the prisoners. There were whole beans in it. My mother explained that those men could no longer digest their food properly. It was August. We had nothing to drink, only condensed water from the engine's boiler. That would have to be clean.

'There was a young woman in our carriage who was ill and kept vomiting. We probably caught what she had, the same virus. My younger sister Rózsa and I got splitting headaches, high fevers and diarrhoea. Mother was a paediatrician, but there was nowhere for us to go. Afterwards it turned out we'd had meningitis. There were no medicines, nothing. Rózsa died from it. I survived, but my spinal cord was infected. We returned to Mezőmadaras in September 1945. The house had been stripped bare by looters. Only the furniture was left. We had to share the house with another family. My grandmother was with us, it was her house, but there was only one room left for her, all the others were taken. The furniture from the whole house was piled up in that one room, turning it into a maze crawling with cockroaches, beetles and woodlice.

'From time to time I had stabbing headaches, but I didn't say anything to my mother because I knew there was nothing she could do. I was almost seven. It was three days after we arrived at my grandmother's house in Mezőmadaras. I'd been playing outside, on a swing, and I went upstairs with a bad headache. From one moment to the next I was completely paralyzed. I had a high fever for six weeks. I've never been able to walk since. I can't use a toilet without asking someone to hold me and wipe my buttocks. That's simply the way it is. I'm accustomed to saying things that other people find humiliating or embarrassing. I don't have any choice.

'My grandfather wrote his will and died. From that moment on my father travelled back and forth between Mezőmadaras and Keresd. He tried to keep things going. We still had fifty hectares of the 30,000 the family used to own, most of which was lost in the land reforms of 1920 and 1945. The expropriation continued steadily, and taxes were high. That's the reason so many people left the country; they couldn't see how they could live, how they could survive. My father did everything himself, since he no longer had any staff. On Saturdays and Sundays he taught the peasants how to work the land. He was an agricultural engineer. A lot of knowledge had been lost in the war. Practically all the livestock had been eaten or taken away by the armies that passed through. Everything had to be done by hand. As a doctor my mother helped anyone she could in Mezőmadaras, without asking for payment. The rest of the time she helped my father on the land.

'I was staying with my grandmother in Marosvásárhely, along with my sister – that's where we were on schooldays – when my parents suddenly appeared at the door with suitcases. That was on the evening of 3 March 1949. They hadn't been taken from their house in the night because the villagers and local officials had protested to the militia and said that my parents must stay in the village. Not until the afternoon were they put into a truck and brought to the militia headquarters in Marosvásárhely. Later they had to undergo the same humiliation as all the other aristocrats, reporting to the militia weekly and waiting until someone shouted out: "The wife of Gábor Bethlen!"

'We were parasites. The intention was to turn all the other classes against the aristocracy. We were demoted. Children were taught at school that the aristocracy had exploited the people. My father was sacked from the factory and from then on he worked as a gardener. He was also an agricultural labourer on a collective farm. He flatly refused to leave the country. My mother would have been happy to go, but she stood by him. Later she taught hygiene two days a week at a technical college. At school everyone was given a biscuit with iodine in it every day, except for my sister and me, because we were exploiters. We couldn't become pioneers; we weren't allowed to join in any of the festivities at school because we were the enemy. As a child that kind of thing bothers you. It was a perpetual humiliation.'

Anikó sits up straight in bed and goes on: 'We lived with my grandmother for a while, but because we were expecting to be moved to a smaller place, we went to live in an apartment building with people my parents vaguely knew. We divided the apartment up. But the husband of that family was a pervert who kept trying to grope us. We didn't tell our parents because we knew they couldn't do anything to change the situation. They couldn't protect us. To simplify his task, the man sabotaged the toilet upstairs so that we all had to go to the latrine in the courtyard, which meant taking eight steps down into the garden. That was impossible for me. I had a chamber pot. All those years. For twenty-two years we lived in those conditions.

'After elementary school we weren't allowed to go to secondary school. My sister went to Moldavia to continue her studies there. In Transylvania everyone knew that the Bethlens were aristocrats, landowners, but in Moldavia the name didn't mean anything to anyone. My father went with her to earn money so that my sister could attend school. He worked near a big lake and after two years an inspector came from Transylvania and said: "Why do you keep that count on here?" He lost his job the next day.'

In the heart of Transylvania I drove past the Renaissance castle belonging to the Bethlen family, which had managed to recover ownership two years before. I recently met a young Bethlen in Budapest, a grandson of Anikó's grandfather's second wife, and I understood from him that the family still hasn't decided what to do and how to share out the returned property. Anikó told me that the last will made by her grandfather favoured his second wife. Shortly before he died the grandfather asked Anikó's father to forget the past and show some compassion for his stepmother.

A ten-kilometre road through a charming valley with hills on both sides shrouded by oak woods leads to Keresd. Driving along it I came upon just one house and three girls on roller skates. Keresd is a village at the end of the world and on its south side, where the asphalt road peters out into a muddy track, is the gypsy district, the *țigănie*. The village is occupied mainly by colonists, Romanians who in communist times eagerly took possession of the well-kept houses built by the Saxons, who had left the village and gone abroad. The Bethlen castle stands on a hill in the middle of the village and above it is the family church, big as a cathedral. Beyond that the hills begin, with meadows and forests.

I could find no caretaker at the castle. There was a brand new green fence topped with barbed wire all around the property. In the corner by the family church I managed to climb over without scratching myself or tearing my clothes. In the grounds stood giant trees. The land had been mown. I spotted the old path winding up from the castle to the church, so I walked down it. The whole castle had a new roof and most of the windows had new frames, already glazed. It was a square Renaissance castle enclosing a spacious inner courtyard and several towers with Renaissance windows chiselled out of white stone. Those too had been restored.

One side of the castle had yet to be renovated, so I was able to get into the courtyard. The round south tower was of the kind that makes the hearts of romantics beat faster, crying out for ballads and stolen kisses. The staircase ended in an open gallery on the first floor, with elegant archways supported by carved sandstone pillars. Smoke curled up from a chimney in a lower section of the castle. I walked back and climbed over the fence again, at the corner nearest the church, and looked out across it all. The evening sun coloured the towers and walls a golden yellow. A hundred metres down to my right, near a small house, a woman was taking washing off the line while an elderly woman next to her split chunks of wood with an axe.

Anikó is one of the few Bethlens still living in Transylvania. The rest of the family is spread across the world, from England to Argentina. During my visit to Anikó she told me how her father's stubborn determination to stay in Romania was explained by some aristocrats abroad as tacit approval of the communist regime. I don't know who is the brains behind the restoration of the Bethlens' 600-year-old castle in Keresd, but it wouldn't surprise me if it's a seventy-one-year-old paralyzed woman lying in a bed in Marosvásárhely, who has inherited her father's indomitability.

Looking at cellars

Marosvásárhely, September 2009

In Marosvásárhely there were at least two hundred and forty-three people who had been given the status of Domiciliu Obligatoriu on 3 March 1949, among them members of fifteen aristocratic families: Teleki, Bethlen, Bánffy, Haller, Huszár, Mikó, Kendeffy, Kornis, Schell, Kuún, Kemény, Dániel, Zichy, Toldalagi and Tisza, as well as many families of untitled nobles, such as Ugron, Betegh, Jakabffy and Fráter. They were condemned to a life in cellars, attics, laundry rooms and sculleries. The book *Vár állott, most kőhalom* by István Mikó lists the jobs held by the great landowners, a stark contrast to what they had done before 1949: foreman, chicken plucker, warehouse clerk, ditch digger, chimney sweep, carpenter, domestic servant, cowherd, cobbler, bird scarer, rodent eradicator, night watchman, gravedigger, ice-cream salesman, typist, home dressmaker, nurse, button painter, sales assistant, cleaner, seamstress. Others worked in sugar factories, roofing-tile factories and brick factories, or were casual labourers on a pig farm or a kolkhoz.

Half the population of today's Marosvásárhely is Hungarian. It's a glorious Indian summer and Anikó Bethlen has just introduced me to Emma P. We're standing in front of a wooden gate on the Strada Liceului, a traffic-free village street. The houses are low, with lime trees lining both sides of the road. The gate is too tall to see over. We knock. Then I try pounding the gate with my fist. A man in camouflaged fatigues appears. He says 'Csókolom' to Emma, the everyday version of the Hungarian greeting 'Kezét csókolom', 'I kiss your hand'.

The man opens the gate to reveal a courtyard with a pile of hardened cement sacks against one wall. He gestures that we are welcome to come inside. He's one of those grimy eccentrics that used to arouse my curiosity but nowadays simply get on my nerves. Before you know it, you're the prisoner of someone else's insanity. On one wall in his living room are several carelessly stuffed animals. A Sunday huntsman, alcoholic and amateur taxidermist. The house gives the impression that renovation work has been going on here for years.

'That wall used not to be there,' says Emma, pointing to a brick wall next to the house that cuts off access to the back garden. Immediately in front of the wall are concrete steps to the cellar. We make our way down. The man waits at the top of the steps. I have to stoop to get through the entrance. I'm afraid Emma might fall. There's a larger space with a sink and two smaller rooms. It's like any unused cellar: dismal. As a child I climbed walls and crept into abandoned monasteries, school buildings and bunkers. This has the same smell of damp and decay. You half expect to find a mattress in a corner with a tramp lying on it, a pile of dried-out faeces or the remains of a fire. In the entire cellar there's just one tiny window with wired glass. It's depressing to think that people lived here. The place is as clammy and oppressive as a crypt.

Emma walks from corner to corner, inching her way. She stops and says: 'My sister had the worst part of the cellar. Not in the sense that the window was small but because of the woman who lived above.' She gestures with her head. 'This was the laundry room. The woman went on using it. She always walked in unannounced, coming in the evening or at night to fetch her washing or to hang it up. It was all my sister had. When it was time for a big wash, my sister had to vacate the cellar. A couple of times a year the woman had a pig slaughtered, and she insisted that had to happen down here too.

'Thank God people like that were rare,' Emma goes on, still talking about the woman who subjected her sister to her every whim. 'Generally people in Marosvásárhely were very good to the deported and tried to help them.'

We climb out of the musty cellar and say goodbye to the man. Then we walk off down the street, or rather shuffle; Emma is unsteady on her feet and I support her. The roads rise and fall steeply in this part of Marosvásárhely, an old district on a hill a stone's throw from the town's central square. She points: 'That's the Reformed church. We were married there in 1957.' Emma beams.

'One of the gifts we received was a cake from a baker who became a friend of ours. It had almonds on top. The children had never seen almonds before; they thought they were little onions. I didn't wear white for the wedding, since we couldn't get hold of an appropriate dress. My husband had a suit and I wore a white blouse and a silver *spitze* in my hair. Everything was borrowed. After church we went to my mother's room. Hers was big enough for a few people. We ate the cake there. After we were married my husband came to live in the cellar with me.'

I help her into the Land Rover. It may be the mother of all off-road vehicles, but for a frail eighty-four-year-old it's far from easy to get in and out. When I bought it I saved on the side steps. Emma is a tall woman, dressed in what you might irreverently call a tent dress, of Eastern European manufacture. Her cheeks are scaly, her coat dusty; a melancholy decay hangs about her. She misses her husband. They lived a life of intense solidarity. He died several years ago

Emma received me in her flat earlier in the day with tea and a dish of biscuits and Smarties. Next to the dish lay the expropriation documents from 1949, photograph albums and her Carnet de Muncă or record of employment, an item of inferior quality, made of rough paper bound into a hard cover. That 'workbook' contained a list of exactly where you had worked and what you had done, with stamps from the relevant authorities. It also gave your parents' names, which was how class enemies were excluded from every job other than simple manual labour.

'The terror of this book!' she said, lifting it into the air. She was keen to show me documentation of what had happened to her. 'You mustn't write only about the big, dramatic things. It's important to write about the little things, everyday things, if you want people to understand life under a regime like that.'

In the 1970s, along with her husband, she was able to buy the flat she lives in now, with a telephone. When they got home they would cover the phone with a cushion, since it was known to be a tried and tested Securitate bugging device. Bugging techniques were introduced in the early 1970s, presumably because it was becoming possible to make the equipment smaller and smaller. From then on, heavy ashtrays, vases and telephones were introduced into Romanian hotels, restaurants and private apartments, and the Securitate files changed. They had previously been a mishmash of notifications from informants, observations of routines and meetings, copies of opened letters and transcripts of conversations, along with conclusions drawn by the Securitate officer in charge, all adding up to a somewhat surreal collage. The file and the facts didn't matter too much, since if someone had to be sent to a labour camp or a firing squad, they'd be sent anyhow. With the introduction of bugging equipment on a large scale, the Securitate files became filled with interminable reports of banalities: people cooking, peeing, snoring, sewing and washing; the rattling of pans; toilets being flushed. The few people I'd spoken to who had seen their Securitate files were disappointed by a vacuousness punctuated only occasionally by an interesting or spicy fact.

In her concrete flat, Emma showed me black-and-white photographs of the cellar she'd lived in, and of her husband, who still resolutely looked like a gentleman even in that time of terror and poverty: jaunty, wearing a threadbare jacket with a bow tie. The flat was full of cardboard boxes, with tablecloths and miscellaneous fabrics hanging everywhere. In the kitchen were piles of pots and pans. The furniture was 1970s Eastern Bloc. The only thing in that dowdy flat reminiscent of a cultivated past was an oil painting of Emma's grandfather.

Emma was born in Kolozsvár in 1925 to a family of ancient Transylvanian nobility. In 1948 she graduated from the Babeş-Bolyai university in Kolozsvár with a chemistry degree. She was brought up by her grandmother. After her father died in 1938, the family's estate passed to her and to her brother and sister. She doesn't want me to give her family name in this book.

Emma whispers: 'There's a famous poem by Gyula Illyés. "*Hol zsarnokság van, ott zsarnokság van. Mindenki szem a láncban.*" "Where there is oppression, everything is oppression and everyone is a link in the chain." As long as I didn't have to show my identity papers, I was a normal person. Until 1952 I lived a normal life. I was in Kolozsvár when the militia took my family from the estate on 3 March 1949. It wasn't until 1952 that I was given Domiciliu Obligatoriu. From that point on I was unable to find work. A friend let me teach some of his lessons at a school, so I was able to work as a chemistry teacher. I was lucky they didn't check my identity papers.

'I had to work to live. Does that make me an accomplice of the regime? No. I worked for the people. In the place where you have to live, you live, whether you like it or not,' says Emma. She's silent for a moment, then she says: 'Ten years after leaving university we had a reunion. I wasn't invited, because one of my fellow students had become a Securitate agent. I was able to attend to the next reunion, since the Securitate man wouldn't be there. Perhaps he'd become too important by then to go to university reunions.

'I always had a guardian angel. I never had to do heavy labour. For years I copied musical notation in the palace of culture, and I worked in a laboratory checking foodstuffs. For my husband it was different. He had to do hard work, first as a day labourer in gardens, later as a workman building bridges. It gave him lead poisoning. He was a very good musician. He played the viola and the piano, and in the Russian prisoner-of-war camp he learnt to play the double bass. He never talked about that camp. I saw a picture of him somewhere, in the camp in the Caucasus, playing his double bass.'

When Emma talks about her husband her voice grows softer. We drive along a street where three elderly sisters lived in a cellar. Strada Justiţiei. Good name. I park at the side of the road. Emma points to a tall old building. That's where they lived. Romanian aristocrats. In the cellar. Emma tells me the youngest of them once secretly returned to the family estate. She stood outside, looked at their old home and then put it out of her mind. She travelled back and none of the three sisters ever saw the family property again after that. They were *grande dames*, well-read; they'd travelled the world. The stairs were too steep for them in old age. For years they didn't go out. The other cellar-dwellers brought them food. When one of the three had to visit a doctor, Emma's husband fixed wheels to the legs of a chair and pushed her to the hospital. The sisters were delighted by the hospital windows. 'So much light!' That outing made them tremendously happy.

Emma: 'The worst thing was the exclusion. You were no longer part of society. Many old schoolfriends didn't want anything more to do with me because contact with me would hamper their careers. The feeling that you're a danger to your friends is atrocious. If I noticed friends feeling uncomfortable, I avoided them from then on. If you found yourself approaching an acquaintance in the street you quickly crossed over. That's why people with Domiciliu Obligatoriu visited each other, so that they wouldn't be a danger to anyone else. Our exclusion created a small but good community.'

I asked whether she enjoyed being with people with Domiciliu Obligatoriu.

'We couldn't speak freely. The Securitate kept an eye on us practically all the time, and invariably one of us would be arrested afterwards. We met at different places to make it as hard for them as possible. The people arrested were interrogated for a long time and they usually made you stand on one leg. Sometimes you were held for days. That was why we played so much bridge and rummy; we could make jokes, laugh, look at each other and flirt without having to say very much. We were shadowed by the Securitate. The phones were tapped. They still are.

'When the revolt in Hungary broke out in 1956 my mother implored us not to say a word about it. When my pupils asked about it, all I could do was to read out a poem by Endre Ady. That was how I tried to make clear what I thought. One time I was accused of saying something bad about Stalin. The father of one of the children in my class was in the Securitate, and he saved me by crossing my name off the list. I don't know which father it was. I didn't want to know. You shouldn't underestimate how severely you could be punished for a thing like that.

'My stepfather Árpád Mikó was picked up. He'd made a remark about the monetary system. In 1952 new money was introduced to make sure no one could use any funds they'd secretly stashed away. Someone betrayed my stepfather for complaining about the system. The Securitate tried to put pressure on him. They wanted him to tell them who had gold, since we weren't allowed to have any. He refused to talk, but he paid for his comment with a year in a labour camp. My mother and I were picked up at the same time and banished to a small cobbler's workshop that faced onto the street. We had to live there with eight deported families, sharing a single toilet.

'The camp my stepfather was sent to was called Bicaz, in the Carpathians. They were building a dam there. After he came back, all he told us was that he'd had to break rocks on a steep slope. Even within the family you didn't talk about those experiences. You don't talk about great suffering. That's how a person protects his psyche. My stepfather's brother, László, was picked up five years later and sentenced to ten years' imprisonment with hard labour in the Danube delta because he knew about a so-called conspiracy, called "Steel Fist" and hadn't told the Securitate about it.'

Károly Orbán was a friend of Emma's from her earliest childhood. He spoke eight languages and was the kind of man who didn't keep his opinions to himself. Emma showed me a photograph of him. He looked like Paulie in *The Sopranos*, a man with a powerful gaze. Once he got something into his head there was no stopping him. Emma turned away as she started to talk about him and turned back to face me only half a minute later. The Securitate followed every step Károly took. Before his arrest he'd had a prostate operation. He suffered in prison; the guards wouldn't let him go to the toilet.

'I had to put it aside,' Emma says of the book that was published two years ago about the show trial to which Károly Orbán and others were subjected. 'I couldn't read it.'

On 3 March 1949 Károly Orbán's family was removed from a property in Mezőmadaras, the village where Anikó Bethlen had also lived. They were banished to an adobe house in Marosvásárhely. When it rained they had to put buckets all over the place because the roof leaked like a sieve. During their Domiciliu Obligatoriu they were forced to move twelve times. Mária, Károly Orbán's daughter, was seven when her mother died. She still remembers Anikó Bethlen, especially the big ginger cat she had. Mária's father tried to keep his family by working as an ice-cream salesman, button maker and private teacher of English. He was arrested and executed when Mária was twelve. She now lives in New York under a different name.* In a book of reminiscences by a number of Transylvanian families she describes the large park around the house at Mezőmadaras. There were two huge silver firs. When they had Domiciliu Obligatoriu and lived in Marosvásárhely, the miller at the old country house came to tell them the silver firs in the park had been felled. It was the first time in her life that she saw her father cry.

Emma shows me where to park. A street with low old houses on the right. She has already told me about this cellar, her eyes glistening: how she did it up single-handed, how colleagues and schoolchildren came to help paint it, how she rustled up furniture from here and there to put in it, and found a stove. She lived in this second cellar for sixteen years, first alone and without a window, later with a window and her husband. They were the happiest days of her life: her own cellar. From 1952 to 1968 she lived there, and after so many years her heart swelled with joy as she talked about it. 'I can't explain to you what it

---

* A great many children of aristocrats and untitled nobles changed their names in the communist period to avoid discrimination. It meant they could study or find a normal job and lead a decent life. Many others were adopted.

meant to me to have a place of my own! I can still remember the first night I spent there. I was able to make tea and sleep in my own bed. It wasn't a cellar. No. It was mine.'

Strada Şcolii. Iskola utca in Hungarian. School Street in English. I watch Emma shuffle along the pavement beside me. Now that we're getting close I have my doubts. She's only just told me that she's never been back. I'm a monster. I stop and ask her if she's sure about this; we could simply go and eat cake in a *cukrászda*. No, she wants to go to the cellar. She's determined. I realize that my casual suggestion has become an odyssey for her.

We arrive at some rusty, chest-high railings. Here it is. On the front gate are several nameplates and doorbells. Beyond the railings lies a garden with an apple tree. We're in the middle of Marosvásárhely, but it's as if we're looking at a little garden in a Hungarian village. The grass is scattered with brown leaves and an old white Dacia is parked on it. Beside the wall of the house is a vegetable plot. Emma pushes the bell. No answer. Maybe it's better that way. I half-heartedly call out 'Hello!', then look at her and raise my eyebrows, but she stands with her bag in her hand as if she's willing to wait here for the rest of the day. People who lived in Ceauşescu's Romania don't worry about having to wait for a while. In the 1980s it took many hours to get food items – flour, eggs, milk. A queue outside a shop was a good sign; it meant supplies of some kind had been delivered.

A small, rotund man appears. He looks annoyed as he picks his way along the garden path. When he recognizes Emma he's awe-struck. He straightens his back and gives a little bow, takes her hand and tilts his head forward in a pleasant, respectful yet not subservient way. He's honoured that she's come. I shake his hand. He's a roguish older man, resembling a likeable headmaster. Emma explains why we're here. He goes ahead of us. After just a few steps down we walk along a short corridor and turn left into a room. It's not really a cellar, more a basement apartment. The room now serves as a student bedsit.

I'd imagined a bigger space, since the cellar was used for bridge evenings. It's almost a closet and I can barely stand up straight: four metres by two and a half, with a kitchen attached no bigger than a standard toilet cubicle. Above the unmade student bed is a window with a view of the courtyard garden. Emma's husband cut it out of the wall, Emma has told me with pride and joy. She stands on the threshold of the room and surveys the mess, then walks slowly to the kitchen and stares at the dirty pans on the stove. She turns away, steps into the room again and runs her eyes over it one more time before walking to the window and looking out. Then she hurries back up the steps.

The man and I follow. He quickly picks up a plastic bag of apples and gives it to Emma. I take the bag from her. Carrying a bag of maggoty light-green apples I follow her out of the garden. We walk in silence to the car. She fiddles with her fingers and says: 'It's become a kind of prison. It was open then; now it feels as if someone lives there who's put themselves in a prison – a bad feeling.'

She shakes her head. I help her into the car, then get in and start the engine. She stares at the black plastic of the dashboard. Suddenly a little girl is sitting next to me. Her hands are folded between her knees, as if she's having to hold herself together. Then she says: 'My house doesn't exist any more. It was mine. I made it from nothing. Now I can take my leave of it. In my memory that cellar was something beautiful and good, it was my dream house, but it turns out it was nothing but a hole in the ground.'

No one in Armenierstadt speaks Armenian now

Gherla, September 2009

The potatoes are being grubbed up, the nuts shaken out of the trees, the storks are flying back to Africa and we, without a permit to see it, are on our way to a high-security penitentiary in the most Byzantine part of Europe. The prison is at Gherla, a small town fifty kilometres north of Kolozsvár, on the banks of the Szamos.

Gherla was originally called Armenopolis, or Armenierstadt in German. In 1700 the Habsburg emperor Leopold gave the Armenians the right to build a town of their own on the Szamos and sold them a piece of land not far from the bishop's palace for the purpose. Armenopolis grew from a village of some seventy families into a town of three thousand Armenian households. It was the first town in the Habsburg Empire to be built as a grid, like New York. Some tens of thousands of Armenians lived in Transylvania, having arrived in several waves of mass migration from the motherland

and from eastern Moldova at the invitation of the prince of Transylvania, Michael Apafi. Apafi gave the Armenians the right to settle at four places in Transylvania: Csíkszépvíz, Gyergyószentmiklós, Szamosújvár (Gherla) and Erzsébetváros (Dumbrăveni).

I'm travelling in the company of Lidis, a Romanian sociologist. I know her from the Central European University in Budapest where we studied together. She has fine features and long black hair. She's caring and considerate, with high ethical standards. It has often surprised me that in the wild East you keep coming upon highly civilized, refined individuals of this sort, like orchids blooming on a rubbish dump.

In the little towns that Lidis and I drive through, the streets are full of people. Women dressed in black throng in front of the Romanian Orthodox churches. Driving through the hills and the villages with their wooden or adobe houses, horses and carts, cows at the side of the road, women and girls wearing headscarves and festive traditional costume, I can barely contain my enthusiasm for all the beautiful things I'm seeing. But to Lidis, a Romanian from cosmopolitan Timişoara, this is simply a backward region. When I point with delight at a flock of sheep on a slope, I realize that where I discern a magnificent archaic landscape, she sees only poverty. I express my disgust at the new buildings in the villages, those shoeboxes painted in garish colours. Lidis doesn't understand why I should object.

'The villagers have a right to a good life, don't they? The people who live here are peasants. Ignorant peasants. They don't have an internet connection, they live in the shit. And the same goes for the majority of the population of Romania, even today.'

Lidis sees the villagers' ignorance as one of the causes of her country's problems. You can put anything over on them; the riffraff are able to stay on their comfortable perches in Bucharest because the majority of the people are stuck in this comatose backwardness. And to cap it all the joyful Dutch visitor is delighted by this whole sink of iniquity!

'Of course these people have a right to running water, sewers and the internet,' I say. 'But they can install decent toilets, bathrooms and kitchens by refurbishing the existing houses. The future for the villagers lies in small-scale agriculture and tourism. The landscape, the wooden houses, the walled churches – a village only needs one orange colossus like that and the magic is gone. Those houses lack all human scale. It's as if they've been inspired by Ceauşescu's Casa Poporului. With megalomania like that you'll destroy your own future.'

Lidis stares straight ahead. We glide through the drab landscape of late summer. I no longer dare to point ecstatically at ox-drawn carts, at bent women turning the rich soil with mattocks, at fields being ploughed with horses, or flocks of sheep swarming across the hillsides. And I haven't even unleashed all my theories on Lidis yet. Like the notion that the insane architecture says something about the country, about being uprooted, adrift from tradition, like a teenage boy who dyes his hair purple and gets himself pierced all over. It might seem merely a matter of appearances, but it's symptomatic of the impulsiveness and lawlessness of countries set adrift.

The former satellite states of the Soviet Union, including Hungary and Romania, are in a moral vacuum. Knowledge of their own past is lacking. They're susceptible to crazy ideas. By systematically crushing, exiling and killing the bearers of tradition, morality and fairness for over half a century, a society makes itself unstable. Population groups that traditionally formed a middle class of artisans and traders – Jews, Saxons and Armenians – were killed or deported, or escaped abroad. The Jews were murdered in the Second World War. After the war, half a million Transylvanian Germans were sent to camps in Russia and several hundred thousand Saxons and Swabians fled westwards. The Armenians knew from their relatives in Armenia, part of the Soviet Union since 1922, what the coming of the Russians would mean and in the last year of the war they fled via Hungary to France, America and Lebanon.

In communist times the Armenian schools were closed. Free trade, by which most Armenians made their living, ceased. Several hundred still live in Transylvania, and in Budapest there's a community of several thousand, with its own church on Gellért Hill. A hundred and twenty Armenians are left in Gherla. Half of them attend the Armenian Catholic church. The Armenians who stayed are no longer traders but engineers and bank employees. The church choir is made up of Armenians, but they don't know what they are singing. No one in Armenierstadt speaks Armenian now. Not even the priest.

Lidis has researched the Romanian system of detention under the communists; she knows the worst prisons and several of today's prison governors. She has already spent two weeks trying to arrange for me to be allowed into the prison at Gherla. First she sent a request to the governor explaining my mission and my motives. The governor answered that she would have to obtain authorization from Bucharest, at the national prisons administration. Lidis sent them an email and received a reply saying her request must be submitted by fax. Her fax went unanswered. After telephoning continually for three days she got a woman on the line who snapped at her, saying the director was on holiday and Lidis should resend the fax. At that point I asked her to give up any further attempt.

I want to see Gherla prison primarily because several of the relatives and friends of people I've spoken to were held there, but also out of a desire to get closer to that 'feeling', to the terror of the totalitarian state. Naive? So be it. I really can't think of a better way. Terror, oppression and torture are unknown to me. I've never experienced them, but they certainly frighten me.

I've spoken to two people who were interrogated by the Securitate for several weeks and spent years in the Romanian gulag. Perhaps trying to sense the oppression and terror is as nonsensical as trying to get to know what pain is by reading about it.

In Budapest I've twice been to the Terror Háza, or House of Terror, the museum devoted to the horrors people were subjected to under fascism and communism. The museum is at Andrássy út 60, the former headquarters of the ÁVH, the Hungarian secret police. The permanent exhibition has been put together with a touch too much theatricality. The information ought to have been presented less sensationally, with nothing but cold facts and bleak statistics. Nevertheless, although I regard myself as a more-or-less sober Dutchman, decades after it happened I can feel the pain and fear oozing out of the pores in the walls. You'd have to be made of reinforced concrete not to feel it. Perhaps I'm secretly expecting to experience something similar at Gherla.

Gherla was one of the three Romanian institutions – along with Aiud and Camp Peninsula on the Danube – Black Sea Canal – where the 're-education programme' developed in Pitești in 1949 and 1950 was implemented. It started in Gherla in the autumn of 1951 and went on until August 1952. In a special wing, prisoners were tortured by fellow prisoners for days, sometimes weeks on end until they foreswore who they were and a new man was born.

The brainwashing happened in four stages. You were shut in a cell with a fellow prisoner who, after you'd got to know him and felt you trusted each other, became your tyrant. Pressured by means of humiliation and torture, in a process known as 'unmasking', the prisoner had to distance himself from everything that was dear to him. The final step that brought re-education to a successful conclusion consisted of making the victim torture a fellow prisoner, preferably his best friend. Students and priests were the groups seen as most in need of re-education.

The programme was based on the ideas of Soviet sociologist and educationalist Anton Marenko and developed by Ludovic Zeller from Oradea and Boris Grunberg from Tiraspol. The subject must be made to understand that he was a *declassé* and that his only hope of salvation lay in gaining the support of the Party, which he could do only by bringing fellow failures to the path of truth by means of 're-education'. The goal was to destroy the personalities of opponents of the regime. Alexandru Nicolski, deputy director of the Securitate, was responsible for implementing the system, which was first used on 6 December 1949 in Pitești, where a group of prisoners trained in 're-education' methods provoked an argument with their cellmates. The guards intervened and took the cellmates to the courtyard, where they had to undress and lie flat on the ground. For half an hour the guards hit the prisoners with iron bars before turning them over to Turcanu, the leader of the re-education group.

The Romanian leadership terminated the programme in 1952, probably because of concerns about bad publicity abroad, or as the result of an internal power struggle. Twenty-two of the prisoners involved in the re-education programme were executed. None of the inventors of the programme were tried. Part of the reason no one speaks about re-education is that the only possible way of surviving it was to torture fellow prisoners. I haven't met any of those who went through it. I did, though, have a phone passed to me one summer's afternoon when I was sitting with friends in a garden in Marosvásárhely eating lunch. It was a Transylvanian who had survived re-education when he was a student. He couldn't meet me, but he had written a book. Freely translated, its title was: *If You've Survived Then You Keep Your Trap Shut.*

In its grotesque sadism, the Romanian re-education programme demonstrates the essence of communism: the insistence on submission to the Party, the creation of a new man by violence, the destruction of the individual, the deep-seated hatred of all independent thinkers. Strikingly – and this actually sums up communism – the new man was defined by his preparedness to become a tyrant himself. A system that produces such a programme is one of unlimited terror.

Behind a cemetery rises a tall building surrounded by high walls, with a watchtower every 200 metres. The structure inside the walls, with its great height in relation to its width, looks like a late-nineteenth-century grain silo. But this is a Renaissance building, converted to become Transylvania's central prison in 1785, under Habsburg rule. Until then it had been Bishop Martinuzzi's fortress.

Around the prison lies a district full of typical low Hungarian rural dwellings, each with an apple tree and a few chickens in the yard. The roads are of mud. In winter, in the shadow of the prison, this place must be a sorry mess.

We stop next to the wall. The guard in the nearest tower steps out of his cubical and keeps an eye on us, a machine-gun slung loosely over his shoulder.

An elderly woman walks up to us. She's lived here all her life. Seventy years. I ask whether she can remember anything about the 1950s and whether she knows this was one of the worst prisons in Romania.

'No,' she says guiltily. 'We didn't really know anything. We didn't know what went on inside the walls. At night you'd sometimes hear screaming. That's why we thought there was torture going on. But we never saw prisoners coming in or being driven away.'

The early 1950s were probably the hardest years in Gherla. The prison governor was a Securitate officer by the name of Gheorghiu, who welcomed the prisoners by telling them: 'This is Gherla University. When you graduate – although I don't think you ever will – you'll be a real man. Until then, I'm your boss.'

Cell 99 was on the fourth floor, in a corner to the northeast, away from the town, with windows onto the prison yard. The screams of the tortured echoed around the yard, which now houses two basketball courts. On that same fourth floor, the smaller cells 96, 97, 98 and 101 were used for 'unmaskings' and the accompanying torture sessions, which sometimes lasted for weeks. Prisoners had to transfer their own faeces from their chamber pots into their eating bowls and were hit repeatedly until they'd eaten everything. People lay on pallets. If anyone fell asleep he was hit hard on the soles of the feet with an iron bar. The night was one long struggle to stay awake. There were also 'playful' means of torture. A prisoner would be made to launch himself off from the shoulders of a fellow prisoner with his arms spread, like a plane, and land flat on the floor. This went on until the prisoner had made a beautiful landing.

The entrance to the prison is around the corner. We are let into a small room. On the left is a glass wall with a counter. It's not much different from the average railway station ticket office. The woman behind the glass is friendlier than most counter staff in Eastern Europe. She listens. Lidis talks and talks, and hands over documents. The woman disappears into another room and comes back after a while with a male colleague. He's wearing the same blue uniform and he tells us that letting a foreigner in without agreement from Bucharest is out of the question.

Via a side door, three men step into the small space. The first is extremely tall with a typically American appearance: a long and narrow face with a perfect set of teeth, slightly sunken cheeks, his hair sleek and neatly combed to the right. He looks like a religious-maniac brother to the actor Steve Buscemi. The guard gestures that we must all go next door, into a waiting room the size of a washroom. I end up next to Steve Buscemi's brother. He is indeed American and he's been visiting prisoners for eight years on behalf of the Baptists. He tells me: 'The progress this prison has made is unbelievable. You should have been here five years ago. It was mediaeval then. They had too many men crammed into small spaces. The prisoners here have long sentences. Most will never leave this prison, but they are open to God.'

The Romanian Baptist community is tiny, and a relatively large number of its flock have criminal records.

'The Romanian Orthodox Church is the most powerful Church in Romania. Financed by the state, it's the official state church. All the priests, monks and nuns are provided for by the state. That was true under communism too; the priests' salaries were paid by the Romanian state. Unfortunately...' The Baptist lowers his voice. 'That meant there were a lot of Securitate among the priests.'

The Baptist and his two Romanian companions are called away. 'May the Lord watch over you,' he says.

A short while later Lidis and I are called. A small man in a suit is standing in the room through which we entered. He doesn't shake hands. He bawls Lidis out in Romanian. She smiles charmingly and speaks calmly. Then the little man seems to explode. He stamps to the door that leads to freedom. Standing outside with the doorknob in his hand he shouts: 'You're getting me into trouble!' He sweeps his arm in the direction of the two guards standing behind Lidis. 'Okay, just let them in!'

A bald guard enters the prison. He speaks English and has all the gaiety and heartiness of a guide on a sightseeing boat. We walk towards the main gate and cross a bridge that probably once spanned a castle moat. To the right are ping-pong tables, surrounded by a six-metre fence. Muscled, bare-chested men shout as they play. From speakers high up comes 'Poker Face' by Lady Gaga.

I shared a bed
with the archbishop
of the Greek Orthodox
Church

Gherla, September 2009

The main gate rises before us. This was once the fortress of Bishop Martinuzzi, that distant ancestor of Judit Hajós. Beside the entrance is a two-metre-tall marble plaque bearing the names of the men who helped to convert the place into a prison in 1785: Degenfeld, Rhédey, Bornemissza, Apor, Lázár, Kemény, Jósika and Mikó – probably provincial governors of the time. With the coming of communism these ruling families became the persecuted. The Rhédey and Lázár families had died out by 1949 and could no longer be rounded up. Carola Bornemissza was fortunate enough to have died a year earlier. I don't know whether there were still Degenfelds in Transylvania then – Ilona had a great uncle, Count Otto Degenfeld, who lived in Vienna, where we visited him once – but descendants of all the other founders still lived in Transylvania, and they all without exception became victims of communism. Several were imprisoned in Gherla. Count

László Mikó was led in through this gate in 1958. Will he have made out the name of his ancestor on the plaque?

I haven't spoken to any of the aristocrats who were held at Gherla. The last of them died in 2005. Through Anikó Bethlen I did make contact with a Hungarian clergyman in Marosvásárhely, László Varga, who was imprisoned here at around the same time, the late 1950s. He wrote in his memoirs that the hardest thing of all was being cut off from the outside world. You didn't know how your parents were doing, your brothers and sisters, your children, your wife.

The Romanian policy was to persuade the wives of prisoners to petition for divorce. Women were put under pressure in ways that amounted to blackmail. They were sacked from their jobs, their children excluded from school. As soon as they filed for divorce the restrictions were lifted. The prisoner would be called into a small room to sign the papers submitted by his wife. Then he was taken back to his cell. It was just another way of breaking a prisoner's will.

László Varga described divorcing his first wife that way. He received me one evening in his modest house in Marosvásárhely, where he lives with his second wife. She was in a wheelchair. He had met her because of his imprisonment and he was still thankful for that. Because of the bonus on his pension for every year he'd been in prison, he was now a rich man. He had this large house and a car to drive her around in. He'd received a life sentence because he and a few friends made efforts to promote good relations between Hungary and Romania, which was naturally interpreted as subversive activity at the show trial in 1957. He had been in the prisons at Gherla, Kolozsvár, Jilava and Piteşti. The difference between the prisons in Transylvania (the first two) and in Wallachia (the last two) was that in the former things were done in a fairly orderly manner. In Wallachia it was a mess.

'In Piteşti we were given only *mămăligă* to eat. In Transylvania we got a kind of maize bread and there were beds. You were usually two or three men to a bed eighty centimetres wide, but at least there were beds. In Jilava we had to sleep on the floor. That's where I saw István Bánffy. Jilava was a transit prison. In Gherla I shared a bed with the archbishop of the Greek Orthodox Church. The company I had in Gherla has never been equalled in my life since. Never again was I surrounded by such extraordinary men: diplomats, senior officers in the military, professors, bishops, aristocrats, poets. I was even in a cell with Count Tisza, a remarkable man. He'd become a Seventh Day Adventist in prison. He adopted a subservient attitude to the guards that didn't suit him.'

Anikó Bethlen told me about a distant relative, a countess who had served time in various Romanian prisons, including Gherla. She was sentenced to eighteen years for typing an anti-Communist manifesto. When she came out of prison she became a Jehovah's Witness, because they were the only people who retained their humanity in the camp, under all circumstances. The people running the camp had eventually managed to turn all the other prisoners into animals.

The prison official leads Lidis and me round to the left and back to a low door. It's as if we're entering a wine cellar. Under the old brick vaulting the space is clammy and dark. This is now the memorial room. There's one narrow air shaft for ventilation. The guide says this was the only place of execution. Lidis will contradict him later, telling me that prisoners were executed at other places too, in the woods outside Gherla for example, and sometimes in full view, in the midst of the other prisoners. In one corner stands a simple coffin made of planks.

Lidis: 'I don't think they used coffins. The prisoners were dumped in a pit, several at a time.'

Lining the walls are glass cases displaying the paraphernalia of repression: manacles, shackles and black aviator's goggles. The guard says the goggles were put on men about to be executed. They had to kneel down with their heads between their knees, hands tied behind their backs, and the barrel was put to their necks. On the wall are plaques of gleaming marble in memory of the people executed, with their names and dates of execution, all in 1958 and 1959. I count the shiny memorial plaques. There are forty-two of them. Lidis whispers in my ear: 'It was many more than that.'

In *The Chronology and the Geography of the Repression in Communist Romania*, Romulus Rusan writes that prisoners also died under torture in Gherla. Then there were the dozens who succumbed to malnutrition or tuberculosis. Romanian Count Radu Rosetti (one of his forefathers had been given a title by the Habsburgs) was held in Gherla. His weight fell from 82 to 48 kilos while he was there. The archives are incomplete. Where reports are available, the cause of death is often given as 'heart failure' or 'high blood pressure'. One method of 'silent genocide' was to have prisoners disappear into mass graves during transport through the *padurea verde*, the green woods. Romulus Rusan makes mention of one such transport from Gherla in the spring of 1950, with thirty-eight prisoners.

'Did anyone ever escape from Gherla?' I ask our guide.

'No,' says the guard, a little too triumphantly. 'But they did while working in the fields. Sometimes prisoners got away then.'

Reverend László told me: 'In Gherla the cells came in different sizes: six-man cells of two by four metres with three-tier bunks; a cell for thirty to forty men and a cell for a hundred. The more people in a cell the better, because it increased the chances of making good friends. We taught each other poems. I had a good memory for poetry. At one point I was in a cell with four poets.

'In prison we communicated via the pipes, in morse code. At first we used Romanian, but it was quickly replaced by English because then the guards couldn't understand. I didn't see see a single printed word in all those years. You weren't allowed to read. If you were caught with anything written you were put in solitary confinement. Below ground they had cells that were always flooded. You'd have to spend three days in a watery cell like that. You couldn't lie down or sit. There was nothing, no chair, no bed, only a floor covered with thirty centimetres of water. In winter it was freezing cold in there. You had only a jute sack to wrap around you. You were deprived of food, given just half a pound of bread and a bit of water. A worse punishment was to be locked in the black cell. It was pitch dark and so small you couldn't move, only stand up bent over. I can sleep anywhere, that's never a problem, but in the black cell it was almost impossible.

'Because I'd been sentenced to life, I wasn't allowed to work. The risk I'd escape was too great. You had to get up at six, at seven you were given a little water with some black dregs and a piece of bread. At one o'clock there was lunch, at eight o'clock the evening meal, at ten o'clock bed. We were in our cells all day. You weren't allowed to lie down. If you did and were caught you got solitary. You were given one piece of soap to last two months. You could wipe it across your hand and then write words on your hand with a piece of bone. That's how I learnt English. If the guards came by to check, you only had to spit in your palm once and all the words were gone. I preached and tried to help others. No, I wasn't a hero.

'After seven years and five months they let me go, in 1964. Thanks to the American government. Ceaușescu needed money and the United States made it a condition that he let all his political prisoners go. In 1964 a general amnesty for political detainees was announced.'

It was the first time I'd heard that explanation. The general amnesty is a known fact; I thought Ceaușescu had introduced it to make himself popular with the Romanian people and to present himself as a moderate leader. For all those with Domiciliu Obligatoriu it was important because many of the restrictions on them were lifted at the time of the amnesty. They were given more freedom of movement, allowed a greater choice of where to live and work, but in practice the discrimination continued, since their identity papers were still marked 'DO'. They retained their pariah status.

We leave the memorial room. I expect to be taken back to the lockers, but we go further into the prison. We have to pass through another barrier with a metal detector. Gates open and close. We arrive at the large prison yard, surrounded by high buildings on its long sides and on its short sides by ten-metre-high walls topped with barbed wire. There are two basketball courts. A man covered in tattoos rams the ball into the basketball fence with an enormous bang. We walk past a group of prisoners who are mooching about like loitering teenagers: two Pakistanis, several gypsies, and a great many muscle-bound men with tattoos and a dull look in their eyes. They're excited by the fact that a young woman with bare legs is passing just a few metres away.

Lidis and I are shown classrooms painted light blue, the walls hung with maps of Romania, Europe and the world. Then a room with a battery of computers, a craftwork class-room and a language centre with headphones. The tour does not have the same oppressive effect as a visit to the underground cells of the Terror Háza in Budapest, but perhaps that is actually the point of the pale-blue walls, the cheerful guide and the carefully tended memorial room. The well-intentioned Sunday-school atmosphere served up to us is a long way from the hell that Varga, Bethlen, Mikó and thousands of others descended into half a century ago.

The PR tour concludes with a visit to Gherla's in-house deejay, an old hippy with a long grey beard like a hermit of the Greek Orthodox Church. In a far corner of the recreation and education floor, in a tiny room lined with egg boxes, he plays the music that you hear blaring everywhere: Lady Gaga, Madonna, 50 Cent. He sits there all day long, on his own, in a windowless cubicle. It's the closest thing I see to the black cell that László Varga told me about.

Enemies of the people

Budapest, October 2009

My meeting with the foremost specialist on the Hungarian nobility in Hungary and Transylvania, Baron János Gudenus, takes place in the Astoria Hotel at the start of the Rákóczi út in Budapest. A hundred metres further on is the house where Ilona's family used to live in the winter, a faded yellow-ochre building, four storeys high and forty metres wide, with the family coat of arms at the top of the façade. The communists tried to chisel out the shield but it was too high up. It's one of the few properties in Budapest still to have the original coat of arms in the front wall. The house has not been returned to the family. In Hungary there is no scheme for returning houses expropriated by the communists to their previous owners. On the ground floor on the street side is a Costa Coffee outlet, and beyond it a dubious-looking currency exchange office and a large pharmacy.

Until the second half of the nineteenth century the city boundary ran through here. Although the Astoria Hotel is no longer what it was (a McDonald's has opened beside the main entrance), with its parquet and wooden panelling, its gleaming brass balustrades and lamps, it still exudes the atmosphere of the old world. Gudenus points through the window to the building across the street which used to house the Nemzeti Kaszinó, the famous club for the Hungarian aristocracy. At its gaming tables family fortunes and country estates were won and lost in the years between the wars. Miklós Bánffy describes in his memoirs how he spent nights on end gambling here with Mihály Károlyi, his cousin and bosom friend from childhood. In the time of the Dual Monarchy, the Hungarians were renowned for their card playing. The unspoken rule was that anything lost at the tables must be handed over within twenty-four hours. Count Mihály Károlyi was manoeuvred into politics by his family to keep him away from the gaming tables.

My appointment with János Gudenus has been arranged by Judit Hajós, an old friend of Ilona's and mine. She will act as interpreter. Through her Transylvanian grandparents she is related to Countess Rhédey and therefore to the British royal family. Judit can sometimes be excessively boisterous, but she more than makes up for that by her joviality and her appearance; she could have been a model for Art Nouveau painter Alphonse Mucha, with her Danube-blue eyes and wild long dark hair.

On 14 January 1947 the nobility was outlawed in Hungary. As well as double-barrelled names, the use of titles and coats of arms was banned, as were distinctions once extended by the king or emperor, such as 'privy councillor to the emperor'. The nobility was outlawed in Romania that same year, along with every way of addressing a person in speech or writing that could suggest a difference in class.

— Mit gürcöl itt bregem? Ez a föld úgyis újra az enyém lesz.
— Tévedni tetszik, installom, mert a temető éppen ellenkező irányban van.

In Hungary fifteen hundred castles and almost three million hectares of land were expropriated. In 1951 mass deportations took place in Budapest, Győr, Szombathely and Székesfehérvár. Titled and untitled nobles, officers, the wealthy bourgeoisie, people in key positions and house owners unfortunate enough to live in houses the nomenklatura had their eye on were put on transports. Among them were survivors of Auschwitz. Some committed suicide, others demonstratively pinned the star of David to their lapels. More than 15,000 people from Budapest, 5,182 class-enemy families (including six princes, fifty-two counts, forty-one barons and hundreds of untitled nobles) were hauled off to so-called 'social camps' in the Hortobágy, an isolated part of the Great Hungarian Plain. The deported were forced to perform hard labour and sleep in stables and barracks, surrounded by barbed wire. Agricultural land was flooded in an attempt to create Europe's most northerly rice paddies.

Between 1949 and 1953, under Mátyás Rákosi – nicknamed 'the bald murderer' – more than 200,000 people in Hungary disappeared into prisons and labour camps. At least six hundred were hanged in that period. How many died as a result of the tough conditions in the camps and prisons, or by torture or in night-time executions is unknown. There were four concentration camps in Hungary in those years: Recsk, Kistarcsa, Kazincbarcika and Tiszalök. Thousands of prisoners were engaged in hard labour there in daytime, in quarries or in coal and iron ore mines. It was all intended to destroy them slowly.

Baron János Gudenus is the author of the standard work on the Hungarian aristocracy, *Összetört címerek* (Broken Blazons). He's a quiet man, not very big. His hair is thin. Under communism he sought out many of the aristocrats in Transylvania in person, since it was impossible to ask them about their family histories by letter. In the 1960s and '70s the standard of living was higher there than in Hungary. 'That changed in the 1980s, when life in Romania became extremely hard as a result of the austerity measures forced upon the people by Ceauşescu. First the Treaty of Trianon, then the war, then Gheorghiu-Dej and Ceauşescu – in three great waves the Transylvanian aristocracy was forced out of Romania.'

Gudenus: 'I've spent my life with women, not the young but the old. I've devoted my life to sitting with decorous ladies and noting down their stories.'

That sounds familiar to me. I too drink more tea these days than I'd choose. The fact is that within families it's mostly the women who pass on the culture, who take upon themselves the upbringing of the young, preserve the continuity of the family and know the stories and the gossip. It's the women who live longest, too. By talking with the old ladies, Gudenus has been able to capture the history of the Hungarian and Transylvanian nobility over the past sixty years. There is no official record. No one else was interested, except for the Hungarian secret service (which from 1946 to 1950 was called the ÁVO before being renamed the ÁVH) and the Romanian Securitate – they wanted to be certain that the power of the aristocracy was broken once and for all and that they hadn't overlooked anyone, or, more importantly, any gold, money or jewellery. After the detained returned from the camps, they were allowed to do only heavy manual labour and had to live in huts or tiny houses. Their children were excluded from secondary school and university. They were banned from living in Budapest – which is why so many ended up in villages close to the capital.

János: 'The aristocracy and the military families were regarded as the main threat. A note was made on our identity papers and school files, saying we were class enemies. They used us in the classroom as a warning to others.'

That's exactly what Ilona's father told me. He and his sister were made to stand facing everyone and the teacher said they were enemies of the people. They were forced to say aloud in front of the class: 'I'm the spawn of capitalists.' Then all the children were invited to spit on them. Ilona's father was and remains quite indifferent to all that. In the conversations I had in Transylvania it struck me that of all those discriminated against at school, the women had found it more humiliating than the men, possibly because girls are more socially sensitive and more ambitious, wanting to excel at school – the kind of ambition that is generally foreign to boys until they reach twenty.

Katalin Mikes told me: 'When you were seven you could join the pioneers; you were given a red necktie then. You had to work hard at school, get good marks and behave well. I had good marks, I was eligible. I remember my teacher. He was young and he said: "Katalin, I have something unpleasant to tell you. We can't let you become a pioneer I'm afraid, because your father is a count." I almost started to cry. I didn't care whether my father was a count or not.'

Anikó Bethlen and Kati Ugron were also extremely angry about being told they couldn't be pioneers. They'd felt excluded, whereas many men were actually proud to have been refused. The discrimination began in 1949 and continued in Romania until the 1970s. In the 1980s Zsolna, the daughter of

György Ugron, was allowed to become a pioneer. The seven-year-old came home delighted, but her news evoked little enthusiasm there. In the 1970s little Kati Ugron in Transylvania received the same treatment as Ilona's father twenty years before in Hungary.

Kati: 'It became clear from an early age that we needed to live a double life. It was better to hide your origins. I went to nursery school. On the first day the teacher asked which of us had parents who did not have working-class origins. Those children had to stand up. When we did, three or four of us out of the whole class, the teacher said: "Look, no one's allowed to play with these children, because they're class enemies." Two months later, just before Christmas, the same teacher asked: "Who goes to Sunday school at the church?" The same three or four children stood up. The teacher said: "See that? I've already told you not to play with these children. They're the enemy." When I was thirty, I spotted that teacher one day on the banks of the Maros. She'd often laid into me, hitting my fingers with a ruler. When I saw her it all came back and my initial impulse was to go over to her and give her a good thumping. But in the end I left her alone. I didn't even say anything to her.'

'The expropriations we had to endure under communism were nothing compared with the actual intention,' says Gudenus. 'To physically destroy an entire class. First with deportations, torture and executions; later through intimidation and psychological terror. They tried everything: excluding us from society, putting us in labour camps, beating us up in the torture chambers of the secret police. But they didn't succeed in dragging us down. Hardly anyone went crazy, or turned to drink, or yielded to the temptations of communism.'

Scapegoats and
informants

Budapest, October 2009

János Gudenus' claim that none of the aristocrats gave in to the communists or went under because of them does not, I fear, hold true. It sounds great and would inspire hope, and for a long time I believed he was right, but as I spoke to more people, and for longer, cracks appeared in the façade. Gradually people started to come up with stories about the other side of life in a dictatorship. I slowly descended into the darkness. The fact that they buckled says less about the people themselves than about the regime they were living under, which wanted them either to bend or to break.

To gain a clearer impression of how it worked in practice I meet young historian Zsófia on a café terrace in Budapest. She works for the Terror Háza, the most visited museum in Hungary.

Zsófia: 'In all Eastern Bloc countries the secret police were modelled after the NKVD, the forerunner to the KGB. The

ÁVO and the Securitate were always accompanied by KGB instructors. In Budapest there was even a Dzerzhinsky Academy, set up in 1950-1951 for ÁVO applicants and named after Felix Dzerzhinsky, a Pole who worked with Lenin and devised the methodology of terror. People were taught how to put a file together, how to prepare a prosecution, how to handle the dramaturgy of a trial. They also received training in techniques of interrogation and torture. The most important aspect was psychological terror. Those subjected to it always say that mental torture is worse than physical torture. You were picked up at night. That's the origin of the Hungarian word *csengőfrász*, "the fear of the doorbell".'

A seventy-year-old countess in Transylvania described that fear to me. After her family's 3 March deportation she ended up with her grandmother, who still had an apartment in the centre of Kolozsvár. It was clear they wouldn't be allowed to stay there. Every night her mother and grandmother took turns to stand by the window looking out at the street. In Romania it was always a Duba, a Land Rover-type vehicle, that came to fetch you. One night a Duba stopped outside the house. They heard men trudging up the stairs. The whole family was terrified. No one knew what happened after they came for you, but they did know the fate of the Russian tsar's family during the 1917 Revolution. That night it was five elderly ladies living in the same house who were taken away, one of them on a stretcher.

Zsófia goes on: 'You were given black goggles or a blindfold every time you were moved, even within a prison. You were kept in perpetual isolation. Denied any news, you lost all sense of time. You sat in a cell where the light was on day and night, and you were systematically kept awake. Each cell had a sofa bed, but you were forbidden to lie on it and if you fell asleep you were beaten awake. During nocturnal interrogations the same question was put to you endlessly, sometimes for weeks.

In the Andrássy út you were given a bowl both to defecate in and to eat from. Each prisoner wore the clothes he'd arrived in, so you became filthy and started to stink. The goal was constant humiliation.'

One of those I spoke to in Transylvania showed me a list of fellow Transylvanian aristocrats who were murdered during the dictatorship, committed suicide or disappeared into psychiatric institutions. In the latter case there is no way of knowing whether they had hereditary defects or ended up there because of the system – in Romania there were at least ten mental institutions of a political nature. The death list I saw was very precise, with forename, surname, title and year of death. The person who showed it to me had known all of them. He went through the list with me and told me slowly, name by name, what had happened. A catalogue of tragedies. I listened, tensed rigid, not making notes. It's all in my head. To protect the relatives I'll leave out the names.

After 1944 there were around fifteen cases of suicide among the Transylvanian aristocracy, many of them prompted by a longing for release from rape, torture, terror or being forced to become a Securitate informant. Death seemed the only way out of the nightmare. A Transylvanian countess took poison after the Russians raped her, another jumped down a lift shaft and a third walked up to the fifth floor of a building and threw herself off. In two cases a woman hanged herself and her husband did the same weeks or years later. In one family a mother and child both committed suicide within a short period. In another family two brothers ended their lives at a young age. One aristocrat hanged himself after returning from the Securitate torture chambers. Another fell or jumped out of a window of the Bánffy Palace in Kolozsvár, which is now a museum. An aristocrat in a Romanian hospital died after her drip was pulled out; it's unclear whether she removed it herself. Two Transylvanian counts escaped from the hell of

Romania but couldn't leave their demons behind. One hanged himself in Argentina and the other ended his own life in Germany.

György Ugron described being followed for years by a Securitate agent in Kolozsvár. Butch, the man was called, and he was putting pressure on György to divulge information. The Securitate usually wanted people to betray their fellow aristocrats by telling them who was still hiding money, gold or jewellery. In later years people were put under pressure to give regular accounts of what others were up to, or to install bugging devices. György was regularly picked up or ordered to report to Securitate headquarters. That was terrible, because you never knew how long they might keep you, what they were going to do to you or whether you'd be thrown into the basement cells. One day the Securitate man was no longer there. György went home and said to his wife: 'The devil has left me!' His wife didn't know what he was talking about, since in all those years he hadn't told her he was being followed. The Securitate man had died a natural death and was not replaced. György Ugron was no longer seen as a priority.

A Transylvanian aristocrat who had fled to Budapest after the war was unique in being spared the Hungarian deportations of class enemies in the summer of 1951. Everybody was a little surprised. He'd been able to travel to Romania and Austria. He had money and he said his business partner could fix all sorts of things, although what kind of business he was in was a mystery. The deportations of the titled and untitled nobility, whether in Hungary or in Romania, could not have taken place without informants, since in the end hardly anyone was overlooked. You could find the large landowners in the land register, but the nephews, nieces and cousins who owned nothing and happened to have titles or patents of nobility were more difficult to trace.

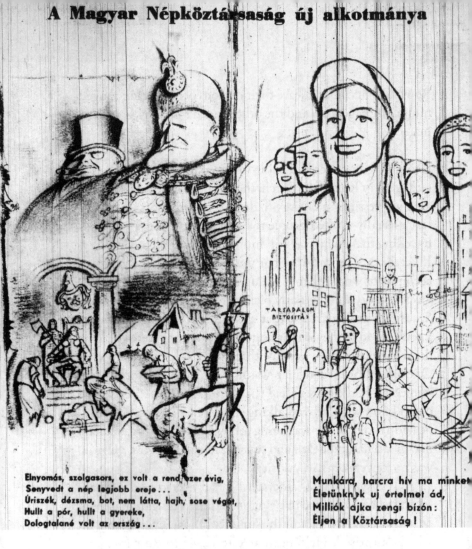

Elnyomás, szolgasors, ez volt a rend ezer évig,
Senyvedt a nép legjobb ereje ...
Úriszék, dézsma, bot, nem látta, hajh, sose végét,
Hullt a pór, hullt a gyereke,
Dologtalané volt az ország ...

Munkára, harcra hív ma minket
Életünknek uj értelmet ád,
Milliók ajka zengi bízón:
Éljen a Köztársaság !

An aristocrat told me: 'I won't say who, but there was an informant. They will have needed someone right in our midst, both in Romania and in Hungary, possibly several people. A baron who gave the ÁVO names for the deportation lists of 1951 later fled to Vienna. He asked for help from a friend of ours, from the same class, who by then had a good job with a big company. Our friend confronted him with his betrayal. The man went bright red and slammed his fist onto the table so hard that he broke two bones in his fingers. The friend found him a job and said he never wanted to see him again. He wasn't allowed to use the company's main staircase, only the steps at the back. That's how it went. Although they worked in the same building, my friend never saw the informant again.'

In Hungary there were several aristocrats once known for their leftist sympathies, including 'red' Count Mihály Károlyi and the anarchist Count Ervin Batthyány. The leftwing Baron József Hatvany attended Cambridge University, where he buckled down to study the ideas of Marx, Engels and Lenin – none of which prevented the communists from throwing him into prison. Then there was Princess Margit Odescalchi, who supported the new regime and was rewarded with the right to keep 150 hectares of land. The story goes that she shared it out among poor peasants before becoming a factory worker. She was the communists' showpiece – a princess who sided with the proletariat! – so they gave her a seat in parliament. She had become an anti-fascist during the war after listening night after night to her brother being tortured by the Gestapo in the cell next to hers. In a book published in 1951 called *People's Democracies*, Australian journalist Wilfred G. Burchett writes of her: 'Margit Odescalchi was a notable and noble exception of her class. In general the Hungarian semi-feudal aristocracy was the most corrupt and decadent in Europe and could only be compared with that of Russia of the Romanovs, in the twilight of the Czarist Empire.'

Burchett travelled through Eastern Europe in 1948 and 1949, staying mainly in Hungary and Bulgaria. A fervent communist, he wrote about the trial of Pál Esterházy and Cardinal Mindszenty. Mátyás Rákosi, the leader of the Hungarian Communist Party ('Stalin's best pupil'), wanted a show trial with a lot of international and domestic press in attendance, in order to put the 'old Hungary' in the dock. He wanted to see Cardinal Mindszenty, the most senior representative of the

Catholic Church in Hungary, and Prince Pál Esterházy, the
biggest landowner in Hungary, publicly humiliated.

The pretext was dealing in foreign currency. One of Mindszenty's subordinates had exchanged dollars. Through a bank,
Pál Esterházy became the buyer of those dollars. Around that
single fact a plot was fabricated. Some twenty people were arrested, Mindszenty first, at Christmas 1948, and Esterházy
a few days later. For weeks they were kept awake in the dun-
geons of the ÁVO at Andrássy út 60, and deprived of food and
water. They had to strip naked for interrogation and were confronted with embarrassing or incriminating behaviour from
the past. Not allowed to go to the toilet, they defecated or uri-
nated in their underpants. They were forced to stand against
the wall until they collapsed and were kicked and beaten.
Their mouths were held wide open with clamps so that their
ÁVO interrogators could piss into them.

Rákosi instructed the head of the ÁVO, 'the fist of the party', on how to make a good show of the trial. He was to ensure
that no traces of violence were visible on the hands or faces of
the defendants. The answers they were required to give were
drummed into them. Vilmos Olti, the presiding judge, posed

the questions in such a way as to make the defendants appear idiots. The trial began on 3 February 1949, a month to the day before the deportation of the aristocrats in Transylvania. The tough repression and physical persecution of the aristocracy were launched almost simultaneously in Hungary and Romania, a year and a half after Stalin had called for the dictatorship of the proletariat to be restored. The show trial of Mindszenty and Esterházy was the starting signal for nationwide persecution of the nobility, the main enemies of the people, whether or not they had titles, or wealth, or land.

The hundreds of thousands of men like Australian Wilfred Burchett who applauded communism in the Soviet Union and its satellite states can at best be accused of extreme credulity. But Burchett was not simply gullible, he was also malicious. In his writing he legitimizes torture and murder: 'They bitterly complain about their poverty, do no work and in general live by selling off bits of jewellery or dealing in black-market currency. They provide a disgusting example of what happens to a privileged class when it is robbed of its privileges [...] Their hope for the future is the third world war, which they fondly imagine will restore them their estates and privileges.'

From 1949 onwards, the nobles of Hungary and Romania were condemned to a life comparable to that of a serf prior to 1848. They could disappear into concentration camps for the slightest of reasons. I suspect Burchett's sanctimonious tone represents the official party line. Cartoons based on the same reasoning were published in the communist weekly *Ludas Matyi*, the Hungarian version of the Soviet propaganda magazine *Krokodil*. The nobility was easy to caricature: big double chins, decadent faces, stuffed bellies, fur coats bulging with jewellery and dollar bills. The nobles were blamed for the things Hitler had blamed on the Jews: enriching themselves by foul means; being black marketeers and warmongers. The class enemy, with its egotism, had called down misery upon itself and was incorrigible, a relentless parasite on the working class. The Communist Party, fair and just, would take upon itself the difficult task of purging society of this sick element.

In Romania the Hungarian nobles were enemies twice over, class enemies from an enemy country. After the war, Transylvanian aristocrats who had served in the Hungarian army or occupied high office were labelled war criminals and traitors by the Romanian government and in most cases sentenced to death in their absence. Their possessions became the property of the Romanian state. For some aristocrats, returning to Transylvania was not an option. The writer Count Albert Wass was sentenced to death in his absence and fled to the West. Erzsébet T.'s brother was another of those who received a death sentence. Baron Endre Atzél returned to Transylvania in 1944 with a three-man delegation, on his way to negotiate with Stalin, and was never heard from again. Géza Kemény, the grandfather of my friend Botond, was dragged out of his house in Pusztakamarás by Romanian soldiers along with his small son and taken into the hills, where a machine gun was put to his head. At the end of the war Béla Bethlen gave orders for the freeing of political prisoners, including many communists, because he feared that otherwise the Germans would execute them. In 1945 he was imprisoned by the communists for ten years, spending some of that time in Gherla. István Bethlen, former prime minister of Hungary and an outspoken opponent of the alliance with Nazi Germany, was taken to Moscow by the Russians and died in prison there in October 1946.

In Romania it was only after the Hungarian Uprising of 1956 that show trials took place. In 1957 the Romanian authorities 'discovered' a plot involving fifty-seven people. The aim was to intimidate the Hungarian minority in Transylvania. Among those convicted were forty-nine Hungarians, half of them Catholic priests, Franciscan monks and titled or untitled nobles. Here too a small group of symbolic leaders was to be brought down in public. Ten of those convicted were given death sentences and three more died after a short time in prison. The harshest punishments were reserved for the clergy and titled aristocrats.

A number of those found guilty had set up a party whose aim was to restore democracy. During their trial they were accused of preparing a counterrevolution, under the slogan 'Long Live Zamora!' The leader of the organization, Baron József Huszár, was sentenced to death. The suspects were tortured over a long period of interrogation. I was given the details by a man who knew the Huszár family. József Huszár had a glass ampoule pushed into his urethra, which was then smashed with a hammer, and boiling oil was poured over his wounds. His torturers made sure they kept Huszár alive so that he could eventually be hanged.

In a mass trial, Count Farkas Bethlen was sentenced to twenty-two years in prison. The court claimed that Károly Orbán, childhood friend of Emma P. and a former large landowner of noble extraction, was due to be appointed ambassador to London or minister of foreign affairs once the communists had been overthrown. The secret meetings Orbán was said to have attended in Marosvásárhely were bridge sessions in cellars. He was executed in the Securitate prison in Timișoara on 1 September 1958.

Baron István Schell lived in a cellar and at the time of his arrest he was working as a foreman. He was given a twenty-five-year sentence, which he served in prisons in Timișoara, Arad, Jilava, Galac and Gherla. Count Zsigmond Kún was an official in Marosvásárhely and it was claimed in court that he had planned to deploy a tank unit to occupy the radio station in Bucharest. He received a life sentence. István Orbán was condemned to death for treason and shot in the back of the neck on 1 September 1958 in the prison at Timișoara. Count László Mikó, former governor-general of Maros-Torda, was a supply clerk in Marosvásárhely at the time of his arrest. He had DO and was forced to report to the militia every week. He chose not to join the organization but received a ten-year sentence because he refused to betray his friends to the Securitate. He served time in prisons in Timișoara, Arad, Galac and Gherla. Baron István Bánffy was condemned to fifteen years' hard labour for being a member of the organization. He served part of his sentence in labour camps in the Danube delta. He is the man with the wooden leg whom we encountered earlier in this book.

I ask Zsófia, the young historian at the Terror Háza, whether she knows what form of torture was used on Huszár. She tells me it was a method often used in both Hungary and Romania, on women as well as men. In the Terror Háza she has some of the glass rods. The ampoule was a kind of hollow pipette about twenty-five centimetres long, slightly wider in the middle, which was inserted and smashed. It was extremely painful, but it left no external marks of violence on the prisoner.

Zsófia: 'Electric shocks were used too. For the mouth and nose they applied a lower voltage. Nails were pulled out; bodies were subjected to burning with flames of the kind you use when you go camping. Cigarettes were often stubbed out on the skin during interrogations, with lips particularly popular because of their sensitivity. They would hit a prisoner with rubber coshes, often on the soles of the feet so that it was hard for him to stand. Often they used a special cosh with beads of lead in it. Victims had to fulfil certain tasks, such as endlessly standing on their toes with electrical terminals placed under their heels. Or a prisoner would be made to clamp a pencil between the wall and his forehead; if the pencil fell he was beaten. The show trials and the interrogation and torture techniques were derived from those used in the Soviet Union.

Methods in Hungary and Romania come from the same instruction manual. Aside from some local inventions, torture methods were identical across the satellite states. The intention was to break a person and rob him of all dignity.'

Kis contesa

Zabola, February 2010

There's snow on the peaks of the Berecki-havasok. We skirt
the worst of the crumbling road surface and pass one of
the churches built by Gergely Roy Chowdhury's family. His
ancestors provided a Catholic church for the Hungarians in
the village and an Orthodox church for the Romanian forestry
workers. Two pillars loom up in the beam of the headlights:
the entrance to Zabola. The dilapidated gatekeeper's house
and the avenue stretching ahead of us under ancient chest-
nut trees hint at the grand life once lived here. The wrought
iron gates slowly swing open. After driving from Budapest
for twelve hours along winding roads – the last stretch full
of potholes – with Gergely, descendant of the Mikes counts,
and Dean, a young Canadian writer, I've arrived in the most
easterly corner of Transylvania.

This is the final destination for my two passengers; for me
it's a stop along the way. The Canadian will be staying at Zabo-

la to work on a book set in Montenegro, in an area some Montenegrins call 'Vukojebina' (literally, 'where the wolves fuck' – the back of beyond). We park under pine trees tens of metres tall next to the 'Machine House' where Zabola's guest rooms are located. Gergely will now have to throw himself once again into the task of restoring the main house, along with his brother Sándor, as well as running the forestry company and the guesthouse.

I first read about this place in *The Snows of Yesteryear* by Gregor von Rezzori, whose father worked for a while as a gamekeeper in the vast forests owned by Gergely's great-grandfather Ármin Mikes.

Gergely Roy Chowdhury looks like D'Artagnan, the fourth musketeer. His brother Sándor and he are the kind of guys who get all the girls nudging each other when they walk into a room. He's a thoughtful young man who grew up partly in Austria and partly in England, where he attended the London School of Economics. His father, Basu Roy Chowdhury de Ulpur, is from an ancient aristocratic lineage in Bangladesh. The family was robbed of its houses, villages and estates during the partition of India in 1947 and Basu fled, ending up years later at a university in Austria. Gergely's mother is Katalin Mikes. During her time at university in Graz she met a man with a comparable family history of dispossession and fell deeply in love with him.

Anikó Bethlen in Marosvásárhely told me that Gergely's father was an extraordinary man, far more at home in Transylvania than in Austria. She said he felt he had a spiritual bond with the region. In the 1980s, along with Katalin, he regularly travelled from Graz to Transylvania in a car loaded with aid supplies – clothing, medicines, toilet paper, chocolate, canned food, coffee – to help families there. Ceaușescu's attempt to pay off the country's foreign debt caused shortages of absolutely everything.

It's winter. First I speak to Gergely's mother. Sixty years after the deportation, Katalin Mikes is back in the small house from which she was taken away, with her grandmother, at the age of four. It's at the edge of the grounds. Zabola is the name of both the village and the sixteenth-century ancestral home. Katalin Mikes' persistence saw the house returned to the family a few years ago. She travelled to Romania immediately after the fall of Ceaușescu and started collecting as many property deeds and other documents as she could find. The family archive at Zabola was thrown out of the windows on 3 March 1949 and burned.

Katalin goes ahead of me up the three steps to the glass front door that was smashed by a gang of heavies that day. She points to the spot where the glass lay when, as a child, she walked out through the door to the waiting truck with its canvas canopy. The living room is simple. Here she lives, modest and indomitable, in a gardener's house on the edge of the park in which the family mansion stands.

Her father died in April 1945 at the age of forty. His house, in the middle of Szászfenes in forty hectares of land, was stripped bare by looters during the war. Where her father grew maize, large shopping centres have been built: Metro; Polus. She has yet to receive any compensation. Katalin consistently talks of a 'house', but on the map of Transylvania her father's property is labelled 'Mikes kastély'.

In the final months of the war, Katalin's parents fled to Hungary. There was a hope that western Hungary would be liberated by the Americans or the British. Relations between Hungarians and Romanians were such that it was sensible to leave before the Romanian and Russian troops arrived. For Hungarian women the coming of the Russians would almost certainly mean rape, for the men a threat to their lives or the risk of being sent to Siberia or to labour camps elsewhere in the USSR. Official figures put the number of women raped by the Soviets in Budapest alone at 100,000. There is silence about the hundreds of thousands of rapes in Hungary and Transylvania. It remains too painful for the women to talk about and unfortunately there is still a preconceived notion that a woman cannot be entirely innocent if such a thing happens to her.

Because of her connection with the Esterházy counts, writer and psychologist Alaine Polcz was able to escape to their mansion in Csákvár in Hungary. Forty-six years after the event she had the courage to write down what she went through. *A Wartime Memoir*, published in 1998, begins with a description of her attempts in 1944 to escape besieged Kolozsvár (the town where Erzsébet T. too was trapped until she managed to leave on a train full of the wounded and dying). The station was in complete chaos; everyone had been advised to flee. There was an exodus and Alaine stopped German trucks in an attempt to get a lift.

At last she arrived with her husband and mother-in-law at the Esterházy estate in Csákvár. Sadly not the British but the

Russians got there first. Alaine describes how she was raped lying on the floor. First she screamed, then for a time she endured it motionless and silent. It went on for days. Her greatest fear was that her back would break, the soldiers were so violent. 'It had nothing to do with embraces or sex. It had nothing to do with anything. It was simply – I realize now as I write it down – aggression.'

Alaine Polcz: 'Every war has a thousand faces. This is mine, as I survived it. How a young woman, I myself, as a wife of a couple of months and aged nineteen and twenty, from the ranks of the Transylvanian minority [...], landed at the Esterházy manor house in [Csákvár]. A woman's life at the front. Hunger, lice, digging trenches, peeling potatoes, cold, filth. This life was not only mine. My husband's white-haired mother was dragged away and raped just as pubescent girls were. Russian soldiers attacked me, beat me, protected me, stepped on my hand with a boot, fed me.'

That movement of hundreds of thousands of Transylvanian Hungarians westwards in 1944 had nothing to do with a preference for the Germans. It was simply the human survival instinct. Katalin Mikes was born in Szombathely in Hungary in the autumn of 1944. They stayed with one of her mother's uncles in the far west of Hungary. The uncle was a retired bishop and he tried to protect as many people as possible against the Russian soldiers in the church's summer palace. It led to his death. Katalin Mikes: 'You could write a whole book just about what happened there.'

She couldn't, or wouldn't, tell me any more than that. She said Countess Kinga Széchenyi knew more. The Russians came in three waves. The first two passed by, the third wave forced its way into the palace. The Russians were drunk. They fired in the air. Bishop Mikes went to the front door with Katalin's father, Sándor Mikes, and his butler Géza Vida and died there.

Katalin's father died less than six months later. He was buried in the family crypt in Maroscsesztve. Katalin came to Zabola with her mother and grandmother at the end of the war, and her mother tried to continue the agricultural and forestry activities on the estate. István Haller and Csaba Apor assisted her. I heard from Anikó Bethlen that Katalin's mother was a beauty, spoke four languages and was highly intelligent, if a little lacking in practical skills. After the deportation of 3 March 1949 this ethereal lady was forced to work in the quarries and in a soup kitchen. On 23 September 1950 she and seventy-five other nobles and rich farmers of the Széklerland were arrested on charges of stirring up resistance to the dispossessions. They were loaded onto cattle trucks in Braşov. They didn't know where they were being taken. After a three-day journey – they kept stopping, always outside villages and towns to prevent contact with the local population – they arrived at a labour camp in Tulcea. They disembarked in a no man's land. Katalin, now fifty, stressed to me that she did not want to speak about that. It had been such a terrible experience for her mother that neither of them had ever referred to it afterwards. From other sources I know they had to build houses out of branches, reeds and mud in an utterly remote location, and work in rice paddies up to their knees in leech-infested water.

Five-year-old Katalin was taken in by a family they had befriended in Szentkatolna, a few villages away from Zabola, where she went to the local school along with the peasant children. The teacher was nice. He was forced to teach the children about the class struggle according to the new Marxist lesson material, which pointed to the aristocracy as exploiters. 'But,' the teacher said to the packed classroom, 'there were exceptions, like Katalin's grandparents. They did many good things.'

Her mother fell ill in the labour camp and was allowed to visit a doctor, which is how she ended up in Marosvásárhely. When her mother was released from the camp, Katalin was allowed to meet her there. The six-year-old took a decision that you'd hardly expect of a girl of that age: 'My mother had thrombosis, she had no possessions and nowhere to live. I travelled back to Szentkatolna without her. That was very difficult for both of us.'

Katalin lived with her foster family until she was thirteen. As a child she went to a church service in Zabola with her foster parents just once in all that time. They put a headscarf on Katalin so that she wouldn't be recognized, but the villagers saw who she was and whispers ran around the pews. After the service the entire village waited outside the church to greet the little girl as '*kis contesa*', the little countess. Katalin assumed they called her that because countesses didn't live the way she did. People brought chickens, turkeys, baskets piled high with apples, apricots and peaches, and she was invited to come and eat at all their homes.

At sixteen Katalin was able to leave Romania. One of her aunts had married an Austrian prince and he did his best to help his niece escape Gheorghe Gheorghiu-Dej's dictatorship. It's possible that an uncle who was an influential German politician (Karl Theodor von und zu Guttenberg, whose grandson later became the German minister of defence) intervened as well. From a muddy village street in Transylvania, surrounded by geese and peasant children, she was put on a train with a photo of her grandmother in her hand so that her aunt would be able to identify her. At the station in Bruck an der Leitha, Princess Auersperg was waiting, an aunt she'd never seen who would take her to a castle in Styria.

For eight years Katalin was stateless. In effect she grew up as an orphan, since from the age of five she had no father and most of the time no mother in any practical sense. Katalin's mother wanted to stay in Transylvania, despite the stigma of DO, despite having been in a labour camp, despite the fact that her only child lived abroad and she had to work in a factory making locks. She refused to leave the country. On one occasion she returned to the family estate in Zabola, but she went no closer than the fence around the grounds. The main house and the outbuildings were an orphanage then. Later the place served as a psychiatric institution.

In 1969, when she was twenty-five, Katalin was given permission to travel to Romania and visit her mother, who was living in a small room in Marosvásárhely along with a pleasant elderly woman. She died in 1978. A great beauty, she had stayed in Transylvania all through the dictatorships of Gheorghiu-Dej and Ceaușescu, and she was buried next to her husband in the family crypt. 'Thank God I was able to attend her funeral.'

In the park at Zabola the villagers erected three wooden Székler crosses in memory of Mikes family members who grew up in Zabola or lived there, GRÓF MIKES KELEMEN 1820-1949; GRÓF MIKÓ IMRE 1805-1976 and GRÓF MIKES ÁRMIN 1868-1945. The last cross is for Katalin's grandfather. Katalin showed it to me. We took a short walk through the grounds and she pointed to where the family chapel once stood. Like the graves, it had disappeared from the face of the earth. Not a stone was left.

I climb into the Land Rover. The heating isn't working. In the recess for coffee cups I've put two fat candles. I light them. My younger brother tells me that if you're snowed in you can survive a night in your car in the freezing cold just by burning a single candle. I leave Zabola behind me. In one little town I drive through I see rusty goods wagons and huts made of scrap timber on frozen mud. Outside the cafés stand carts drawn by scrawny horses that stare at the ground, waiting for their bosses to stagger back out to them. Packs of stray dogs chase after each other on the station platforms. This place must once have been a hive of activity. On the fields and meadows lies a dusting of snow.

The visit has exhausted me. I feel the pain that lies under the surface, but you don't talk about the things that really hurt. Noblesse oblige learnt at their mothers' knee makes people phlegmatic and evasive even when it comes to the greatest of tragedies. One of the Transylvanian aristocrats I spoke to said: 'A gentleman doesn't trouble others with his problems.'

Back in Budapest I follow Katalin Mikes' advice and approach Kinga Széchenyi. She is the author of a book about the victims of communist terror in Hungary. After we've mailed each other a couple of times, she sends me an account of what she remembers of the final days of the Second World War, when she was staying in the same house as Katalin Mikes: 'We spent the whole winter and early spring of 1944-1945 with my great-grandmother's brother, János Mikes, the retired bishop of Szombathely, at his residence in Répceszentgyörgy. This was the last, devastating period of the Second World War. The reason for our long stay was that the region where our estate was located, the county of Békés in the southern part of Hungary, had already been occupied by the Russians in the autumn, and Budapest, where the family usually spent the winter, had been under a terrible siege. So mother (Sarolta Wenckheim Széchenyi) decided to take us twins (Erzsébet and Kinga Széchenyi) and our governess Eta to our uncle's place, close to the western border of Hungary. The bishop's palace was packed with relatives, friends, acquaintances, and later with people from the village. All of them came because they felt safer under the protection of Bishop Mikes.

'I remember Bishop Mikes, Uncle János to us, as a very kind, loving person with an extremely good sense of humour. I remember how he loved to watch us and how he laughed at the funny things my twin sister and I did as small kids, while discovering a whole new world. It must have been unbelievable, it occurs to me now. In the huge park we could enjoy wonderful peacocks walking around, while the sky was filled with aeroplanes on their way to bomb our country, and later we heard the rumbling and rattling of firearms as the front line approached.

'Just a few days before the front line came close to Répceszentgyörgy, we turned four years old. The Germans left and the Russian army was expected any minute. This was a night I'll never forget. Now I know it was 28 March 1945. Lots of people were crowded into a huge, dark room of the palace. By that time the electricity had been cut off. I was trying to sleep in an armchair. After a long silence, there was a horrifying noise. The bishop went down the stairs leading to the entrance to calm the noisy, drunk Russian soldiers, who were firing their weapons. But as we heard later, when he tried to come back up, he collapsed and died. He had a serious heart disease and was not supposed to climb stairs. The Russian soldiers overran the whole building, smashing and looting whatever they could. Thinking back, I can still hear the noise they made as they crushed and trampled on everything in the room with their heavy boots.

'After that, only pictures come to my mind. Uncle János very pale, dead, laid on a bed. Then we are in a room with mother, Eta and some younger women, surrounded by Russian soldiers. We are ordered to leave the building. Mother frantically throws some of our belongings onto a blanket and makes a bundle. When all of us tried to leave, the Russians let mother, Eta and the two of us go, but not the other women. To this day I don't know what happened to them. Mother pretended that one of us was Eta's daughter. Later I was told that the Russians didn't harm mothers with small children. The next picture is of a small house in the village, where my sister and I are munching on some sour-tasting leaves. Some Russian soldiers are sitting nearby, cleaning their weapons.'

A workers' paradise
without workers

Bucharest, February 2010

On 2 March 1949 a law was adopted under which all estates of fifty hectares or more and all model farms were nationalized. The deportation of the nobility and wealthy farmers in the early morning of 3 March 1949 was no small operation for the Romanian Communist Party. The militia and the Securitate had been set up only a few weeks previously. In those days the Party, helped into the saddle by the Soviets, needed above all a loyal assault division to get its regime of terror, torture and intimidation up and running. The deportation of large landowners was only the second major operation by the militia and the Securitate. It was important for it to go well.

The collectivization of agricultural land was announced at the congress of the Central Committee of the Romanian Workers Party in Bucharest of 3-5 March 1949, which adopted a resolution concerning 'efforts to strengthen the alliance between the peasants and the working class and the social-ist metamorphosis of agriculture'. The subject under discussion was how to bring twelve million peasants together into the GAC (Gospodării Agricole Colective, or collective farms, the Romanian equivalent of the Soviet *kolkhozy*) and the GAS (Gospodării Agricole de Stat, or state farms, the equivalent of the Soviet *sovkhozy*). Ana Pauker, chair of the Agrarian Commission, favoured the Santa Claus approach: the good get treats, the naughty the rod. In practice the emphasis was on the rod. The Communist Party intended to push through collectivization by force. The former large landowners were a rewarding and obvious first target for persecution.

My friends in Bucharest have explained to me how to recognize a Securitate agent: he barely looks at you, and you can read little from his face. He wears an ill-fitting dark suit. He has no opinions and often keeps silent to give you a chance to talk. He mainly asks questions, and if he tells you anything then it's information that's generally available, which he will do his best to present to you as if he's divulging something important. He'll never share anything new with you. In short, they're sponges that cling on and suck as much information out of you as possible. They're friendly and they continually scan their surroundings. Based on such descriptions, I imagine a slightly neurotic type of man in a cheap suit, peering around like a junkie wondering whether his dealer is in the building yet.

I'm sitting at a small table in the Rembrandt Hotel on the Strada Smârdan in the old part of Bucharest, opposite the Romanian Central Bank. It's freezing cold outside. This space is used as the breakfast room, but you can sit here all day drinking coffee and cognac. I'm alone, waiting for a man to arrive. I estimate the likelihood of his being a current or former Securitate agent at ninety per cent. It's my first appointment with a man from the security service. His name is Virgiliu. A professor in London put me in touch with him, writing that he was deputy director of the Securitate archives. From many sides I've been assured that the Securitate still has full control of the files. To be deputy director you would have to be an agent.

There he comes, up the stairs. He's stout. I stand up and shake his hand firmly. If you're going to associate with the Securitate, it's no good starting out with a feeble handshake. He looks me straight in the eye, not glancing around even for a second. He asks hardly any questions. He talks practically nonstop and tells me all kinds of things I've never heard or read anywhere before. This is an old stager, I think for a moment. Dyed in the wool. But then I begin to have doubts. He's cordial, but that's really the only thing that fits with the profile sketched by my friend. I ask him about the deportations of 3 March 1949. He's carried out extensive research into that episode in the Securitate archives.

'The crucial question for the Romanian Communist Party was how to create a working class,' says Virgiliu, looking at me. He leaves a long silence. I say nothing.

Good question, indeed. If you want to create a workers' paradise then, naturally, somehow or other you need to have workers. Romania was an agrarian country with hardly any industry. In 1949 seventy-five per cent of the sixteen million Romanians lived in the countryside and worked the land. The majority of peasants had no desire at all to be collectivized. In 1952, according to official Romanian sources (which are incomplete and therefore give a very conservative figure), 80,000 peasants were in jail for actively resisting collectivization. Class war was an essential ingredient for the creation of 'the new man'. Collectivization was not driven by economic motives, it was carried out for ideological and political reasons. The main priority was to follow Soviet guidelines. The Romanian communists were under direct day-to-day supervision from Moscow.

'A working class could be created only by collectivizing agriculture. The social fabric of the villages would have to be ripped apart, the younger generation taken out of the villages and put to work in the brand new heavy industries. Their parents would work on collective farms. That way every Romanian would become a worker. Except that no one was in favour. The man responsible for collective farms was the deputy minister of agriculture, Nicolae Ceauşescu.'

According to *Transforming Peasants, Property and Power*, Gheorghe Gheorghiu-Dej, leader of the Romanian Communist Party, decided collectivization should be directly linked to a frontal attack on the *chiaburi* (the Romanian term for rich farmers). The concept of a 'rich farmer', like 'class enemy', was relative and flexible. Gheorghiu-Dej said openly of those who resisted: 'Don't these people deserve to have their necks and backbones broken for perpetrating counter-revolutionary actions? These people deserve to be beaten up really hard. Have no pity on them, for they show no pity for our regime.' Nicolae Ceauşescu had been paying attention and he used violence on a large scale. He personally opened fire on protesters and had Securitate troops and the militia do the same. Officials would snap at local communists who didn't achieve collectivization quickly enough: 'Just you wait till Ceauşescu comes here to sort things out!'

Virgiliu: 'The Communist Party had mountains of work to do in those days. Before it could press ahead with the process of Stalinization, it would have to undermine the existing society. Traditions needed to be ripped out root and branch, the elite needed to be destroyed and no sign of its values could be allowed to remain, whether physical or symbolic. The link between the peasant and his land had to be severed. All enemies, real, imagined and newly created, had to be removed.'

Virgiliu is right. Depriving people of their financial capital – estates, houses, money, jewellery, paintings; everything they possessed – was not enough. Social and cultural capital needed to be destroyed too. So the nobles were deported as a way of unravelling the social fabric, exiled to workplaces where they knew no one. To destroy their cultural capital, as many libraries and family archives as possible were burned, as happened to those of the Mikes, Kemény and Bánffy families, and at Erzsébet T.'s castle. The most tangible things were destroyed. A definitive and permanent wall had to be built between past, present and future. Then the old world could live on only in people's heads, or in stories.

All symbols had to be removed. Family coats of arms were chiselled off façades and gravestones shattered and used to make roads. The looters and graverobbers were by turns Russian soldiers, Romanian communists and local petty thieves. Crucially, those in power made clear that everything associated with the old establishment was outlawed, and that therefore the looting and destruction would go unpunished.

In Zabola the Mikes' family chapel was demolished and all the ancestral graves were removed. In Dornafalva Erzsébet T. pointed out to me the houses, built in the 1970s, that now cover her family's graves. Kati Ugron could only cry when she first visited the family crypt in the woods at the Laposnyak estate. All the graves had been broken open. The graverobbers had gone to work like jackals, searching for jewellery.

Zsolna Ugron told me that the family crypt in Pusztakamarás had been spared, but that the gravestones of members of the Ugron family were broken in two and their names chiselled off. Years ago an attractive Hungarian great aunt of Ilona's, in her youth the spitting image of Ingrid Bergman, showed us her family's mausoleum, a white temple on an island in a large lake in the park behind the house. It was virtually a ruin. Russian soldiers had looted it in 1945, pulling the coffins out of their niches and leaving them in the water.

Where once swans glided between the fountains, the coffins holding the remains of her ancestors bobbed on the surface.

Virgiliu: 'The large landowners had to be destroyed ideologically, symbolically, economically and physically, to overturn the old stratified society once and for all. Their removal was crucial and relatively simple. It was a matter of a little over two thousand families in the whole country – everyone who owned more than fifty hectares or a model farm. After the removal of the large landowners, their agricultural labourers would be left, along with the land, the tractors, the agricultural equipment, the buildings. It would make an ideal starting point for the first collective farms. Everything was there: labour, land, machinery. So it was important to take the owners away – not to prisons but to provincial capitals – and to make sure they couldn't come back.

'It was a carefully conducted operation by the Securitate,' Virgiliu says of 3 March 1949. 'Preparations began in early February. A list was compiled of all the major landowners in the country. That was a simple administrative task. The many laws and taxes introduced since 1945 meant that most large landowners could barely survive, which reduced the likelihood of resistance. It was all meticulously prepared. As class enemies they represented a major threat, so the operation must not be allowed to fail. Village by village a timetable was put together, detailing which families must be picked up and in what order.

'It was led by the Securitate and the militia, but a large proportion of the manpower consisted of armed workers, party members. On 1 March the activists were taken by truck to the places where the operation was to be launched. In Oradea, for example, the muster station was the national theatre. Two hundred armed men slept there.'

I'd often driven through Oradea. Later, after hearing Virgiliu's account, I stopped there one time on my way back to Budapest. The centre of the city was full of the most beautiful

Art Nouveau houses with ornamental turrets, arches and balconies, and façades decorated with coloured rosettes and sunflowers. Close to the bridge over the Sebes-Körös stood the national theatre, as announced in two languages on the tympanum: TEATRUL DE STAT – ÁLLAMI SZÍNHÁZ. There the men slept in the seats and in corridors. With its neo-Classical exterior and neo-Rococo interior, the building was a prime example of bourgeois architecture. On the roof was a silver-painted statue of two cupids holding a man-high laughing mask in their four hands.

'They had enough food with them for twenty-four hours, so that no one needed to leave the theatre and nothing about the operation would leak out. Those two hundred men were responsible for picking up eighty to ninety people. They made sure they always arrived at a house in force,' says Virgiliu. In some cases, however, information did leak.

State farms were set up with names like Red Star, Red October, Lenin's Flag and Freedom. After the large landowners were deported, years of systematic dispossession of smaller famers began. The nationalization of their land was accompanied by mass deportations and terror. A standard method was to shoot dead the men who put up most resistance and leave them lying on the ground so that their families had to bury them.

If everything went smoothly there was no violence. A district would be singled out and its party committee would call together each village's People's Council, the village police and the teachers at local schools to discuss how collectivization could be achieved. Party activists were sent to the villages to compile inventories. A former party activist explained in *Transforming Peasants, Property and Power* how it went from there: 'We would rarely do our persuasion work inside the peasants' homes, because peasants would talk disrespectfully to us if they saw us on their property. We would therefore summon them to buildings of the People's Councils or to the school, because there we were in control. We made them sit in the classroom and listen to long boring lectures and discuss propaganda brochures. Party chairmen of factories and of cadres were all at our disposal. We used as many of them as we needed. We organized them into agitprop teams. They did their job; they knew by heart what their duties were.'

This gives an insight into the psychology of the oppressor, which generated a cocktail of unfamiliar territory, mind-numbing lectures and brute force.

Gheorghiu-Dej had earlier set out the overall party philosophy concerning expropriation: 'People must be told they won't escape the collective farm just as they won't escape death.' In April 1962, thirteen years after the start of the collectivization campaign, he announced in a speech to the people that the socialist transformation of agriculture was complete.

At the end of our talk in the Rembrandt Hotel, Virgiliu gives me his card, shakes my hand heartily once again and walks away down the stairs. When he's out of sight I look at the card.

He's a researcher for the CNSAS. Its full title is there, in English: 'National Council for the Study of Securitate Archives.' This isn't the man in charge of the Securitate files! He's the deputy director of an independent organization that is researching the Securitate archives, or at least the documents the Securitate is willing to release. In short, the professor who sat across from me and spoke nineteen to the dozen is almost certainly not a Securitate agent at all. He was simply introduced to me inaccurately. The next day I check with Coen Stork who the people at the CNSAS are. He too believes they're legitimate. But of course in paranoid Bucharest you can never be sure.

The
Danube – Black Sea
Canal

Bucharest, February 2010

Toni Tartar. That's what my driver and interpreter is called. He has two bottles of mineral water from Borsec ready in his car. We're driving from Bucharest to Cernavodă, 175 kilometres to the east. As well as being the site of the fine Saligny Bridge over the Danube, Cernavodă is at the westerly end of the Danube – Black Sea Canal, a project approved by the Politburo on 25 May 1949. The canal is sixty-four kilometres long and runs from Cernavodă to Constanţa. The Danube winds for 400 kilometres before flowing hesitantly, triple-branched, into the Black Sea. It was Stalin who insisted a canal should be built. He could use it to move troops, thereby reaching recalcitrant Yugoslavia relatively quickly. Stalin was also an advocate of putting enemies of the people to some use before killing them. The Danube – Black Sea Canal soon came to be known as 'the grave of the Romanian bourgeoisie'.

It's a bleak day. The landscape to the east of Bucharest is flat. There is hardly a tree, only cabbages, their floppy leaves drooping, as if even a cabbage gets depressed in these parts. Not a house or a village in sight. Ninety-five per cent of the deportation camps in communist Romania were in these dispiriting lowlands to the east and northeast of Bucharest. The coastal strip has always been sparsely populated, and not without reason. It's said that the cold wind from Siberia blows straight across here. Dobrogea and the plain of Baragan were the Romanian Siberia.

Tulcea lies in the Danube delta, a thoroughly wet and forsaken region. The prisoners lived in barracks, in barns, fifty to a room, and worked in rice paddies ankle- to knee-deep in water, without stout shoes, without proper clothing. Katalin's mother fell ill and was fortunate enough to be removed from the camp. In the same camp were Baron László Apor with his wife and daughter, Baron Péter Apor with his wife and child, Béla Teleki's wife with three children, the wife of Károly Orbán (the childhood friend of Emma P. who was later executed) with one child, and dozens of other former landowners from the Széklerland, a total of seventy-six Hungarian class enemies – kulaks and both titled and untitled nobles – who were accused of inciting rebellion among the peasantry.

The Danube – Black Sea Canal marks the southern boundary of a windy plain that was dotted with deportation camps. There were fourteen labour camps alongside the canal. By the spring of 1952, 19,000 political prisoners were working on the canal along with 20,000 volunteers – people who had been designated 'volunteers' by factories all over the country – and 18,000 soldiers. Practically all the aristocratic families I spoke to had at least one member who'd been in a prison or labour camp. Mihály, grandfather of Gábor Teleki, was in a camp next to the canal. Béla Haller's father was in a camp in the mountains, near Bicaz, as was Arpád Mikó, stepfather to Emma P.

The man with the wooden leg, István Bánffy, was sentenced to fifteen years' hard labour in 1958 and sent to a labour camp in the Danube delta. Of all the aristocrats in the camps, hardly any are alive today. Their children have said little about it.

In Marosvásárhely a friend took me to see Dezső Bustya, a Hungarian church minister. As a political prisoner he was sent to the Danube – Black Sea Canal in 1952. They were welcomed by the guards with the words: 'We'll send you lot home in an envelope.' The clergyman had a kindly disposition and he stressed that even in the camp the good in a person might come to the surface unexpectedly. Privileged prisoners were sometimes rewarded for good behaviour with permission to send a postcard of a maximum of five lines. Dezső Bustya did not belong in that category. One day he saw a soldier he knew from school. He wrote a note and hid it in a shoe-polish tin along with the address. He kneaded the tin into a lump of mud and when he got the chance he pushed the lump towards the soldier with his foot. The soldier later picked it up. Because of the willingness of that soldier to risk his life, Dezső's parents learnt that their son was still alive.

A report by the Romanian ministry of foreign affairs dated 27 February 1954 says of the labour camps: 'Many prisoners have been hit with iron bars, spades, shovels and whips for no reason. Many died as a result of the blows they received, while others were disabled for life. A number of prisoners have been shot dead; others have been refused medical treatment when sick and forced to carry on working against medical advice, some of them dying as a result. Prisoners are put into isolation cells in winter naked or scantily clad. Some have been forced to stand in icy water until dinner time as a punishment, while others have been put outside naked in summer with their hands tied, to be bitten by mosquitoes.'

Toni Tartar's father was an army tailor. They lived in Bucharest close to military unit number 0746. His father made uniforms for the soldiers in the camp and suits for the officer in charge. When the revolution broke out in December 1989, Toni's father told him to keep his head below the windows at all times. Army camp 0746 chose to side with the people. Toni has printed a map showing all the penal camps along the canal. It includes all those I've heard of, all but Coasta Galeș, which I later discovered was called Galeșu. Eight hundred priests were imprisoned there.

Cernavodă has a mosque with an ancient minaret. The canal was dug beside the railway line from Cernavodă to Constanţa, which was laid in 1860 by the Ottomans. In this coastal region, the Dobrogea, a Muslim minority resides to this day, composed of Tartars and Turks. A tall, ugly bridge straddles the canal. To the left, half a kilometre away, flows the Danube, wild and furious. You can see the canal branching off from it. Somewhere here must have been Km 0, the first penal camp on the canal. The next is camp Km 4, followed by Saligny, Satu Nou, Km 31, Poarta Albă, Ovidiu and Peninsula. It was in the last three of these camps that Dezső Bustya was held.

Cernavodă is empty. The town is now famous mainly for its nuclear power plant, which generates seventeen per cent of Romania's electricity. The canal brings cooling water to it from the Danube. Toni Tartar believes it's not sensible to eat agricultural products from the surrounding region. The whole area reeks of old-school communism: the wide empty road with its crash barrier and cracks in the asphalt; the abandoned traffic tower at the intersection; the fences; the industrial, dehumanized landscape. Apart from an absurd number of crows there's not a living creature to be seen.

After Cernavodă it gets even more gloomy. I'd been expecting charming rural villages, each with a church, perhaps a café, elderly ladies on benches along the road, like in Transylvania. I've told Toni we'll be searching the villages for elderly men and women, for priests or village schoolteachers, to ask what they knew about the penal camps. But we drive through an utterly depressing and empty land. To the right is the railway to Constanța, beyond it from time to time the grey sheen of the canal, to the left and right of the road undeveloped land with houses that are little more than huts. Almost every front garden has a well and behind or next to each house is a privy knocked together from scrap timber. Nowhere a church, nowhere a village square – it looks as if no one has taken the trouble to build anything here since the Ottomans scorched and abandoned the region in 1878. Apart from a nuclear plant.

I met Dezső Bustya at his flat in Marosvásárhely. He speaks Dutch, having made friends with Dutch ministers who studied in Kolozsvár during the communist era. Dutch Protes-

tants have always been active in Transylvania. Their faith lies somewhere between Dutch Reformed and Presbyterian. As a schoolboy in 1952 Dezső helped set up an anti-communist organization whose members were Hungarian and Romanian children. In August that year, at the age of seventeen, Dezső was arrested. I know what a seventeen-year-old boy is, a combination of man and child. My eldest son is seventeen.

Communism would bring paradise on earth. That was the idea, Dezső said. They witnessed the sufferings of their parents. The schoolchildren spent whole afternoons in the hills around Kolozsvár with forked sticks, looking for snakes. They wanted to tap the venom and use it to poison the communist leaders. They lifted stones in hope. For lack of adders they produced a pamphlet. 'People! Fight with all your strength against the communist rulers who are destroying your families!' The pamphlet was copied two thousand times and left on benches in the park and on the steps of government buildings on the night before Mayday. On 1 May the children strode triumphantly through town.

Four months later they were arrested, thirty-five children in total, all aged between fifteen and seventeen. Dezső's future wife, Erzsébet, who put coffee and a plate of biscuits in front of us, was among them. She was fifteen. They were interrogated for six weeks in the cellars of the Securitate building in Kolozsvár. Across from me sat a man full of energy, his eyes twinkling.

'We were four men to a cell. The cell was so low that you couldn't stand up straight. We had one spoon and one plate between two. In the cell was a concrete seat and two steel-framed beds, no window, only an air vent the size of your hand. The hunger and the lack of oxygen were our biggest problems. At night the interrogators came. You were given black glasses so that you couldn't see where they were taking you.'

Those must have been the pilot's goggles I saw in a glass case in the commemorative room in Gherla, the goggles prisoners wore when they knelt down to be shot in the back of the neck. Obscene things, entirely black: the frames, the lenses, the rotting rubber. Pitch dark glasses, darker than welding goggles. There must have been thousands of them in use in Romania. The general rule was that prisoners always wore goggles when they were moved, so that they couldn't get their bearings or communicate.

'In the interrogation room, lamps were shone in your face. You were blinded by the light. The officers sat in the dark. They ate, drank beer, smoked cigarettes. They took turns; sometimes you were interrogated all night long. It was like in those books by Solzhenitsyn. They used the same methods in all Eastern Bloc countries: the night-time interrogations, the temptations, the false promises. If someone said something they liked, he was given a cigarette. Or you might be told you'd get only a year in prison instead of five, or that you'd be allowed to see your parents. All lies. One of us was weaker than the others.'

I asked whether the interrogators used violence.

'There was intimidation. We were hit. We were given electric shocks.'

He offered me the plate of biscuits. I knew the whole arsenal of techniques. He said nothing about them.

'Prison enriched me. I found a wife there, and a profession. When I came out the only thing I could do was to go to the theology faculty. There were tiny holes at the bottom of the cell door. One day I was looking through them and I saw the clothes of one of the girls passing by, so I knew they'd been arrested. I thought: I must marry one of these girls. I'm responsible for their suffering. We were taken to the state prison. From there all the juvenile prisoners were sent to Gherla. Erzsébet went to Mislea, a women's prison. She was with interesting people there, aristocrats and the wives of former political leaders. Meanwhile I'd turned eighteen. So I was sent to the Danube – Black Sea Canal.'

In Gherla the 're-education' programme was stopped in August 1952, around the time the children arrived there.

To the right of the road I can see wooden barracks. Toni turns carefully onto the frozen mud road. The long barracks are roofed with corrugated asbestos. People are living in them. All the land far and wide in every direction is undeveloped. It looks like a swamp, and the settlement resembles a leper colony. There's washing hanging to dry; a few chickens wander about. No smoke rises from the chimneys.

In the camps the barracks were where brigades were assembled, arranged according to their sentences or by social back-

ground. In barracks A were ex-military and ex-party members and in barracks G the liberals and peasants. That made it easier for the guards to know who they were dealing with. Many of the prisoners had no real idea what the accusations against them were. The boss of the Securitate had told each province how many arrests would be needed to fill the quota for the canal.

Two hundred metres to the right is a low brick workshop. Several men are leaning over a car. My initial assumption is that people here specialize in switching number plates. We get out, Toni Tartar and I, simultaneously, like detectives in a film noir. The men stand up from behind the car bonnet. It's icy cold, a cold that penetrates to your bone marrow within three minutes. The workshop is minimally furnished. There's no heating and hardly any tools. A man with an empty tube of sealant is rummaging around near a delivery van that's missing half its engine. A Romanian Orthodox priest with a brown leather jacket over his black cassock steps out of the shadows. He has a gaunt face. There are lumps of dried mud on his shoes. His cheeks are taut with cold.

He tells us that the wooden barracks we passed were for the volunteers. They were far better built than the accommodation for political prisoners and they've been occupied by homeless people for twenty or more years now. He doesn't know where the prisoners' barracks were, but in the village graveyard he's always coming upon the bones and skulls of people who were thrown into unmarked graves.

A Securitate investigation in 1967 concluded that there were 1,304 undocumented deaths in the Danube camps. Corneliu Coposu, secretary of the Peasants Party and himself imprisoned for seventeen years, wrote that after 1947, 282,000 people were arrested, of whom an estimated 190,000 died in custody. In an instalment of the Romanian documentary series *Testimonies of Suffering*, made by Lucia Hossu Longin, one of the prisoners held in the Poarta Albă camp says that the number of deaths among the political prisoners was alarming. He remembered being sent to the washroom that served as a mortuary. Twenty-four corpses lay jumbled on the floor as if dumped there like a heap of firewood.

Dezső Bustya: 'We slept in wooden barracks, fifty men in two rows. Four brigades slept in each barracks. We had to take turns to keep watch so that other prisoners didn't steal our things. Each watch lasted two hours. I used to recite the Heidelberg Catechism twice over, questions 1 to 129. By the time I'd said it twice, two hours would have passed. We wore prison clothes, worn-out rags. Track had been laid along the bottom of the canal and the rocks and earth were carried away on tip trucks. I had to help to move the rails. We pulled the sleepers out of the ground to burn them in the barracks. Earth and stones were also moved out in wheelbarrows. You had to shift four cubic metres a day. If you didn't manage that much, you were punished mercilessly. The winter of 1953 was very harsh. At night the canal often filled with snow. We had to remove that first. The aim was not to dig a canal but to destroy a generation.'

The prisoners got up at five. They washed at a couple of standpipes and for breakfast they were given coffee made of roasted rice and a hunk of bread or *mămăligă*. Next came the morning roll call. There were thousands of prisoners, so it took more than an hour. Then they marched to the canal, forced to sing communist battle songs on the way. At the end of the day they were counted again. The evening meal usually consisted of potato soup.

Dezső told me that one of the Hungarians worked in the kitchen and from time to time managed to get hold of some extra food to give to the others. On Sundays they secretly held church services: 'In ordinary life under communism, you didn't dare say anything, but we had nothing left to lose. Without jokes, without laughter, you couldn't survive the canal. We made plans, formed a new government, created a new legislature and fantasized about the punishments we'd impose on the people responsible.

The largest penal camp was at Poarta Albă. It's now a prison on a vast walled terrain. Everything that belongs to the prison is freshly whitewashed and some of the window frames are bright blue, giving the whole place something of the look of a Greek holiday camp. The wall is fenced off with barbed wire, and on the outside it has a watchtower with a guard at each corner and every 200 metres. A policeman with puppy fat on his cheeks, wearing sunglasses, stops us at the entrance. In 1952 there were

35,000 prisoners in this camp. Dezső Bustya mentioned that the guards' children call him 'Domnu Bandit', 'Mr. Bandit'.

In Poarta Albă the canal cuts through a hill. There are high cliffs below a seventy-degree slope. A giant mosaic has been set into the rock face. Muscled workers stand energetically digging while two officers, one in a flat cap, the other in a hard hat, their chests stuck out, study a map. They have the angular bodies of Ken, the male version of Barbie. The mosaic shows the canal behind them crawling with ships of all shapes and sizes moving both upstream and downstream.

The cold is piercing. Between me and the towering mosaic lies the canal: dreary, seventy metres wide. There's not a ship to be seen, left or right, not a boat, not a fisherman, not a duck – nothing, as far as the eye can see. In the six hours we spend driving alongside the canal I see one tug, the Temixron 2. For lack of industry or war, the canal is completely redundant. I ask myself how long I could have held out in the hell seven metres below my feet. The water laps at the edge. On the embankment behind me a goods train passes, laden with coal.

The Romanian Workers Party lived up to its slogan for the project: 'Cu partidul nostru mare, Duc Dunărea la Mare!' ('With our great party we are bringing the Danube to the Black Sea.') The grey canal flows into the sea near Peninsula penal camp, which is indeed on a peninsula. It functioned until 1977 and after that it was used mainly to hold people caught with weapons or who had tried to flee across the border. Prisoners not set to work on the canal were used for quarrying. According to *The Chronology and the Geography of the Repression in Communist Romania*, there are mass graves here. Up to eight thousand prisoners at a time were held in Peninsula, which was also known as 'Extermination Camp no. 1'.

Toni Tartar tells me about the memoirs of an ex-prisoner, George Andreica, who writes that in Camp Midia, which was close to Peninsula, four barracks were fenced off. The inner

camp was called 'death' by the prisoners. Former soldiers were locked up there and left to slowly starve. Inside the fence the grass and flowers had disappeared. Everything that chanced to go inside the fence was eaten: insects, snakes, mice, rats. When masses of frogs washed up there one day, they were devoured alive. Prisoners who died were eaten by their fellow captives. One day a dog belonging to the camp's head butcher disappeared. Inside the fence around 'death' the guards found the bones of a medium-sized animal. At that point all the prisoners in 'death' were executed.

The gate to Peninsula is half open. I can see a road barrier beyond it. A gypsy boy warns us there's a guard in attendance. It's starting to get dark. We walk onto the terrain. After 200 metres, on the camp's central exercise yard which boasts a high tower topped with massive floodlights, a large fellow approaches us, a woollen hat on his head and a cudgel in his hand. His jacket bears the words International Security Protection. He's friendly, speaks English and takes us to where the prisoners lived.

The perimeter fence is full of holes, but the barbed wire still runs all around the terrain. The barracks are locked. I peer through the broken windows: empty spaces, like long class-rooms. The guard says they lived twenty men to a room. The bars have been stolen. Grass is coming up through the tiles. The weeds are tall. Everything is rusted and broken. The low walls of the ruined buildings and around the periphery are fragile. It's all so shabby, so mundane. I don't detect anything guilty about the place. I might just as well be walking around the grounds of a textiles factory bankrupted long ago.

When I get home I start reading about the re-education pro-gramme in Camp Peninsula. Barracks 13 and 14 were used for 'unmasking'. Professor Simionescu was tortured in Barracks 13. He was a well-known doctor. After endless torture sessions he threw himself onto the barbed-wire perimeter fence and was shot dead by the guards. The news of his death reached his wife, who went to the ministry of internal affairs to complain. The fact of her visit there was picked up by the BBC and Radio Free Europe. Attention from the West was one of the reasons why the ministry ended the re-education programme.

The barbed wire around the camp has turned dark brown and brittle. As we leave, Toni gives the gypsy boy, who is still standing by the gate, five lei. Across from the camp entrance is a row of drab houses and at the corner a grocery store with ten or so products on its shelves. The places where the com-munists re-educated their unwilling citizens were chosen for their isolated locations, so that not too many people would be kept awake by the screaming at night. The lights of Constanţa shine on the horizon.

Peninsula was the last camp that Dezső was held in. He tells me work on the canal was stopped in 1953 because the calcula-tions were inaccurate. The engineers had repeatedly given too rosy a picture. I imagine that Stalin's death on 5 March that year made it possible to halt the money- and oil-guzzling project. For form's sake, a number of the Romanian engineers were sentenced to death and several more to hard labour. In 1976 Ceauşescu restarted work on the canal. Instead of political prisoners he used ordinary criminals as well as soldiers and workers. It was completed in 1987, two years before his downfall.

Along with thousands of others, Dezső was transferred from the Danube – Black Sea Canal to Jilava, a hub that every prisoner transport passed through. In 1954, two years after Dezső was arrested, all the boys and girls of Illegális Kommunistaellenes Szervezet (Illegal Anti-Communist Organization) in Jilava were brought together and given a talking-to by a party bigwig, who expounded upon the eternal goodness of the party and the workers' paradise. They, as young people, had slipped on a banana skin. But fortunately the party was forgiving by nature. Tomorrow they would all be comrades. In the future they could even become ministers. They were freed.

It wasn't until years later that Dezső discovered the true circumstances of their sudden release. The father of one of the children was a nurseryman. He bred a very special plant. Every year it won him a socialist medal. Gheorghiu-Dej came each time to pin it on him in person. In 1953 the nurseryman said to Dej: 'I don't want that medal. I want my son back.'

Conversation
in a hotel lobby

Marosvásárhely, February 2010

In Marosvásárhely lives a woman of noble blood who was held in the deportation camps in Baragan and Dobrogea. I heard about her from Anikó Bethlen. Every time I visit Marosvásárhely, Anikó helps me to speak with as many people as possible. She's convinced it's important for the stories of the deportations to Baragan to be written down. On each occasion up to now she has approached this woman and asked her whether she'd like to speak to me, and now, at the very last moment, on my final visit to Marosvásárhely for the time being, she's willing to meet me.

I wait in the lobby of the Concordia Hotel in the late afternoon. I've told the young man at reception where I'm sitting and that perhaps an elderly lady will arrive. I've spoken to her on the phone. She definitely did not want to meet at her house, since she was determined to keep a distance between her memories and her current life. Anikó has told me that she hardly

ever talks about her experiences in the deportation camps. I'm
sitting in a red designer chair, a notebook and recording equipment on the circular table in front of me. I've ordered a café
latte. The lobby is empty, apart from three noisy Romanian
bodybuilders a few tables away.

A woman of my mother's age comes in. I stand up and
shake her hand. She's wearing a shawl and she has that same
dignified unpretentiousness I've come upon so often in Transylvania in this group of people, and which I find extraordinarily likeable: an unhurried attitude that has nothing to do with
being posh or with haughty silence and everything to do with
giving another person space. It's a meekness I associate with
the deeply religious, rather than the aristocracy. Her clothes
betray both poverty and class. She has the face of a careworn
woman who never gives up.

She doesn't want me to turn on my audio recorder, nor to
make notes. She wants me to sit and listen.

They'd already been deported from their estate in 1949,
but on 23 September 1950 they were transferred to the Baragan plains along with seventy-five others. They were stuffed
into windowless cattle trucks. The doors were slammed
shut and locked. She was eleven years old. They sat for days
in there, under a burning sun. The train never stopped in

a town, so they couldn't make contact with anyone. She didn't know where they were going. She shows me photographs of where they ended up, where they lived. Flat open land with what look like dog kennels, untidily knocked together. A slum for Lilliputians.

The woman speaks very intently, bending her head forward slightly as if to help her descend into her memories. I sit in the bright red chair diagonally opposite her. When she looks up she doesn't seem to see me. There's one unfortunate thing: I can only half understand what she's saying. She speaks Hungarian and no other language. I generally understand the Transylvanians better than the Hungarians, since they tend to speak a beautiful archaic Hungarian that I find easier to follow than the torrent of words in Hungary. A Transylvanian friend once told me that twenty years ago the old ladies often still spoke Hungarian with a French accent and enunciation, since French was the language of their youth, but this woman uses words I don't know, and her sentences join themselves up into incomprehensible streams of sound.

I've conducted a number of interviews in Hungarian, but I recorded them. I understood enough of what was said to follow the narrative and ask questions. I learnt the details later. Now I'm powerless. What she's telling me will be lost. Perhaps that's her intention. This is not an interview. She tells me about her husband, who was also in the camps. For a long time. He's taken to drink. He's aggressive, not just at home but at work. Rough. She gabbles on and on, in melodious Hungarian, like a bird.

Sometimes she looks up at me and I nod. From time to time she gives me a longer look, which means I need to say something. I try 'yes'. Occasionally she asks whether I can follow her and every time I answer that I can. Sometimes she asks me a question. Now and then I try to explain something. Such as my old theory: that you pass on all the problems you've been unable to solve in your own life to the next generation. Just try explaining that in Hungarian in a hotel lobby.

She speaks almost nonstop for over an hour. In an aside she tells me that the place we're in, this huge neo-Classical building that now houses the Concordia Hotel, belonged to her family until 1949, but clearly she doesn't give a damn about that. She's no desire to drink anything. My coffee gets cold. I don't take even a sip, since what she's telling me is so important. I look at her. Slowly she comes to her real pain.

Her son. My age precisely. A talented boy, but he stays home. All day. Doing nothing. He's apathetic. She has trouble getting through to him. Nothing interests him. He sees no purpose, no future. He can't find a way to live in this world. She holds her hands tightly entwined in her lap and looks up at me. She too wants her son back.

Vécsi vár.

Part 3

They were found wanting

És híjjával találtattál

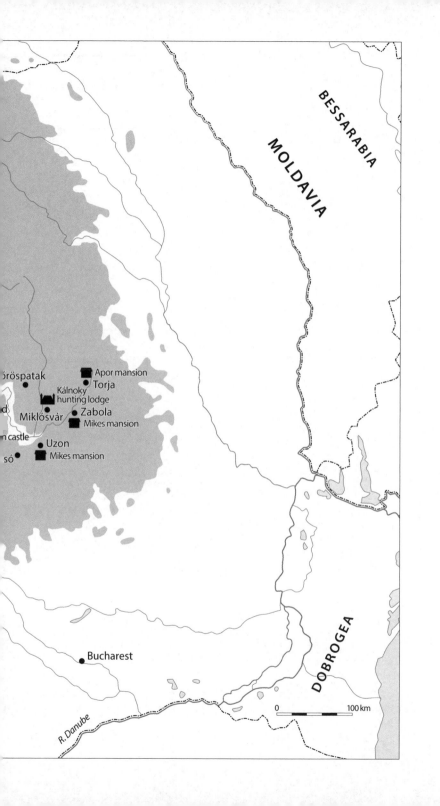

Beetroot
and champagne

György Ugron: 'You might say that communism destroyed three generations here: the generation of my grandparents, that of my parents and my own. My parents' generation had a great childhood and could learn languages, but had a tough time after that. My generation had a pretty tough time too.'

On 19 March 1965 Gheorghe Gheorghiu-Dej died. Three days later his protégé, Nicolae Ceauşescu, was chosen as First Secretary of the Romanian Communist Party. Two and a half years after that, in December 1967, Ceauşescu announced that the class struggle in Romania was over. He no longer needed to target the aristocracy or the bourgeoisie, since both had been virtually crushed. So he turned on minorities. He wanted to put an end to the multi-ethnic composition of Transylvania and he tried as far as possible to drive minorities out of the country. He sold the Jews and Saxons to Israel and Germany for hard currency and bragged that Romania's three most successful export products were Germans, Jews and oil.

György Ugron left Transylvania in the summer of 1989 with his wife and his daughter Zsolna. 'We arrived in Budapest by train. Twenty-nine relatives were waiting for us at the station. It was a tremendous feeling, as if we were the Hungarian ambassador and family. Life under Ceaușescu in the 1980s was hard. To pay off the national debt, practically everything the country produced was exported. Shelves in the shops were empty. Wherever Ceaușescu went on a visit, all the stores were filled with specially delivered products. He came to Kolozsvár a couple of times while we lived there. The whole city was closed off and a day before his arrival the sale of alcohol was banned. People lined the roads, clapping. In the fields along the route, potatoes were buried ahead of his arrival and they were harvested by children as he passed. Whenever he visited state farms, they would make heaps of vegetables and fruit out of painted polystyrene, with a few at the front that were real, just in case he picked one up. He lived in a fantasy world.'

György's daughter Zsolna told me she always came home from school to a cold, dark house. In the 1980s electricity and gas were available for only a few hours a day. The first thing she did on getting home was to put a cushion over the telephone. You were obliged to use state-issued phones, which worked as eavesdropping devices twenty-four hours a day. Zsolna also said that a queue at the baker's or the supermarket was a good sign; you always joined it immediately. There were no luxury articles at all, and almost all basic products were scarce. There was hardly any toilet paper. The only things you could nearly always get were beetroot and cheap Romanian champagne.

The ration card for Brașov in 1987, for example, shows the amounts of food each family had a right to buy, a semi-starvation level of nutrition that was presented to the Romanian people as a 'scientific diet'. In Brașov a year's ration amounted to 8.5 kilos of meat (23 grams a day), 2.5 kilos of flour (7 grams a day), 10 litres of cooking oil (27 millilitres per day), 10.5 kilos of salami (29 grams per day) and 10 eggs (1 egg per 36 days). Diesel for cars was cut back to a minimum. It was this grinding poverty, with no prospect of improvement, that drove the Romanian people to the verge of despair and eventually, even in the perfectly controlled police state that Romania then was, provoked them to rise in revolt in December 1989.

It looks as if it's been filmed in black-and-white. The twenty people on the balcony are all dressed in black, with occasional shades of grey. They line the bottom of the image. The building rises powerfully behind them. The angle is low, a worm's-eye view. A good deal of thought has gone into the camerawork. On the façade of the robust grey building are pillars many metres high, emphasizing man's insignificance. The dictator is wearing a long dark coat and a high black hat, standing against the backdrop of a window with net curtains. Next to him is his wife, one of two women on the balcony.

It's 21 December 1989. On the square, called the Piața Republica, are 80,000 workers drummed up from Bucharest and the surrounding districts, holding banners bearing jubilant slogans and portraits of Nicolae Ceaușescu. They look up at the balcony of the building that houses the Central Committee of the Romanian Communist Party. As ever, there are many Securitate officers among them. The gathering has been organized to reaffirm the authority of the great leader. As Ceaușescu finishes his first few sentences, the bussed-in workers, keeping almost perfect time, set up a slow Stalinist applause that resounds with oppression and death.

Eight minutes in, workers from Turbomechanica outside Bucharest start chanting 'Ti-mi-șo-ara, Ti-mi-șo-ara', the name of the city where deaths have occurred in riots over the previous few days. The crowd takes up the cry. Ceaușescu falters. As the protest swells, his mouth falls open.

It's the ultimate image of a dictator losing his grip. Louis de Funès could not have portrayed it better. Nicolae Ceaușescu actually resembled him in a way, especially when frivolously clad in his white summer suit with matching flat cap, off to inspect kolkhozes, his belly sticking out, vacant and self-satisfied, eyes fixed on machinery, on scale models and above all on the camera, or in boots and a tasteless hunting costume with a big breakdown lamp and no gun, standing next to a slain brown bear. He's right in the middle of practically every photograph, unambiguously presented as the centre of the Romanian universe. Despite his absolute power as a man in a position to decide at random on the life or death of any of his twenty million subjects, his gestures, posture and physiognomy betray his cramped and primitive nature. However high the pedestal, however far he has climbed and no

matter what suit or uniform he has put on, he always makes you think of a gherkin.

A man wearing a hat opens the door behind him and beckons to the dictator. Judas. But Ceaușescu remains standing there behind the six microphones into which he is desperately shouting 'hello'. You could almost feel sorry for him. He shouts it at least twenty times. The camera has turned away from the leader and the people massed below, and all this time it's been focused on the sky and the upper floors of several important buildings. The microphones are still on. In the background you can hear the crowd. Elena whispers that he must promise a wage rise. Meanwhile the desperate 'hello, hello' echoes against the backdrop of that series of buildings and the grey sky.

Four days before this extraordinary scene, on Sunday 17 December 1989, Elena and Nicolae Ceaușescu spoke to the interior minister, the head of the Securitate, the supreme commander of

the army and the minister of defence about the unrest that had started in Timișoara. When the minister replied that the militia and the Securitate hadn't opened fire on the crowd because they had no ammunition, Elena said it was alarming that the interior minister didn't know the right thing to do.

Nicolae Ceaușescu took up the theme: 'A few troublemakers want to destroy socialism and you make it child's play for them. Fidel Castro was right. You don't silence an opponent by speaking to him like a priest but by destroying him.' Ceaușescu added that they, the leaders of the Securitate, the militia and the army, were cowards and he was taking over supreme command himself. 'You know what? I'll put you in front of a firing squad. You can't keep order with rubber truncheons. From now on everyone will have weapons and ammunition.'

Eight days after that, he and Elena were executed, after a show trial in the best Soviet tradition in a small building at the military base in Târgoviște. One of the paramilitaries, a member of the firing squad who helped to tie the hands of an uncooperative Elena Ceaușescu behind her back, later testified that she didn't smell good: she'd shat her pants. Of the actual execution all you can see is gunsmoke, and then Nicolae Ceaușescu's corpse, legs folded under him. His greatest fear had been realized. The man who built a career in the party primarily by means of brutal aggression, who personally opened fire on farmers protesting at losing their land, who was so paranoid that even after the British queen shook his hand he carefully cleaned his fingers with alcohol, was dead. Those images of the dictator as a rag doll were replayed endlessly on Romanian television.

Zsolna Ugron watched the balcony scene on television in Hungary, along with her father. Her parents couldn't believe it. What if it's not true? What if it's all a fabrication? They'd escaped Ceaușescu's oppression only a few months before. When the first reports of fighting in Timișoara leaked out, Zsolna and her mother, a cellist, were in the Ferenc Liszt Academy in Budapest. Someone came into the auditorium during the performance and whispered in Zsolna's mother's ear. They immediately hurried home to watch the story unfold on television. In the days that followed there was a constant stream of phone calls and a buzz of rumours. Eleven-year-old Zsolna wrote a poem about the dictator's death.

Béla Bánffy junior was in Kolozsvár. He was twenty-two and employed at a metal works, along with his brother. They regularly listened to the Hungarian radio station Kossuth and to Radio Free Europe, so they knew what was going on in Timișoara. At the end of the working day there were whispers at the factory that they were all going into town to demonstrate. Several hundred people gathered in front of the factory. The director tried to stop them. The route to the centre of town was blocked by tanks, as was the bridge over the Szamos. The demonstration swelled to several thousand people and they didn't stop at the line of tanks. The soldiers let them pass. Then from the top floors of the houses came gunfire. Béla ran into a doorway. Everyone fled into courtyards and stairwells. The shooting continued. In Kolozsvár that day some twenty people were killed.

Gergely Roy Chowdhury, twelve years old, was in Graz, Austria, at school. He doesn't remember much about the events, except that his mother Katalin Mikes, brought up in Transylvania, was extremely on edge. She travelled with the first convoy of aid supplies sent to Romania by the Austrian branch of the Order of Malta, a sovereign Catholic order of knights set up in the twelfth century to provide medical treatment during the crusades. A truck filled with Maltese in blue uniforms came to their house in the middle of the night to pick up his mother.

Tibor Kálnoky was twenty-three and living in Munich. In 1987, with his father, he'd come to Kőröspatak for the first time, the village where the Kálnoky castle stands. He watched as the villagers embraced his father, who had decided before coming that this would be his last visit to Transylvania but was so overwhelmed by his reception in the village that they returned in 1988 with Tibor's younger brother, Boris, who was just starting out as a journalist. He became the first Western journalist to write about the uprising, in an article published in *Die Welt* in October 1989, two months before the revolution: 'Romanians, awake!' Three days after Ceauşescu's execution, Tibor Kálnoky arrived in Romania with his father and brother and forty tonnes of humanitarian aid.

The first two months after the revolution were euphoric. The Romanians openly thanked the Hungarian minority for saving them from the dictator (since the Romanian revolution started in Timoşoara at the church and home of Hungarian pastor László Tőkés), but three months later Romanian nationalism raised its head and Tibor, his father and two Hungarian journalists barely escaped lynching during a meeting of the Greater Romania Party in Alba Iulia, which was attended by four thousand people. They were dragged to a lamp post by a mob shouting: 'We drink Hungarian blood.' Someone had fetched a rope. Just in time to avoid being hanged, Tibor was able to show them his American passport and his father produced a French identity card. Three weeks later, in March 1990, at a similar meeting in Marosvásárhely, eight Hungarians were lynched. The number would have been far greater were it not for the gypsies of Marosvásárhely, who came to their rescue shouting: 'We will help our Hungarian neighbours!'

Gábor Teleki was twenty-one and staying in Brussels with his family for Christmas. The television was on all the time. His mother cried as she watched and kept asking herself why she wasn't there.

Zsigmond Mikes was twelve years old and at boarding school in Germany. He saw the television pictures of the revolution without understanding quite what they meant. Suddenly, as a boy with his origins in Romania, he was the centre of attention among his fellow school pupils. Briefly, at any rate.

Castles returned

Gernyeszeg, September 2009

On the edge of Gernyeszeg stands a low house with a sign outside that reads, in large red letters, COUNTESS FASTFOOD. There's nothing very aristocratic about the greasy sausages and potato soup, but perhaps the name is an attempt to make a connection with the Teleki counts. In Gernyeszeg they employed one of the best cooks of the Dual Monarchy, Mihály Brezsán, later taken on by Rudolf von Habsburg, the crown prince who shot himself in the head at Mayerling. The eighteenth-century baroque Teleki Palace described by Miklós Bánffy in his Transylvania trilogy under the name 'Var-Siklod' is in Gernyeszeg. It's now a home for children suffering from tuberculosis or whose parents have problems such as alcohol or drug abuse. The castle has been given back to the family, including the home full of children. The family has not yet decided what to do with the castle.

Gábor Teleki is the only member of the Teleki family currently living in Romania, in Bucharest, but he is not the only heir. Born in 1968 and schooled in Kolozsvár, Gábor is one of the people I know from the Piaf Bar. He remembers a happy childhood in Romania. His grandfather Mihály was born and brought up in Gernyeszeg and had four children. He was taken away in 1949 and spent two years in labour camps at the Danube – Black Sea Canal. After he returned from the camps he worked in a garage and lived in a cellar with his four children.

Four men are standing at the gate to the park, talking in Hungarian. I greet them. No one stops me. The palace is clammy inside, dark and empty, like most institutions in Eastern Europe that rely on government funding. All around it are tall plane trees. A stone bridge crosses the moat. The water is so green with scummy algae that it looks as if you could walk

straight across. The winding moat flows into a lake surrounded by baroque statues. Gábor's grandfather was not allowed to swim in the lake, but he could always go down to the Maros, 200 metres away, where there was a bathing spot used by the family, with a jetty and a diving board.

The palace looks out on extensive grounds. The view includes an obelisk at the place where the Margit spring used to be, where all the water needed at the castle was fetched. The house was heated by tiled stoves and lit by paraffin lamps, with silver candelabra on the dining tables. The staff wore blue-and-yellow tunics with buttons bearing the family coat of arms, which was also displayed on the coach. The servants had lunch at twelve o'clock, the family at one. For the servants the bell rang once, for the family three times. In the dining room, where the Habsburg emperor once dined after the hunt, there are now long tables where gypsy children with big eyes sit eating potato soup from tin dishes. Above them hang the remains of three Murano chandeliers and the television in the corner is always turned on. In a year from now the children's home will have to leave the castle. The Romanian government has not yet made any arrangements for the children.

The park at Gernyeszeg lies neglected. Empty plinths indicate where statues must once have stood. The statue of Juno is missing. Large sections of the moat are dry, its marshy bed overgrown with reeds and willows. No one has mown the grass. Paths have been trodden through the tall weeds in areas where the children walk, like tracks made by wildlife. At the far end of the park is a lawn with playground equipment. Close to the house are cow-pats – someone must have been given permission to keep his cows in the garden of a tuberculosis clinic. A fat dog lies asleep in front of the entrance.

On an earlier trip, in Koltó further north, near the place where the Lápos flows into the Szamos, I visited a more modest house owned by the Telekis. After it was returned to them by the Romanian government, the family donated it to the local community. It houses a school, a nursery for toddlers, the village library, the post office, a surgery for a doctor who visits once a week, the annual vaccination centre for children and pets, the village cinema and a small museum devoted to the Telekis.

The guide showed me a lime tree that was three hundred and twenty years old and told me in Hungarian that Ferenc Liszt and the writer Mór Jókai once came to stay. Sándor Petőfi, Hungary's most famous poet, spent six weeks of his honeymoon in the house and it was there that he wrote 'End of the September'. A little summerhouse with a memorial bench has been built in the park to commemorate him.

In the museum I was shown the Teleki coat of arms, copied by a local amateur painter. The first quarter features a squirrel, the second quarter a lion with a sword in its front right paw. In the centre of the shield, flanked by two lions and two eagles, a goat standing on its hind legs holds a fir branch. I'd seen a multitude of animals in the coats of arms of Transylvanian families: unicorns rampant, lions waving sabres, eagles with wings spread, wolves with geese in their jaws, bears with scimitars between their teeth, bulls with arrows through their noses and snakes with gold balls between their fangs. The one thing they had in common was that they were all dangerous-looking predators. This was the first coat of arms I'd come across with prey depicted on it. What was this storybook animal doing there? I asked my guide.

'The goat with the fir branch symbolizes the attachment of the Teleki counts to Transylvania; the branch stands for the forests, the goat for the mountains,' the guide explained. 'The family was always both illustrious and hospitable. This house was built in the mid-eighteenth century by Mihály Teleki. János Teleki decided on his deathbed in 2008 that it would be given to the village, for use by the community, and a small museum would remain here.'

Between 1991 and 2005, in the run-up to its accession to the EU, Romania adopted more far-reaching restitution laws than most of its neighbours. In Hungary in the mid-1990s, anyone with documentary evidence that he or his forebears had been dispossessed was given special vouchers with which to buy land at auctions. You were allowed a maximum of five million forints' worth of vouchers, or around 20,000 euro, depending how much property had been taken from the family. Some of my friends in Budapest still complain about this injustice. You could buy only land with the vouchers, not a town house, country house or castle. There was a lively trade in them. Smooth-talking Hungarians went to visit elderly people, bought their vouchers for a song and got their hands on large estates.

In contrast to Hungary, the Romanian restitution laws give all those who were dispossessed or whose families were dispossessed between 1946 and 1989 the right to reclaim property. More than 750,000 claims have been submitted: houses, gardens, agricultural land, forests, shops, offices, banks, businesses, palaces, castles. Returning property confiscated sixty years ago is an extraordinarily complex process. The new owners may since have renovated the property, demolished it, or sold it on.

The Romanian government has therefore set up a fund, the Fondul Proprietatea, to take charge of nationalized industries, airports and harbours, and to look into monies owed to Romania by reliable, creditworthy states such as Iraq and Zimbabwe. When a request for restitution cannot be honoured, for whatever reason, compensation takes the form of shares in the Fondul Proprietatea. Among the hundreds of thousands of claims are quite a few from the Hungarian aristocracy in Transylvania.

In 1996 Count István Mikó published a book called *Vár állott, most kőhalom* (Where a castle stood a mound of stones remains) about the fate of the Transylvanian nobles under communism. It includes a list of the fifty most important castles and palaces owned by the Transylvanian aristocracy in 1945. They belonged to a total of thirty families. I have visited ten of the houses on the list; three were in good condition, the rest in a bad way. The buildings are disintegrating rapidly, generally speaking, and there are hundreds of them. Until 1989 the majority housed schools, old people's homes, orphanages

or hospitals, or functioned as the offices of agricultural cooperatives or as army barracks. After the overthrow of communism, countless institutions of this type were closed down or no longer funded. The abandoned buildings were looted, the tiles removed from the roofs, the rafters sawn up for firewood and the bricks used to build new houses, garden walls or pigsties. The Romanian government has given every appearance of acquiescing in this destruction, secretly pleased that the cultural heritage left to remind people of the Hungarian presence in Transylvania is disappearing from the face of the earth. The crooks who run things in Bucharest certainly don't care. Only where people of noble descent have succeeded in recovering family property has the destruction been stopped or curbed. As far as I can see, only the following twelve aristocratic families have until now been successful, or partially successful, in their restitution claims: Apor, Bánffy, Béldi, Bethlen, Haller, Horváth-Tholdy, Jósika, Kálnoky, Kemény, Kendeffy, Mikes and Teleki.

Despite the fact that the Bethlens are still unable to agree among themselves who is the real owner of the renaissance castle in Keresd, the building has meanwhile been renovated – as has Bonchida, property of the Bánffys, restored by the Transylvania Trust (whose supporters include the Prince of Wales Foundation). The ruin of Bonchida has been turned into an educational institution for European restorers. Zabola has been done up to perfection by the dynamic Roy Chowdhury-Mikes family. Erzsébet T.'s comprehensively looted Dornafalva is still to come. The ancient Transylvanian country house of the Apor family in Torja is very slowly being renovated under the leadership of Kata Apor's grandfather, now almost ninety. Tibor Kálnoky has not yet gathered all the paperwork needed before he can set to work on his ancestors' castle and hunting lodge.

A castle near Hadad was recovered by the Bánffys, who then sold it on. The second castle returned to them, in Aranyosgerend, is in an abominable state. The Bánffy family as a whole is in the process of reclaiming 28,000 hectares of woodland that once belonged to them – an endless process. On paper they have regained ownership of 10,000 hectares, but since this is Romania, they still have a long way to go to achieve actual restitution of those hectares. Béla Bánffy junior runs a travel bureau and on the side a company producing hand-made paper (a small firm, of which he is director, ad-

ministrator and worker) as well as a small printing works. Béla tells me that the castle at Hadad was sold three years ago by the three brothers and two sisters of his father's generation. He did all he could to prevent the sale. Restitution, like inheritance, can be a source of conflict. A majority of the relatives needed the money. Like all the other estates systematically neglected over sixty years, it was a project for an enthusiast. The buyer was a nouveau-riche Transylvanian Hungarian.

A third Bánffy-Jósika country house, in Várfalva, has been inherited by Bánffys who live in Germany, where they own a pharmacy. They have restored it with, I'm given to understand, rather Bavarian taste. They use it as a holiday home. Farkas Bánffy dreams of renovating his grandfather's house in Fugad, but he is as yet unable to cover the costs.

A castle of the Tisza counts in western Transylvania, not far from the Hungarian border, has been returned to the Tiszas. They want to sell it. In the Ceauşescu years it was an infamous orphanage where children were tied to beds and

locked in cages. The house has a thermal spring capable of warming the entire building.

In Uzon a castle has been returned to the Béldi-Mikes family, its ownership passing to several heirs including Gergely's mother. She has given her share to her nephew Zsigmond, since he is the only male descendant of the Mikes line.

The Zichy counts have attempted to recover own-

ership of a castle near Magaslak, so far without success, I believe. These Zichys are second cousins of mine (their mother is my grandfather's niece) and they live in Spain. I've never met them, but a Hungarian Zichy recently showed me a photograph of Imre Zichy, one of the unknown cousins, who has clearly inherited characteristic facial features from his mother that can be traced back to the region of Twente in the east of the Netherlands where I come from. Next to the castle, which was used by Ceauşescu as a hunting lodge, is a six-hundred-year-old Orthodox Oltenian church. The Zichys are not a typical Transylvanian family. In 1874 they bought 20,000 hectares of forest in the vicinity of Magaslak, and ever since they have had a bond with the region.

Pál Lázár and his cousins, including Kati Ugron, have reclaimed Laposnyak, along with the grounds and an adjoining hundred hectares of forest. Kati's father has had the outside of the house renovated. A beautiful wisteria climbs along a wire to the four pillars supporting the tympanum over the front door. The far side of the park is filled with elongated stables that have the subtle signature of socialist architecture, and in

between them several carts and agricultural vehicles are rusting away.

On paper at least, the Kemény family has recovered possession of the castle in Marosvécs, which currently operates as a care home for the mentally handicapped. Here too there are numerous heirs, so it's difficult to reach decisions. The Keménys have an agreement with the medical director that the current residents will leave the castle as soon as possible, but no date has been set.

After the fall of Ceaușescu, Botond, my friend in Budapest, went back to the village of Pusztakamarás where his grandparents used to live. It lies a little to the north of Marosvásárhely. His grandfather's house was completely demolished in the late 1970s. (The house that belonged to his grandfather's brother, Béla Kemény, came through the communist years more-or-less intact, but after the revolution in 1989 it was abandoned and since then it has been slowly vanishing.) When Botond said he was the grandson of Géza Kemény, the older villagers started crying and telling him stories about his grandfather. The fami-

ly home had become the office of the local kolkhozes. There he found two bookcases, two chairs and a writing desk that had belonged to his grandfather. He bought them back.

András, a very distant relative of Ilona on the count's side of the family, has claimed ownership of a renaissance castle that belonged to his Transylvanian grandmother. Ceauşescu had taken it over as one of his hunting lodges. Nicolae never went there, which did not prevent Elena Ceauşescu from re-fitting the interior to suit her own taste. András is now caught up in a bureaucratic battle with the Romanian authorities, determined to recover his ancestral property. I asked him what he was planning to do with the house.

András: 'I'm like a dog running after a car, growling and barking. If the car stops there's not much more I can do than piss on the tyres.'

András articulates clearly and unsentimentally the reality for most descendants: they feel an obligation to their forefathers to go after stolen family property, so that those who stole or were given it are prevented from holding on to it for good. But when they get it back there's usually little they can do. Property, houses centuries old, can really only be renovated with foreign money, which means either the support of foreign funds and foundations or the help of families who have returned from abroad with large sums to invest. There is hardly any assistance available from the Romanian government. Romanian Catalin Bogdan wrote an article on the subject several years ago for *Magazine Istorie* entitled 'SOS Heritage!'. 'But it's not only the money that's lacking,' she wrote. 'There's also a certain lack of interest in relics that are not strictly speaking Romanian. There's still a latent attitude of exclusion and indifference towards buildings that remind people of a time when the Transylvanian elite was largely non-Romanian. Perhaps the moment when the Romanian government puts money into the restoration of the former residences of noble Hungarian families, like the Bethlens, Bánffys or Mikós, will mark the point when a blinkered nationalistic mentality is truly on the retreat.'

Hunting for truffles
with the new generation

Kund, September 2009

I'm driving through the dark to the old Saxon village of Kund. Jonas Schäfer, who used to run a German record company, decided a few years ago on a radical change of life. He resigned from his job, spent eighteen months training in the kitchens of a restaurant with a Michelin star and bought an old Saxon farmhouse here. He restored it and started a restaurant. Quite mad, you might think. From the south, Kund is difficult to reach along eight kilometres of unsealed road. When I get out at what I suspect – based purely on the lights – to be the restaurant, an enthusiastic man comes to greet me. This must be Jonas. I then greet Gergely and Zsolna Roy Chowdhury. Gergely is a friend from Budapest who has returned to the old family seat at Zabola, and he has invited me here, knowing I was in Transylvania. Gábor and Iris Teleki are coming as well.

The old farmhouse is built of wood, and with its veranda on all four sides it's slightly reminiscent of a Wild West saloon.

Here, in the midst of the wilderness, in a village of a hundred souls, where the cows wander freely and there are more horse-drawn carts than cars, Jonas prepares the most delicious food: autumn salad with avocado drizzled with apple and grenadine syrup, home-made ravioli in a cantarelle-gorgonzola sauce, barbary duck in the pan with fresh grapefruit, and truffles, chocolate mousse and raspberries. He talks passionately about his East German wine merchant, a man with an unbelievably good nose.

Gergely sits across the table from me, Zsolna to my left and next to her a large Romanian with an impressive face, heavy as a bull but with the eyes of a dog. His wife sits opposite him, to his right on the bench are two small children and on the table is an open laptop that he looks at continually, typing something from time to time. He doesn't really talk to anyone. Next to Gergely is another Romanian, Goron. He buys forests for one of the richest families in Britain. A Swedish family; he's willing to divulge that much. He needs to protect his clients' privacy. Gergely immediately guesses which family he means. They're buying up forests as a sustainable investment.

Gábor and Iris Teleki arrive with their children. The toddlers have to be settled into bed, but that's done in no time. Iris comes to sit with us. The Romanian to Zsolna's left is still looking at his screen. His wife has meanwhile put their children to bed and is staring slightly mournfully into her glass. At the start of dinner I thought for a moment that the laptop was there to keep the children quiet, but the father of the family is still stroking the touchpad with great feeling. I ask him what he's doing.

'I've got a very demanding boss,' he answers.

'Ah, an American no doubt,' I guess.

'No, a Romanian,' he replies, smiling, looking up with his dog-eyes. 'I've worked on Wall Street, so I know what Americans are like. But this is something else again; this is really hard work.'

'Who is your boss then?' I ask.

'Ion Ţiriac.'

'Never heard of him.'

From all sides this hiatus in my knowledge is filled by my dining companions. It seems it's hard not to know this living legend.

'He owns the third largest bank and the largest insurance company in the country. He also has a number of dealerships and he's one of the biggest importers of cars.'

'A former tennis player. He was Boris Becker's manager for years.'

'His fortune is estimated at a billion and a half dollars.'

'He and Nastase beat Roland Garros at doubles.'

'He lived in Germany for a long time, but after the fall of Ceauşescu he was the first to set up a private bank in Romania.'

'And he was in the Romanian national ice hockey team too. He played in the 1964 Olympic Games.'

'He was the first Romanian ever to make it into the Forbes 500.'

'Okay,' I say. 'Clearly a man who likes to win.'

The large Romanian nods apologetically at his laptop. 'Well, yes. Hard work, as I say. I'm in charge of his companies. We have banks, insurance firms, import-export businesses and leasing companies. And we trade in real estate.'

I can understand why anyone in those branches of business would have reason to worry these days. On this my final evening in Transylvania I'm sitting around a table with the new generation of owners of Transylvania's 'green gold': a businessman who represents the interests of a man said to be the second richest Romanian and one of the largest owners of real estate in the country; a Romanian looking for forests for a hugely rich Swedish family to buy; a descendant of Count Mikes who has come back from Austria to manage several thousand hectares of forest along with his brother; and Gábor Teleki, descendant of one of the most famous families in Transylvania, who has recovered some hundreds of hectares of family land near Gernyeszeg. We are under the wing of a German who is deploying Michelin-grade cuisine to breathe new life into a depopulated Saxon village, and an Armenian born in Syria who now lives in Brașov, where he devotes himself to his passion, hunting for truffles.

I sleep in a farmhouse. Jonas has forty beds available, mostly with villagers, so the locals too have something to gain from the strangers who arrive in the dark on Friday evenings in their four-wheel-drives and BMWs. Jonas says the next morning: 'What I do would be impossible without the support of the community.'

'Do you earn enough from your guests?'

'Yes, it's going better all the time. We're regularly full. They know where to find me. Occasionally I provide a catering service, like last year for the first Transylvanian Ball that Gergely and Zsolna organized. I'm doing it again next year, in July. Come with me. I've made something nice for breakfast, Tuscan crêpes.'

At breakfast I sit facing Goron, the forest-buyer. Most of the company from last night are busy attending to small children. Goron is a fairly short man who looks like the salt-of-the-earth type. Later in the day, during the truffle hunt, one of the others will point out to me that, given his excellent contacts in Bucharest, he must be a former Securitate agent.

'How much does a hectare of Romanian forest cost nowadays?' I ask.

'It varies. Between 1,800 and 3,000 euro.'

'And what determines the price?'

'First of all the trees, the quality of them, whether they're firewood or timber and how old they are, but also their accessibility. That's generally the problem in Romania: good forests, bad roads. Laying roads is very expensive.'

'And what do you look for if you're thinking of buying a forest?' I ask.

'Good ground. The quality of the ground. You don't just want soil, there has to be gravel in it as well, so that the roots have a footing and air. Then the trees can grow big. You look at the tree density too. You want the forest to be thick because then the trees have to grow tall to reach the light. Best is oak surrounded by firs, for firewood, because they get tall quickly and then the oaks grow nice and straight. From that point of view diversity is a good thing, a mixture of hardwood and firewood.'

How many contracts did you need to close to buy that 6,000 hectares of forest?'

'Not many. About ten.'

'Unbelievable. I know someone in Hungary who had to sign more than six hundred contracts to get his hands on 2,000 hectares. So there must be quite a few people or parties that own large areas and are prepared to sell. Who are they?'

'That's confidential.'

'But I assume they're private individuals who've had confiscated forests returned to them. Do you buy from Hungarians who've got their forests back, or from Romanians? Or directly from the state?'

'Mainly Romanians. There are a lot of Romanian families who own several hundred hectares. Often they bought them in the early part of the twentieth century, up to the Second World War. It's amazing. From the deeds you can sometimes see who the owners were right back as far as the twelfth or fourteenth century. Some areas were royal forests hundreds of years ago. But let's be clear; we're not selling history. We buy forests that will make a good investment. And those that have now been returned to the Romanian royal family are not exactly prime.'

'Several Hungarian families have managed to get large forests back, do you do business with them?'

'Not as yet.'

'So how do you know which forests are for sale?'

'That's my secret. I can't tell you that.'

Jonas, smart in his neatly buckled chef's jacket, brings us his Tuscan breakfast specialty, pancakes of some sort. When I came to Transylvania in 2006 I thought forests might be going for a song. In Budapest I'd heard stories about families that were reclaiming their forests. The heirs to the Kendeffy counts recovered 13,000 hectares of woodland near Déva and they are now fighting for the restitution of another 36,000 hectares. Eight thousand hectares and a mediaeval castle have been returned to the former Romanian royal family.

'Who are the biggest owners of forests in Transylvania now?' I ask Goron.

'The Romanian state is still the largest owner by far,' he says. Private and state ownership are about equal. After the state, the Romanian Orthodox Church is the second largest landowner.'

'Ah, so that's how they can afford to build all those new churches.'

'I'm not sure about that. They have 200,000 hectares, I believe. After the Romanian Orthodox Church, Harvard University is the biggest investor in Transylvanian forests, with more than 40,000 hectares. Then there's a large Finnish investor, Tornado, then the Romanian royal family and the Kendeffy family. And then you've got the Swedish family. They now own more than 10,000 hectares of forest and farmland.'

'Is that good, all those foreigners?'

'Yes, it's fine. They're all parties that take forestry seriously. I think things are moving in the right direction with Transylvania's forests. It's much better than a few years ago. In the first few years after *die Wende* the worst aspects of democracy came to the surface. People thought they could take anything that belonged to the state; illegal felling was the first thing everyone did. Even now, thirty to forty per cent of the Romanian timber trade is on the black market, partly because of the large number of small owners and the bureaucracy involved. You need stamps for everything and you have to plan your forestry ten years ahead. The ITRSV, the Romanian government inspectorate, checks whether the ten-year plans have been carried out. But the small owners, the villagers, often elderly people who live on very little, they need the money. They fell their own woods and sell the timber on the black market. The buyers and dealers are mafiosi, real mafiosi, professionals. They sell the timber abroad. Every trunk of a hardwood tree officially needs a stamp at the top end, otherwise you're not allowed to transport it. When it's loaded onto a truck, all the stamps at the end have to be visible. A good system in theory, but the dealers hide timber inside truckloads of firewood. Firewood doesn't have to be stamped.'

'Does the timber mafia fell trees as well?'

'It usually goes like this. They arrange for a permit to fell a piece of woodland, ten hectares, say. They go into the forest with trucks, sawing equipment and tractors and fell all the good timber in a huge radius around those ten hectares. Then they drag it to the stretch they have a permit for and take it out from there. It's very hard to monitor.'

Outside three men with dogs are waiting for us. They're truffle dogs. We stand in a circle around them. It's crucial to give the dogs plenty of space. We're most likely to find *Choiromyces meandriformis*, known locally as the yellow dog's nose truffle, which is very common in Transylvania and not of much use. The Burgundy truffle, which looks like a black ball on the outside but is veined a coffee colour inside, is also found fairly often in Transylvania. More rare is the Piedmont white truffle, the most expensive kind, with a market value of between one and two thousand euro per kilo. Large quantities of the Piedmont white truffle have been found in Eastern Europe recently.

After listening to the explanation and whispering to the dogs that today they must concentrate on Piedmont white truffles, we make our way to a steep beech wood.

The Transylvanian Chambord

Kund, September 2009

After two hours spent searching for truffles I climbed the steep hill and took one more look at the magisterial forest of oak and beech. The dogs were zigzagging, noses to the ground. My companions – miracle cook Jonas Schäfer, Gábor and Iris Teleki, Gergely and Zsolna Roy Chowdhury, the Romanian forest-buyer, the tennis billionaire's manager, the Armenian truffle man and his three Romanian assistants plus all the accompanying toddlers – continued their search for the Piedmont white truffle of which, after four hours, they had found three.

I'm driving through unspoilt valleys: high wild grass, narrow strips of maize, groups of cows with long horns, a road made of loose chippings for many kilometres. All I come upon between Kund and Dumbrăveni are two men with a metal handcart. Dumbrăveni is mediaeval and people walk the streets or simply hang around. It's the birthplace of Michael Apafi, prince of Transylvania, and one of the four towns where Apafi invited the Armenians to come and settle freely. There's not a car in sight. I manage to find the approach to Mediaş, a road lined with nut trees. Suddenly it's time to pick them. I can see swarms of people in the tall roadside grass, men with long notched sticks and very dark gypsy girls pouring the walnuts they've collected in the front panels of their skirts into sacks, which are then moved by handcart. Occasionally someone lifts a bulging sack onto his shoulder.

At Brateiu, a small village on the way to Mediaş, the roadside verge is covered in gleaming new copperware: pots and pans big enough to roast a whole sheep in; stills made of a closed, cone-shaped cylinder on legs with a copper pipe affixed to it, curling upwards like a pig's tail.

Between Mediaş and Târnăveni I take the little road for Bazna, passing through villages where girls and young women are fetching buckets of water at one of the village wells. The set of a woman's body as she lugs a bucket of water in one hand is magnificent, the way her body tenses as she leans to provide a counterweight is simply inimitable. And it seems that until they turn thirty, women in Blăjel, Bazna and Boian don't waste any money on bras. Not the water-carriers at any rate. It's an almost biblical scene. I'm still on an unsealed road, passing through overwhelming valleys, dragging a cloud of dust behind me. From time to time I slow down and cautiously overtake a wooden horse-drawn cart.

Suddenly, in the middle of open country, the stony track gives way to a beautiful, jet-black, broad asphalt road. The village begins half a kilometre further on. They've dug a fresh ditch and new cables and sewer pipes are being laid. Enormous reels of cable and sections of pipe lie ready alongside the road. It's a major project. I've arrived in Cetatea de Baltă, or Küküllővár in Hungarian, where I intend to go in search of a castle that until 3 March 1949 belonged to the Haller counts. Béla Haller has described it as a small Chambord, a version of the sixteenth-century renaissance castle on the Loire.

Down below, in the village, the bridge is being repaired. All the verges have been dug up for new cables. Drainage ditches are being replaced with concrete culverts. The asphalt here is brand new or still being laid. In the distance stands the castle, on a hill, looking out across the valley. It dominates the village. A castle wall stops me from getting close. It's the first time I've seen a castle in Transylvania that has been renovated to such an extent. There's an enormous main gate made of wood, large enough to drive a truck through.

If I take a few steps back, onto the marvellous asphalt, I can look over the wall and the gate and see the castle towers rising above me. Somewhere in there, Béla Haller's grandfather was shot dead by his Romanian chauffeur. He was hit in the stomach and taken to hospital, but nothing could save him. There are far better treatments for wounds like that nowadays, Béla told me in his house in Marosvásárhely, so today he would probably have recovered. The chauffeur's wife also worked for Béla's grandparents and she'd warned them repeatedly about her husband, a Romanian nationalist and a hothead with a grudge against Hungarians. One evening he came to the grandfather's bathroom with a revolver. He was convicted of murder but released within two years by the Romanian government. After her husband's death, Béla's grandmother ran the castle and the estate by herself. Later her son, Béla's father, took over. He was the chatelain, thirty-two years old, when the militia roused him from his bed on the night of 3 March 1949 and loaded him onto a truck.

The castle is plastered with dark-grey stucco. It's smaller and less graceful than its French counterpart, but it too has a round tower on every corner. It looks more robust than the real Chambord, which is rather a fairytale palace, built for

concerts, masked balls and flirting amid the box hedging. The French original is white and stands on an open plain – it's not built to be defended. We used to travel through France with my father in the summer when I was a boy, and when I saw Chambord it made a deep impression on me. I wasn't exactly captivated by most of our obligatory visits to castles, historical gardens, museums and mediaeval towns. Usually we all refused, my brothers and I, to get out of the Peugeot 504 station wagon, where we sat in three rows behind one another like galley slaves refusing to row.

A charming little structure has been set against the castle wall. It has a covered terrace, surrounded on three sides by a wooden balustrade, with steps at the front. Here wine tasters are received, so that back home they can report that they've tasted the wine at Castel Jidvei, as the chateau is now called. They don't actually need to be allowed inside. Clever. On the asphalted area in front of the castle gate there's enough space for tourist coaches to turn round. A security camera has been mounted high on the castle wall.

Below me a gleaming black off-road vehicle tears up the drive. A hundred metres short of the gate the car toots out a tune. An outsider, uninitiated in local mores, might think it was a suicide squad: a four-wheel-drive with blacked out windows, the boot no doubt packed full of ammonium nitrate. It doesn't ease up. I hear scrambling noises from beyond the gate and through the cracks between the hardwood planks I can see hasty movement. The gate flies open. A tall grey-haired man in a blue doorman's uniform clings to the still swinging gate as the vehicle, without slowing down, races into the courtyard.

I ask whether the owner is around. I put the question in English, since just as in France you don't make a good impression by speaking German, you should try to avoid speaking to Romanians in Hungarian. There are many places where the mutual aversion between Hungarians and Romanians is still very much alive. Béla has warned me this village is very nationalistic. It's one of the reasons he felt he couldn't settle back here with his family.

The gatekeeper goes for help and returns a short while later with a woman in a floral print dress. I shake her hand, tell her I'm from the Netherlands and am working on a book about Transylvania, and ask whether I could have a quick look around inside the ramparts. She's friendly and tells me that the family is in residence. She won't let me set foot inside the gate, but she is willing to fetch something for me. She disappears. In the park three children are racing around on quad bikes with bored looks on their faces. After a while the woman comes out with a man. She nods to me that she won't be long and then stands talking endlessly with the man, next to a four-wheel-drive. I don't feel like waiting at the gate with my arms crossed like a tradesman, so I stroll around a bit.

There's a notice board in Romanian, English and French, giving a brief history of the Bethlen-Haller castle. Béla Haller has told me that it belonged to the family for only a very short time – and anyhow was won at cards – but here I read that the new owner Eugen Haller restored the castle in baroque style between 1770 and 1773. Surely there are a hundred and seventy-nine years between 1770 and 1949. It says a lot that such a period is regarded as less than impressive by members of the old Transylvanian families. 'The castle was in the family for only a short time; it had no particular emotional value,' were Béla's words. On the notice board I read that it was built between 1615 and 1624 by Gabriel Bethlen and that in 1949 it became the property of IAS, State Agricultural Enterprise Cetatea de Baltă.

Béla didn't see the castle until he was twelve, in 1965, after Ceaușescu came to power and officially abolished the status of Domiciliu Obligatoriu 'because the class war was over'. The stigmatized were allowed for the first time to travel outside the municipal boundaries of the cities and towns where they had been sent. Béla told me that in the late 1970s they found out that the castle had never been officially confiscated; the property deeds were still in his grandmother's name. In the 1990s there were problems with the renovation. The legal owner was obliged to bear the costs. At that point Béla's father decided to sell the castle. Béla said that suited him fine. He didn't regard himself as capable of running the place. It would require a practical cast of mind that he, a teacher of French and Italian, did not possess. The decision denotes an admirable sense of reality, but looking at the centuries-old castle walls, the corner towers and the magnificent view I become vicariously covetous.

At last the woman has reached the point of being able to talk to me. She gives me two vacuous folders about the Jidvei wines and tells me that eight of the castle's rooms have been completed to house the family. The ground floor has already been refurbished; now they're working on the first and second floors.

Nowhere on the notice board does it mention the name of the current owner. The lady talks only of 'la famille'. It's quite remarkable that I can't find any reference to them on the internet or in the brochures the woman gives me. The owner is keeping a low profile, the way I've noticed the new rich in Eastern Europe – the robber barons of capitalism – tend to do. The new bosses wrap themselves in clouds of mystery and stay well out of reach. On the few occasions I've been in close proximity to Eastern European oligarchs, at receptions or parties, I've been struck by their churlish reticence. I think their crude xenophobia arises from the fact that ninety per cent of them, whether in Romania, Hungary, Albania or Montenegro, acquired their wealth by illegitimate means in the chaotic transition period from communism to a 'free market' economy. Evasiveness suits them. Their property is usually spread across a network of private partnerships and holdings, in the name of wives, children, brothers and sisters. For obvious reasons the companies are often registered in Cyprus or Malta.

The toot of a horn from back along the drive and a silver S-class Mercedes charges up the hill. The doorkeeper sprints to the gate. The car does not reduce speed and the gate opens in the nick of time. I estimate that this Mercedes, like the last, must have flown into the courtyard at sixty kilometres per hour. If a car sounds its horn at a distance of 100 metres at that speed, then the man on the gate has six seconds to open up. Wonderful, that blind faith in an underling. How often must this family habit have led to splintered gates?

'I see everything's being restored to its old glory,' I say to the woman in the floral print. 'The family is clearly re-establishing the aristocratic traditions.' As I speak I nod to the uniformed servant and to the park, where the spoilt brats are still horsing around on their quads. 'So I wonder: how have they decorated and furnished it? Is the house being returned to its original condition inside as well?'

The woman lets that pass and looks down her nose at me slightly; she's not really supposed to tell anyone anything about it.

'The entire castle has been restored in mediaeval style,' she says eventually. 'The interior included. That too is mediaeval.' She then tells me that at harvest time two thousand people work for the company. They don't just get wages, they're given a loaf of bread every day. The castle has 2,400 hectares of land. A Transylvanian friend will later tell me he is convinced the owner comes from a Securitate family.

'*Notre patron* also pays the university fees of fifty-two local children.' She tells me how many bottling plants, how many wooden casks and how many steel casks there are, and how many hectolitres are bottled every year, but I can't listen to her any more. The thought of hundreds of square metres of castle being renovated in its entirety – *totul* – in mediaeval style by a nouveau-riche Romanian oligarch from Constanța makes my imagination run riot: a jumble of suits of armour, halberds and swords that you wriggle past to reach gleaming armchairs studded with brass tacks, polished monastic tables – all lit by fat, dripping candles on heavy, overly elaborate wrought-iron brackets. Like a cross between Hearst Castle and a theme park, crammed with replicas.

A little later I'm humming over smooth new asphalt in the direction of Kolozsvár with two crates of Jidvei wine in the boot. In the fields along the way are rows of white sacks. Hundreds of people, gypsies and old women in black with large straw hats, are grubbing up potatoes. Would these be the same people who take a loaf of bread home with them every day in the grape-harvesting season? I've not found a better road anywhere in Romania than the stretch between Cetatea de Baltă and Târnăveni. A large sign in the village of Ádámos tells me that the Romanian government is financing the rebuilding of the road for a sum of 3,562,037.22 lei. It has to be said: *notre patron*, the new chatelain of Castel Jidvei, knows how to crack the whip.

Take the battery
out of your phone

'In the last few years, when I was working on deals that
were crucial for the Romanians, a few seconds after every
phone conversation you'd hear a click,' Dario tells me. An Italian banker based in Vienna, he has supervised many transac-
tions in Romania. Friends of mine in Budapest involved with
Romanian investments and take-overs confirm what he says.
The top people in their companies have strictly forbidden
them to talk about important matters on the phone when
they're in Romania.

Dario: 'In take-over negotiations by the Romanian tele-
coms company Romtelecom, the company boss put his mobile phone on the table, took the battery out and demonstratively laid it next to the phone. He looked around the table
and nodded to everyone to follow his example. Few people realize that turning off your mobile isn't enough. You can still
be listened to. The Romanian state telephone company knows

what it's talking about. It was their most important line of work for years.'

Marius Oprea of the CICCR (Centrul de Investigare a Crimelor Communismului din România), an organization that researches the crimes of communism in Romania, explained it in his flat in Brașov like this: 'In Ceaușescu's Romania the Securitate was all-powerful. It controlled the citizens, the contacts, all foreign trade, the press, telephone traffic, flows of money, foreign bank accounts and Ceaușescu's bear hunts. As far as all that's concerned, nothing has really changed, with the exception of the bear hunts. If the system took against you, then until 1990 you were arrested. Nowadays you're sacked. The communist party no longer exists in Romania, but Securitate officers and former communist activists are hugely influential. A certain continuity in families has arisen as a result: sons of Securitate members are now officers in the secret services, sons of former communist magistrates are lawyers and prosecutors, sons of former members of the militia are in the police, sons of party activists are managers of large companies. You have to remember that in 1989 Romania had 400,000 Securitate informants. Those people have families. Can you imagine how many voters that adds up to? They want the past to remain undisturbed. People say we need to let the dead rest in peace, to let bygones be bygones. Ex-Securitate agents and party members have maintained a conspiracy of silence about the communist past.'

I ask Larry Watts how much influence the Securitate has in today's Romania. Larry is an American historian who has lived in Romania almost continually since 1981 and has made a special study of the interactions and conflicts between the secret service and the army. He was involved in Romania's accession to NATO. We're sitting in his apartment in a wealthy district of Bucharest. He has plonked his young daughter in front of a video in the next room.

'As a secret service, zero. From an economic point of view, vast. The biggest blunder after the Romanian revolution of December 1989 was the dismantling of the Securitate. It's a mistake the Americans could have avoided making in Iraq. Keep the secret service and the army intact, just those two institutions, and you'll be able to control the country. If the Romanian army had fallen apart as well, there would have been civil war in 1990. The Securitate officers all set up in business for themselves. This country is still suffering as a result. As long as you have them in your pay, you've got a certain amount of control over them. That whole battalion of Securitate, more than 15,000 strong, was suddenly unemployed on 25 December 1989. They still had all their contacts and access to the files. No one else knew anything in Romania. People still think there were far more of them. Sure, there were 400,000 informants, all diligently lending their services to the secret agents, but the Securitate was small. It was probably the smallest secret service in the Warsaw Pact. Until 1961 all its officers received their training from the KGB. Later only those above the rank of captain were trained in the Soviet Union.

'Eighty per cent of today's Romanian oligarchs are former Securitate officers or had close ties with the Securitate. Even after it was dissolved, the Securitate tried to retain a monopoly on information. The media are in the hands of three Securitate tycoons. One is a member of a famous Securitate family, the other two used to be Securitate money men, the people who controlled its Swiss bank accounts. The Romanian oligarchs had little reason to want to join the EU. Oil is the real source of wealth here. The oligarchs are trying to keep it quiet, but nowhere is the oil more than 6,000 feet down, whereas in the US, for example, it's at 15,000 feet. The potential is enormous. Except that all the money leaves the country; that's the tragedy. The Romanian oil fields have been sold on via a Dutch holding company.'

Dinu Patriciu, an architect and the son of a man who was on the board of Romanian Shell before the war, managed somehow or other to get his hands on the national oil company Rompetrol after he returned to Romania in 1990, and via a web of holdings he sold it to Kazakhstan. He is said to have earned 1.5 billion euro from the sale, which went through before the financial crisis. Whereas the other Romanian oligarchs saw their newly acquired wealth – in insurance, banking, leasing companies and real estate – shrink because of the crisis, Patriciu can buy the whole world.

Larry: 'It's no wonder Ceauşescu was so scared. Beginning in 1963, the KGB tried to murder him three times. The Russians have carried out a large number of liquidations on Romanian territory, often using heavy goods vehicles to force people off the road. When Soviet troops left Romania in 1958 it was bad for the Hungarians in Transylvania in particular, because up till then they'd enjoyed a certain amount of protection. In 1963 the KGB advisors officially left the country too, so then the old anti-Hungarian political resentment had free rein. When it comes to Romania the secret services of the Soviet Union and Hungary have always cooperated. The Russians have never been wild about the Romanians. In the Second World War they were the only ones who really fought hard against the Russians alongside the Germans. The other countries sent two men and a dog.'

Larry gets up and puts another video in the machine in the neighbouring room, to keep his daughter quiet.

'From 1974 onwards the Securitate went sharply downhill, because Elena Ceauşescu believed all its officers should have working-class backgrounds. The Securitate was already a fairly primitive organization, set up to oppress its own population and not capable of doing much else. The Hungarian secret service was far more sophisticated, since it grew out of an imperial tradition and had an international approach. In December

1989 the Hungarians on the Romanian border had units of the Bornemissza brigade on standby to protect the Hungarian minority in Transylvania, in collaboration with French commando units. Mitterrand would have been perfectly happy to give Transylvania back to Hungary.'

For years rumours have been circulating that the Russian secret service played a major role in the Romanian revolution. In the weeks leading up to the fall of the regime, 30,000 Russians are said to have entered the country as civilians with tourist visas, all of them athletic young men, three or four to each small car. My uncle, Coen Stork, has heard the stories but never seen any firm proof. He thinks it was a genuine revolt by the Romanian people and all the rest is a typical Eastern European conspiracy theory. I ask Larry Watts.

'In the weeks before the 1989 revolution, thousands of Speznatz agents did indeed enter Romania. Gorbachev had predicted that Ceauşescu would come to a bad end. The Russian units entered the country without consulting Gorbachev, who heard about it only after they arrived here. He refused to give them orders to help overthrow the regime, so all through the revolution there were tens of thousands of Russians in the major Romanian cities without a mandate – a ridiculous situation.'

As for Coen Stork, Larry says: 'The Dutch ambassador in Bucharest was the doyen of all ambassadors. He had a huge influence. It's impossible to overstate his contribution. Stork often made contact with dissidents. In Romania there was a special situation because of the lack of an official Russian presence. Dissidents didn't need to protest against the Russians, only against their own government. Some of the dissidents were in contact with Moscow, it's important not to forget that.'

By the time I take my leave of Larry Watts my head is spinning. I thought I was beginning to understand a little about the situation in Transylvania, but this man has turned everything upside-down. Hungarians, Frenchmen, Russians, dissidents and ambassadors – everyone was working for and against everyone else. Watts is a specialist on the subject; his interest in covert links and secret agendas verges on paranoia. He talks about countless conspiracy theories and emphasizes Coen Stork's part in the revolution to such an extent that I start to ask myself who Coen's paymasters were. The next day I ring my uncle and ask him straight out whether he was working for the CIA.

He replies: 'Are you mad! A lot of my Romanian friends used to think things like that and they'd ask me. They usually wanted to know whether I was working for the British secret services, because I had close contacts with the British ambassador. But no, I wasn't working for either of them. In fact it's worse: I was never even asked.'

The Romanian nouveaux riches anno 2010

Bucharest, February 2010

D ario, the Italian banker, has advised me to take a good
look out of the window while landing at Aeroportul International Henri Coandă so as not to miss the parking area where
they keep the returned lease cars. I see a slab of asphalt with hundreds of gleaming black vehicles. The global financial crisis has
hit even harder in Romania than elsewhere, but the Romanian
leaders are fortunate; people here are accustomed to suffering.

I ask the taxi driver to drive past one of the leasing companies. There are rows and rows of Jaguars, Range Rovers, Land
Rovers and Mercedeses, as well as dozens of white golf-buggies.
The asking price for a practically unused black Range Rover is
59,000 euro, the Mercedes S350s go for 40,000 euro, the Porsche Cayennes 27,000, and the Chrysler 300Cs are on offer
for 23,000.

I'm in Bucharest for three days to gain an impression of the
lives and mores of the new Romanian elite. The positions oc-

cupied for centuries by the aristocracy have been taken over by people who come from nowhere, or as Erzsébet T. puts it 'by people whose grandparents ate with a spoon, the meat with their hands'. In Hungary, and even more so in Romania, a private club has emerged of people who control all the information, the raw materials, the wealth, the sources of income and the contacts. These countries seem democratic but aren't. The Romanian oligarchs and the Hungarian elite run their properties like small independent principalities.

The hallmark of the new rich is that they don't quite know how to behave. At the same time that's the nice thing about them. They're unrestrained, unhindered by rules and driven by a fanatical urge to prove that they've made it. They move through the forest of life with the confidence of elephants. In most countries there's a social stratum they can model themselves after, which they often aspire to. It has something of a grip on them as a result. In this region the example is set by clips of rappers on MTV and life in Dubai. In Bucharest and Budapest you soon notice the lack of a frame of reference, and the excesses that result: flying U2 in for your birthday party; spending a weekend in Odessa with fifteen bought women; giving your fourteen-year-old daughter the latest Louis Vuitton bag at the start of the new school year.

The first time I heard about Romania's new rich was at home in Budapest at the breakfast table. During a sports tournament we had two of those lanky boys from the Bucharest International School staying with us. They told me about Romanian children with blow-dried hair and Chanel clothes who were brought to primary school in the mornings by the security firm BGS in cobalt-blue Hummers. At high school too there were examples of pampered offspring, the most extreme case being a sixteen-year-old boy who bought Maseratis and Lamborghinis on the internet with his parents' approval and credit card.

Dario lives in the midst of the Eastern European nouveau-riche environment. He says the custom among wealthy Romanians is to place their businesses in a foreign holding company with its head office in the Netherlands, or on Cyprus or Malta. Investments are generally made through Dutch holding companies. They buy holiday homes on Caribbean islands. A private plane with a pilot goes with the territory (or did until the crisis hit), along with a yacht in a Cyprus marina. As for their homes, they cluster around Lake Snagov just outside Bucharest in houses built close together, just like the old nomenklatura.

Dario has also heard, from a banker in Liechtenstein, that the largest holdalls stuffed with banknotes being carried into that little state do not come from Romania but from Hungary. Putting your money out of sight, or at least out of sight of your own tax authorities, is not an exclusively Eastern European phenomenon, but the huge scale on which it is taking place has to do with the history of these countries and the fact that much of their newly acquired wealth has been obtained by dishonest means. András Gerő, professor of history at the Eötvös Loránd University and at the Central European University in Budapest told me: 'The rich of today have their roots in the upper ranks of late socialism. They weren't the top functionaries, they were sixth-rate but with good connections. The communists confiscated all property and these people got their hands on it. They're all little Khodorkovskys (a reference to a Russian tycoon jailed by Putin). Members of the new elite don't feel safe, knowing they could lose their positions at any moment. Now they're at the top but they might suddenly find themselves at the bottom.'

Hence all the holdalls of cash steadily vanishing into Liechtenstein.

Dario: 'Vast fortunes were made in Romania from 2000 onwards. The smart guys had already amassed property, but it was only after 2000 that they could cash in. With accession to the EU approaching, money was streaming into the country from all directions; investors had the confidence to take Romania on and prices went through the roof. You only had to get hold of a piece of land somewhere in Bucharest and suddenly you were swimming in money. People went crazy. They no longer knew what to do. The price of keeping a mistress soared. A nice apartment in the centre of Bucharest, a credit card and a white Porsche Cayenne were the minimum if you wanted to maintain a reasonably stylish girlfriend on the side. You could see even really nice guys succumbing to it.

'I was once invited to the sixth birthday party of the daughter of an important client. They'd hired an expensive restaurant in a Bucharest park. The children were in gala dresses and all of us, even the five- and six-year-old nippers, had a seven course dinner that went on until ten at night. It was all rounded off with a huge fireworks display with the name of the little girl, Mirela, written across the sky.'

An Englishman who has lived in Bucharest for many years is going to show me the city's nightlife. He knows why I've come and he says: 'The big boys are all abroad now, in Switzerland, France, Monaco or the Caribbean. They don't return to Bucharest until later in February.' Dario has given me a list of places he recommends for seeing the population I'm interested in: a meal at Isoletta, Balthazar, Casa di David or Uptown followed by drinks at Bamboo, Fratelli's and perhaps Downtown as well.

He tells me about the BBC motoring show *Top Gear*, which revealed that one of the rumours about Ceaușescu and his Palace of the People is true. In September 2009 the *Top Gear* team came to Bucharest and staged a race in the palace's network of underground passageways between a Ferrari California, a Lamborghini Gallardo and an Aston Martin DBS. You saw mainly concrete, darkness and headlights flashing past, accompanied by an enormous roar of engines, but it was enough to make clear that below the building are many kilo-metres of tunnels spacious enough for cars to get up to impressive speeds.

Over the course of the evening it becomes obvious to me that the Englishman is not completely satisfied with the turn his career has taken. Previously he was his own boss and worked in the rather more distinguished newspaper business. He left because the job was made impossible for him: 'Everything is in the hands of three oligarchs. Any journalist wanting to write something that doesn't suit the establishment will be silenced. It's sad, but there's no independent press in this country.'

After drinks at Fratelli's we go to Downtown. The first thing I notice are the women dancing on the bars and tables. I saw them in Moscow too, but since all the women here are wearing the same brand of snow-white underwear, if in different styles, I suspect this is not a spontaneous affair. A shame they aren't secretaries or archivists who've had a glass of sangria too many. They move mechanically, looking bored.

We finish our drinks and a little later we find ourselves at a bar in a cellar, at a party put on by the new Romanian elite and its children.

The singer they've hired is hugely famous in Romania and the man to whom she addresses her *'Je ne regrette rien'* was one of the presidential candidates in the last election. The pianist plays like a wild thing and the girl with bobbed hair climbing onto the table is intending to dance, not to take off her clothes. With her raised shoulders, shaking head and long legs in black tights she whips up the partygoers. Everyone carouses and smokes like a chimney and the atmosphere in the cellar is decadent, à la Berlin 1930. A ravishing blonde floats through the crowd in a tall hat, a bearded young man in a dinner suit at her side.

After six years in this region I realize that cultures change slowly, if they change at all. In Hungary I have the feeling that as a foreigner I'm not really welcome. People don't appreciate interference and they resist Western European influences, except when it comes to externals such as fashion, music, makes of car, and the influx of capital and European subsidies. They want to keep things the way they were. Hungary and Romania are façade democracies. Both countries have a feudal tradition that they are continuing to perpetuate. The tycoons of the region will pass on their positions of power to their children or protégés.

The girls are beautiful and the boys are cool. This could be a cellar full of festive twenty-somethings in any world city, but the difference is that these children, whatever their talents or lack of them, will form the new elite. They are indistinguishable from people of the same generation in Paris or Tokyo and their material desires are derived from America, but unless they spend a couple of years studying abroad or have strongly independent characters, they'll adopt the same ethic as their parents and take the same nepotistic route as so many others in this region. They can hardly do otherwise; their clan is their only security.

A few years ago I thought that Hungary and Romania would resemble the Netherlands within about twenty years, as far as their standard of living, development and mentality went. Now I think it will take at least a century, if they get there at all. One of my Transylvanian friends believes it will be at least a hundred years before Romania once more has a thoughtful, civilized elite that knows what leadership means and bears in mind the interests of the population as a whole.

Everyone talked
about that fairytale

Practically all the land next to the road is unworked, but from time to time there's a pasture or a ploughed field. The small surface area of the plots is striking. I take the A30, the secondary road from Oradea to Kolozsvár, driving through villages where the main form of recreation consists of sitting on a bench in front of your house and watching the cars go by. I'm on my way to see Farkas Bánffy. Three years ago, two days after graduating, he moved from Hungary to Fugad in Transylvania to become a forester.

Say what you like about Romanians, at least they flash their headlights to warn you of police checks. I like that, their fraternal anarchism, and I participate with enthusiasm. It's one thing they have in common with the French, Italians and Spaniards. Aside from the Romanian Orthodox Church, the Romanian identity, as far as I can see, is based on the myth of Latin origins. You could do worse. It renders up a lively chaos.

Fifty kilometres short of Kolozsvár, I drive into Bánffyhunyad. Not far from this small town are stretches of forest that have already been returned to Bánffy ownership. To the left and right of the road are huge dwellings with gleaming roofs, some twenty of them. You'd think extraterrestrial beings had landed. The houses are reminiscent of India. They have little turrets, monumental staircases, oriental roofs, pagodas, kitschy balcony pillars, concrete columns and extravagantly decorated gutters and drainpipes. It's as if someone with a love of gleaming ironwork had tried to combine the Maharaja's palace in Jaipur, J.R. Ewing's South Fork Ranch and Ludwig II of Bavaria's Neuschwanstein Castle in a single building made of poured concrete and materials available at Romanian builder's merchants. The result is grotesque and hypnotizing. Someone is trying to make a point here.

Not one of the houses is finished. And perhaps that's just it, perhaps these houses must never be finished. They've been built by the Kalderash, a gypsy tribe known for its ironwork. Here in Bánffyhunyad they are the Gábors. A Romanian once told me they're not blacksmiths but beggars, sending their children in rags to all the cities of Europe and building these palaces back home. I wasn't convinced. The Gábor gypsies with their broad-brimmed hats take their name from Gábor Bánffy, who brought these hardworking, deeply religious tradesmen to central Transylvania centuries ago. It's odd that a group of people known for their nomadic existence should build such vast houses, but because they're unfinished, they still have something transient about them. The Holy Roman Emperor gave the gypsies the right of free passage in 1416. They were fleeing Islam in a period when Europe was under pressure from that religion. In nomadic times a group was usually composed of forty to fifty people moving around in ten or so carts. They slept in tents at the edge of the forests. Their survival strategy was to be able to switch quickly between visibil-

ity and invisibility by disappearing into the woods. One theory is that these houses represent the primeval forest into which you can vanish.

I have all this on the authority of *Kastello – Roma Palaces in Romania*, which talks of the visible signs of illiteracy and a combination of Ceaușescu-style architecture and the cheap trademarks of a consumer society. The book's subject is the gypsy palaces that can be found in various parts of Romania, but as far as I'm concerned the same applies to the palaces the Romanian new rich are having built for themselves. They stem from the same desire to make a statement, to show the world you've made it and can no longer be ignored. The difference between the houses built by the gypsy Bulibashas and those of the new rich is that the former, for all their hysteria, do possess individuality and creativity, characteristics completely lacking in the monstrous edifices erected by today's Romanian tycoons.

I've told Farkas Bánffy I'll arrive at the end of the afternoon. I take a narrow road southwards. It's an unfamiliar route. In Transylvania the minor roads are great; they're so full of potholes that no one who doesn't need to get to where they lead ever takes them. Chickens and cockerels peck at the verges. Women wearing headscarves, their boots buckled with leather straps, walk along the road on bandy legs. I see gypsies in black leather jackets and flat, fur-trimmed boots. With their lined faces they make me think of Sioux women. 'They look stunning until the age of fifteen,' says a friend who visits the gypsies a lot.

Amid the desolation, a gypsy woman is hitching a lift. I stop. She heaves herself with difficulty into the car and smiles at me. She has several teeth missing. With a friendly nod to each other and an exchange of smiles we continue along the road. She points ahead. I understand that she needs to get to the village after next. The road winds onwards. Two villages further on she indicates that I must stop where the houses start. From under her many skirts she produces a few crumpled lei, which she tries to thrust into my hand. I refuse. She removes something from the proffered sum and pushes one lei, one of those untearable notes, into my hand. I nod my gratitude. She gets out. I wave and move off.

The gypsy district, here as almost everywhere, is on the edge of the village, a shanty town built in the mud. The houses are five by five metres with washing lines slung between them. There are no fences in *țigănie* since there is no property that needs demarcating and no one is worried about cattle or toddlers wandering off. A photographer friend who often takes documentary photographs of gypsies told me that local legends warn about them stealing children. The fear is based on more than mere fable, since under communism the Romanian gypsies would sometimes take surplus children from families unable to care for them. Far from theft, it was a way of helping desperate parents. In Transylvania you sometimes see gypsies with red hair and freckles.

There are more wooden horse-drawn carts than cars, sometimes seven or eight moving in convoy. I drive into a village with a sign next to the road announcing '*Târgul de animale*', trade in animals, so I stop and walk onto the muddy terrain. This too is Europe. It has a simplicity that cheers the heart. Sacks of potatoes are on sale, sacks of grain, sacks of oats, harnesses, bells for harnesses, sausages, wooden laths, pigs, calves, cows and horses. I don't think I've left anything off the list. There's a blacksmith shoeing horses. Fat pigs lie in trailers behind them, waiting for a buyer. There are horses everywhere, most of them bags of bones. Horse-trading is in the hands of the gypsies, who no doubt still get the animals drunk to quieten them on the journey, and whiten their teeth with paint to drive up the price.

Out of curiosity I ask a horse dealer for a few of his prices. I give him a notebook and pen so he can write down the numbers, but that doesn't work. The asking price for a little black horse is tapped into a mobile phone for me. Outrageously high. In the end the blacksmith sells me two bells and two red woollen balls to hang on the harnesses of our carriage horses. A gypsy boy tries to sell me a shiny length of stovepipe he's wearing as an extension to his arm. I'm quoted nine thousand euro for a skinny horse, probably three or four times the real price, but even so.

Later, back in the car, I ring Anikó Bethlen and ask her what pensioners are paid in Romania. It's difficult to say, there's a wide range, she says. Soldiers and judges have good pensions, for example, and often Russian language teachers too, at about 1,500 lei (a little under 400 euro). Any pension above 800 lei (200 euro) is good. Many people get around 1,200 lei, but the peasants in the villages are often living on no more than 400 lei (100 euro) a month. They will be de-

pendent for the rest of their lives on the charity of their families or simply have to keep at it, tending chickens and working the land.

Parallel to the road runs a narrow railway, and from time to time there's an abandoned station. In Transylvania I've trained myself to look at the rails before crossing: if the steel is shiny then the line is still in use. This one has small trees between the rails, indicating that no train has been along for at least ten years. There's something beautifully melancholic about it, an abandoned railway line, hinting at chances not taken. Given the current price of steel, it amazes me that the rails are still here. Next to a station platform, in a deserted cutting, are several wagons, as if the stationmaster might blow his whistle any moment and the train, cheerfully decorated with weeds and ivy, set off for an unknown destination.

Farkas Bánffy and I have arranged to meet at five in the afternoon at the MOL petrol station in Aiud, which belongs to the Hungarian oil company. A clapped-out Golf stops next to me. There are two young men in it and one of them, wearing a large hat, gets out. That must be Farkas Bánffy. I follow the swerving Golf on a journey along narrow little roads to the village of Fugad. It's the village of Stefánia Betegh's childhood, where she and her mother were saved from deportation by the villagers. There's a country house here that was built by Farkas' grandfather, who later became minister of agriculture in Hungary and was thrown into jail by both the Germans and the Russians. For a while he earned his living as a coachman.

Farkas ('wolf' in Hungarian) does indeed rather resemble a wolf. He's tall, bony and coarsely shaven. He's a good singer and dancer and he now lives in a farmhouse close to the empty family seat. He renovated the farmhouse himself – the floors, the water pipes – working on it for four months. It feels comfy, even though you can see at once that it's occupied by a bachelor. The building is warmed by a tiled stove and from time to time Farkas walks outside to fetch hunks of wood in a home-made crate.

Farkas: 'The village is a hundred per cent Romanian except for me and my assistant. The villagers are the first generation to live here. The neighbouring village of Magyarlapád is a hundred per cent Hungarian. The locals regard me as a UFO that landed here for incomprehensible reasons. They probably think I'm stinking rich. When I came to live here I wanted to do something for the community, so I started a folk-dancing group in Magyarlapád. I already had a lot of contacts there. People said: "The baron's son is back!" Everyone in Magyarlapád is eager to help me. My mother asks whether I'm eating enough, but I can't walk along the village street in Magyarlapád without being invited for a meal. I've got twenty-five children at the folk dancing, from around twenty families. I take them to Hungary by bus, to festivals. They're aged between fourteen and twenty. I tell them: "Listen, I'm pretty easygoing, but no one's getting back on the bus drunk or pregnant!"'

When I asked Miklós Bánffy, Farkas' father, whether his son's talent for dancing came from him, he answered: 'Oh God no, I can dance the way a stone can swim.'

Farkas: 'I grew up in Leányvár, a village not far from Budapest. As a child you knew everything about the old days: how many horses each family had, how many people would come to a ball, how my grandmother's brother pinched food from the kitchen with a fishing rod. My grandparents were always talking about Transylvania. It was where they all came from. Everyone talked about that fairytale.

I ask Farkas why he moved to Transylvania. 'I love to resolve problems. Did you see the movie *Pulp Fiction*? When they go to the problem solver and he introduces himself, he says "I'm Mr Wolf, the problem solver." Well that's me. A problem solver called Wolf. There were seven of us kids, I'm number five. I was always the naughtiest. I was kicked out of school. Romania is perfect for me. You have to be a bit of a rogue here; if you're too nice to the Romanians they'll walk all over you. I knew how much property we had and I knew you could build a life for yourself here. I like it. It's about my family, my family history. For the first six months I lived in an empty room. That was fine. My mother says: "He could live on an ice floe."

'When there were floods this year I helped organize relief. Everything had been washed away: chickens, fences, cars, parts of houses – all taken by the flood. We received aid supplies from the US, Finland, Sweden, Norway, Austria, the Netherlands, Hungary and Romania because my family has so many contacts. This is our village. There's a big difference between how things work nowadays and how it used to be. Before, when somebody's pig died my grandfather would arrange for the owner to get a new one. Do you think any of the big companies care nowadays whether someone's pig has died or not? In those days you had a responsibility. I think when you help people they're grateful and they'll repay you in some other way. I supervise our own forests and do the same for a number of other families that have got their woodlands back: 400 hectares for us, 230 for other people and another 170 hectares at Bánffyhunyad. I'm doing a two-year forestry course in Sopron. Every month I have to go there for a week. The most important thing is to prevent illegal felling. You have to walk through the woods and check whether you can see the sky, because that's a sign that trees have been taken. If the branches are growing upwards even though there's space between them, you can bet that a tree has been felled. Usually the illegal loggers don't clear away the branches anyhow, so that's another sign.'

When I ask Farkas how he's related to Anikó Bethlen he starts to laugh. His grandfather, Dániel Bánffy, was a brother of Marianne Bánffy, Anikó's grandmother. It makes him laugh because everyone is related to everyone else. Béla Bánffy in Kolozsvár is a second cousin, Gergely and Sándor Chowdhury are third cousins, Zsolna Ugron is a fifth cousin once removed. Clementine, the daughter of Gergely and Zsolna, isn't just his goddaughter but a fifth cousin once removed, and Zsigmond Mikes is a third cousin. Farkas rattles through them and says, laughing: 'If you want the full picture you'll have to ask my father or mother. They'll know. By the way, my mother isn't just my mother, she's also my fifth cousin once removed!'

Bear Hunting
with Ceaușescu

Zabola, March 2010

Katalin Mikes pays tribute to her parents by trying to get back what was taken from them. In the meantime she's giving her children what she missed out on herself: parental love. Her two sons are fighting for the restitution and restoration of Zabola along with her. For the past three years the *kis contesa* has lived with them, as have her two daughters-in-law (one current and one to be, that is) and two grandchildren, on the centuries-old family property, surrounded by extensive forests.

Katalin's son Gergely moved to Romania in 2001 to live on the estate, which dates back around five hundred years. At that time it was still in use as a psychiatric institution. While he and his mother battled the Romanian government for the return of their property, he chatted every day with one of the patients on a bench in the park. It was several weeks before Gergely found out that the friendly man of his regular morning conversations had committed patricide. He'd smashed his father's skull during a family quarrel in a Romanian village and then cut him into pieces.

After years of litigation, Gergely, his brother Sándor and his mother finally managed to recover the house, the outbuildings, the park and several thousand hectares of forest. Helped by his wife Zsolna and his mother and brother, Gergely now runs the place. Guests stay in the Machine House on the estate. Out here in the middle of nowhere, they are repairing, step by step, the damage done by forty years of demolition and neglect.

The forests returned to them include several hunting lodges once used by Nicolae Ceaușescu. The head of the Securitate allowed Nicolae to shoot only from a raised blind, since he regarded firing from ground level as too dangerous. To put the 'genius of the Carpathians' in a good mood, the blinds, known as *Hochsitzen*, were made as comfortable as possible, rather in the way that Hollywood stars are pampered on film sets in luxury caravans. The expropriated country houses and hunting lodges that once belonged to the aristocracy were intended to serve as accommodation during bear hunts.

Ceaușescu is said to have been an extraordinarily unsporting hunter who shot as many bears as he could in a day. His record was twenty-four. Several Romanians have sworn to me that when he pulled the trigger, Securitate snipers with silencers on their weapons would open fire. You might find seven bullets in a bear supposedly killed by Ceaușescu with a single well-aimed shot.

I've visited three gamekeepers who went on bear hunts with Ceaușescu. They took me to see two of the *Hochsitzen* from which the Conducator hunted – if you can call it that. They are identical to the structures Gergely now has in his forests, wooden huts with two rooms, sometimes up on poles, sometimes on the ground. One of the rooms was for storing food and champagne, and perhaps for additional Securitate officers during the hunt, and in the other room was a bed, a wood-burning stove, a table, several chairs or a sofa, and a hatch through which you could take aim at the bears. Everything would have been extremely clean and neat, the bedding delivered in sterile plastic packaging. The bears were fed at fixed times of day so that Ceauşescu's hunt could proceed as efficiently and predictably as possible. The bears were fed the cadavers of horses and cows, but they were also given a highly nutritious mixture of maize, chicken-feed and blood, to make them grow big and fat. Ceauşescu was obsessed with the idea of shooting the largest bear, not only the largest in Romania but in the whole world.

In Braşov I visited Marius Oprea of the CICCR (Centrul de Investigare a Crimelor Communismului din România). Marius has repeatedly received death threats; his wife and child now live in Germany for their own safety. To perfect the Stalinist *mise-en-scène*, at each of the entrances to the block of flats where he lives stood a man who clearly had nothing to do. When I got inside I asked Marius why they were there. 'They're from the security service,' he told me. 'They're here to identify everyone who comes to visit me.'

Oprea: 'Ceauşescu's formative years were during the Stalinist period. Stalin didn't just kill during the hunt, he killed party members and anyone else he wanted dead. In all the Eastern dictatorships, including Romania, the communists believed that the power over life and death was where the leader derived the necessary aura. So the hunting parties were above all symbolic. Ceauşescu killed not because he was a hunter but to show that he was a great leader. He wanted to shoot the biggest bears in Romania and the country's top officials were forced to watch.

Gamekeeper Dénes Pintyó is an old man now. On 19 November 1977 Ceauşescu came to hunt in Homoródszentmárton. 'Ceauşescu arrived from Bucharest at ten o'clock, in an Alouette helicopter. He had a retinue of party members with him.

Ceaușescu was the only one who did any shooting. He had two rifles and a loader. He was a good marksman. The bears were driven to twenty or thirty metres from him. Elena was bored, walking back and forth along a country road until it was over. At two in the afternoon Ceaușescu left. In the intervening four hours he'd shot sixteen bears from his *Hochsitz*, including twelve of a prize-winning size and weight. I've been hunting for fifty-two years and I can tell you: this wasn't sport, it was a bloodbath.'

The second gamekeeper I spoke to admitted to me that he had occasionally thought about shooting Ceaușescu. He took me to a *Hochsitz* in the mountains near the once closed town of Zărnești (in the communist years, missiles were made there in a building disguised as a bicycle factory). Nowadays they use chunks of chocolate from the chocolate works in Brașov, stuffed into a hollow tree, to entice bears. On the lookout for bears, he confided to me in a whisper how it worked. 'Every provincial governor sent invitations to Ceaușescu to come and hunt. Their plans were assessed by Ceaușescu's staff. Securitate officers would come to check whether there were enough large bears and whether everything was in order. The roads and paths had to be in perfect condition and there had to be landing places for two helicopters. The road to and from the helicopter pads needed to be checked as well, since a fire engine would be parked there as they came in to land. The path leading to the *Hochsitz* had to be of a specific width, surfaced with gravel and no longer than 100 metres. It was great for us as gamekeepers, since we were given all the cars, people and resources we wanted. If the bear hunt didn't go well, the governor of the province and the provincial head of Securitate would both be sacked.

'The governor was told the date of a hunt only three days in advance. Ceaușescu was terrified of assassination attempts. The forest was cordoned off by the army, and there were Securitate agents and soldiers among the drivers. All the wild game from all the surrounding hunting grounds was driven towards him. Ceaușescu often lay in bed in the *Hochsitz* until the bears appeared. He was very weak in his final years. The first time I was selected as master of a hunt I had to go to Bucharest, where I was screened by the Securitate. They investigated three generations of my family. When I went hunting with Ceaușescu I was allowed to keep my loaded rifle with me, but there was always a Securitate man behind me. I was instructed that if Ceaușescu was in danger I had a right to kill. From time to time a Securitate officer came to my home while I was out on the hunting grounds. They searched the house and interrogated my family. They told my wife they were friends.'

The third gamekeeper I visit tells me he led the very last of the Conducator's bear hunts, on 4 April 1989. He unbolts the hut and I try out Ceaușescu's bed. Very saggy. It's covered in dust and dead flies. As in Ceaușescu's house in Snagov and in 'Extermination Camp no. 1', the Peninsula re-education camp, I'm unexpectedly overwhelmed by the banality of evil. Next to the bed is a pile of yellowed books – clearly not Ceaușescu's, since they're in Hungarian. Suddenly I realize that the best hunting grounds in Romania are in what used to be Hungarian territory. All the gamekeepers I talk to belong to the Hungarian minority.

Gamekeeper András Szász: 'You were allowed to speak to him only if he asked you something. On that last late afternoon we sat here and he said hardly anything. I was keeping watch at the window. He lay on the mattress until the bears appeared. He shot five times, but the last bear pulled its head in. He missed. We couldn't tell him that, of course, so we confirmed that he'd shot five bears. That night we had to go into the pitch-dark forest and shoot a large bear so that there would be five laid out for the photographs the next morning. Ceaușescu shot his last bear only in his imagination.'

I've been told by one of the gamekeepers that the hunting museum in Posada holds part of Ceaușescu's hunting collection. No one mentions it, but you can identify his trophies from the labels bearing his initials. There are more than three hundred bears in the depot on the first floor, the gamekeeper assures me. The museum's regular collection includes several huge stuffed bears, and there are bearskins stretched out on the walls. Ceaușescu had a special stretching machine developed to stretch the skins, thereby increasing his chances of claiming the world champion bear. I don't know whether the CIC, the international hunting organization that gives out the medals, saw through his plan. Sometimes his stretching machine tore the bearskins in two. By means of a small white lie, I manage to get into the secret depot. I walk up the stairs with two of the museum staff and find myself in a long room, fifteen by thirty metres. It's so full, with hundreds of bearskins piled up and innumerable stuffed heads, that there's hardly enough room to walk between them. A mass grave, and each of the bears has a metal tag with the initials NC.

Ceaușescu had a monopoly on the hunting of large bears, whose diet was supplemented while the people of Romania were close to starvation, surviving on good stories and a sense of humour. One story doing the rounds was that on a particular bear hunt no bears came close. None approached the carcass laid at the feeding place and none at all were spotted in the forest. The master of the hunt had a serious problem. Ceaușescu had already been flown in from Bucharest in an Alouette to shoot a bear. This might cost the hunt master his head, quite literally. In a nearby village a travelling circus had a brown bear that could juggle. The hunt master, assisted by Ceaușescu's retinue of Securitate officers, dragged the bear out of the circus – while the dictator was taking a nap in his blind – and used long sticks to prod the tame animal towards the place where a dead horse was waiting for it. But before Ceaușescu could take aim and fire, the bear jumped onto one of the gamekeepers' bicycles and cycled for its life, away into the forest.

Staying with the
Prince of Wales

Miklósvár, March 2010

I'm on my way to see Tibor Kálnoky, who has a lot in common with Gergely Roy Chowdhury. Tibor moved to the Eastern Bloc a little earlier than Gergely, from England. Working for a number of different companies, he first learnt Hungarian and then Romanian. He too comes from a family of counts that was persecuted in Romania and deprived of its property in the post-war years, and he too is now trying to restore all that was lost with no means at his disposal other than his own boundless energy, and to stimulate the local economy in the process.

When he was nineteen Tibor Kálnoky found a suitcase in the attic of his family home in Paris. It was one of the few things his grandfather had been able to take with him when he fled Transylvania before the Second World War. The suitcase was full of love letters between the grandfather and a Bavarian baroness who had somehow ended up in Transylvania, a few villages away from the Kálnoky estate. The letters told of a vanished life in Transylvania and the experiences of the two lovebirds in Kőröspatak. Tibor's grandfather no doubt fled in 1939 because as a journalist he had openly campaigned against Nazi Germany and the Romanian fascists. Abroad he married someone else. When Tibor read those letters he found himself longing to go to Transylvania. Three years later he left to try his luck, and within a few years he had married there and decided to stay on.

I travel through the hills from Zabola to Kőröspatak, where the Kálnoky castle stands and where Tibor is waiting for me at the edge of the village. I've visited him twice before. Taking a shortcut, he goes ahead of me to the village where he has his guesthouses. All I have to do is follow him. As soon as we race out of the village at top speed I get the feeling I'm being tested, as if we're on horses, spurring them on for a race. It's twenty kilometres as the crow flies to Miklósvár, but via the road around the forest it takes more than an hour. To our left is a fairly steep downward slope. The road is

made of snow-covered mud, flattened by tractors and heavy trucks, and in many places it's treacherously slippery. Tibor's Range Rover flies along as if he's driving on asphalt in summer, while my tyres spin hopelessly. His rear lights disappear. He can probably find his way along this road with his eyes shut. I feel like a fawn about to lose sight of its mother's white rump. Drifting, slipping and sliding I drive on through the ancient forest. Every time the car, with its high chassis, starts to skid, a burst of adrenaline floods through me. It's uphill at first, so gravity works in my favour, but soon the road will no doubt plunge just as steeply downhill and then all this slithering and sliding will be a good deal less fun. Only occasionally do I catch sight of the rear lights of the Range Rover, flashing past the tree-trunks somewhere a kilometre deeper into the dark forest.

Powerfully aware of the approaching descent, I reach the top. Tibor's car has vanished completely, but fortunately there is only one clear path through the snow, crossed by the tracks of wild boar and deer, both hinds and stags. I drive carefully. After a while I leave the forest behind and find myself on a broad sloping plain. The grass under the snow must be dun-coloured by now. These are the wide grassy slopes where flocks of sheep graze in summer, accompanied by shepherds doing their best to fend off the wolves and bears. The road descends gently and brings me to Miklósvár. In the village I know the way. Reaching the old white wall around the property, I turn left and drive up to the gate. The Range Rover is inside the fence. I compliment Tibor on how great it all looks here, ask whether he often comes upon game on the forest road, and drop my hand to one wheel of Tibor's vehicle. Keeping my eyes on him, I feel the treads on the tyre.

'Yes, a lot of game. Mainly deer, hinds and stags, and wild boar. In May I almost drove into a bear. It was early morning and I had a car full of workers who needed to get to Miklós-

344

vár – it was a close call.' Little nodules on the treads tickle my palm: spikes.

We're in the middle of the old Kálnoky region, in the Széklerland, where the population is ninety per cent Hungarian, even though it lies deep inside present-day Romania. The Kálnokys have had links with the area for more than five hundred years, aside from a recent interruption of half a century. The title 'count' was given to one of Tibor's ancestors because during a bear hunt he saved the life of King Lajos I with a well-aimed shot from his bow. On the edge of Miklósvár stands the hunting lodge that once belonged to the Kálnokys, in grounds enclosed by a rusty fence. It's seriously dilapidated. The roof is still on, but there's no glass in the windows. The shutters are hanging loose and the brass gutters and drainpipes left with the gypsies one day. The hunting lodge has not yet been returned to the Kálnoky family. So far the Romanian government has only been willing to give it back on a long lease.

Tibor leads me into a stately upper room, invites me to help myself to a drink and leaves. There are some crystal glasses on a table and a carafe of *pálinka*. I pour myself a glass and sit down. The fire is lit and it's as if I'm back in Twente, in Aunt Mini's sitting room having a secret drink. After a while Tibor comes back.

Tibor has bought several old Székler farmhouses with courtyards and barns and done them up beautifully. He's furnished the rooms in peasant style, with a perfection no open-air museum could match. They are now wonderful guesthouses with wooden floors and ceilings supported by heavy beams. In the evenings the guests eat together near the open fire on the ground floor of the main building. By the light of candles and flickering flames, the gathering looks like something out of Agatha Christie, except for the relatively high proportion of men with beer bellies wearing Iron Maiden or Black Sabbath T-shirts. They're British and they're here because of Vlad

Țepeș, alias Dracula, the fifteenth-century Wallachian leader who managed to scare off the advancing Ottoman army led by Sultan Mehmed II by filling a valley with a forest of wooden stakes bearing the impaled corpses of 20,000 captured Turks.

The surprisingly large number of British tourists to be found in this remote corner of the country is not purely a result of the mystique of Dracula and the vampires. It also has to do with the rather sexy fact that Prince Charles has formed a connection with this breathtaking region. His Royal Highness has Transylvanian blood, as he is well aware. Several years ago he bought an old farmhouse in the Saxon village of Viscri and asked Tibor, whom he knew from England, to have it decorated and furnished for him.

After an extremely pleasant stay in Miklósvár ('No, you can't go on a bear safari – the bears are asleep.') I'm on my way to Prince Charles' house, with an introduction from Tibor. Viscri is an isolated place. I drive through endless snow-covered hills, along a road that leads nowhere else. To the right and left I see groups of deer. For half an hour there are no other cars, only a cart piled high with tree trunks, drawn by a skinny horse. The main road is unsealed. On both sides are Saxon farmhouses painted snow-white, powder-blue and mint-green. All the farmhouses have walled courtyards with gates tall enough for a cart piled high with hay. The courtyard walls and the walls of the houses form a continuous row. In the village street I see only horse-drawn carts and one car, a battered yellow off-road vehicle full of children, with ISKOLA painted on the side, Hungarian for 'school'. Geese and chickens wander along the road and on the verge a horse is tethered to a tree.

I report to the house where a woman lives who holds the key. After a bit of knocking and calling she appears. I tell her I've come for Prince Charles' house, that I'd like to take a look at it. The woman disappears and comes back with a bunch of keys. She gives them to me and lets me go alone, with my large shoulder bag, to the house that belongs to the Prince of Wales. When I arrive at an airport these days I have to remove my shoes and belt, and decide whether to dispose of my contact-lens cleaning solution or drink it there and then.

It seems Prince Charles really enjoys being here, taking long walks in the hills. The house can be rented for part of the year, since the prince spends no more than a week in Viscri. It's a cobalt-blue house with green shutters, all done out in peasant style like Tibor's cottages in Miklósvár. The passageways are low. I'd say they must be about chest high to the prince. It's a mystery to me how he sleeps in a peasant bed; diagonally, no doubt, with his feet overboard. There's old embroidery on the walls with edifying texts in German.

> *Wo Fried und Enigkeit regiert*
> *Da ist das ganze Haus geziert*
> [Where peace and unity prevail
> They make the whole house beautiful]

Tibor tells me that Prince Charles has bought a second house in the area. He's madly in love with this unspoilt countryside. On his latest visit, Tibor arranged for him to meet some of the aristocrats who still live in Transylvania. The prince was in tears as he greeted those distant blood relatives who survived forty years of communist terror. I don't know how Tibor went about choosing whom to invite, but it strikes me that virtually every Transylvanian noble claims to have blood ties with the Windsors. The Ugrons are the only family I've never heard mention it. Charles laid a wreath at the grave of his great-great-great-grandmother and took a trip on a wooden horse-drawn cart, to the utter amazement of the Hungarian peasants of Miklósvár.

Prince Charles feels a bond with Transylvania and the Saxon villages because of their cultural heritage and the beauty of the landscape. He supports the Mihai Eminescu Foundation, which works to preserve them and their surroundings by combining tradition with sustainable economic development. Many of the Saxon villages still have their fourteenth-century layout: a wide main street with a grassy strip next to it (broad enough to hold markets and local festivals) and on both sides the smallholdings, with the houses on the street side and behind them the barns, stables, storage areas and chicken coops, and then finally a small orchard. At the end of the main street is a church, on a natural rise and with a wall around it, built in a dominant position in the Middle Ages so it could be defended against the Tartars and other robber bands that moved across Transylvania looting and killing. There was room for all the villagers within the walls, along with their livestock. They couldn't withstand a long and determined siege, but they could survive a visit from brigands or an army marching through. The churches, fortified and plastered white, can be regarded as a symbol of Transylvania: a sanctuary for the persecuted, although only as long as all they're up against is an army on its way elsewhere, not a gang of robbers that stays for forty years like the one headed by Gheorghe Gheorghiu-Dej and Nicolae Ceaușescu.

In a sense the dictatorship put much of the Romanian countryside into a coma and protected it against any radical change. Now that the population of Transylvania has been rudely awoken, it needs to decide which direction to take. It could opt for hysterical renewal and quick money, lurid purple tower blocks and German cars in metallic greys, presuming that to be progress, or it could hold fast to its own traditions, adjusting them and combining them with modern technology so that the astonishing beauty of Transylvania can be preserved. The future of the region may well lie in small-scale tourism and sustainable agriculture and forestry. At the same time I have to admit that after hours of bumping over potholes, rocks and frozen mud, the thought of smooth asphalt is more than a little appealing.

I have to look into her soul for the secret

Uzon, March 2010

In an ice-cold castle I meet Zsigmond Mikes, a large, circumspect man, born in 1977 in Oradea, the Romanian town not far from the Hungarian border, who now spends part of his time in Germany and the rest in Transylvania. He's a second cousin of Katalin Roy Chowdhury-Mikes, mother of Gergely and Sándor. He and his family have managed to reclaim this Transylvanian castle and land, but unlike Farkas Bánffy, Gergely and Sándor Roy Chowdhury and Tibor Kálnoky, all of whom have breathed new life into their family properties, he remains uncertain what to do with the estate returned to him.

I have a theory about this, a fairly obvious one. The first restitutions of castles and large areas of forest to be implemented involved families that had fled abroad. They have more faith in the observation of official rules than people who grew up in Romania under dictatorship. They fight more determinedly for their rights under law, they have more resources and better lawyers to pursue their claims, and they are less susceptible to intimidation or to the little jokes played by Romanian mayors and officials. People who grew up in an authoritarian state often have a more passive attitude to government than their relatives from the free West.

That is the practical explanation, but there is a psychological side too. The older generation (those aged over seventy-five) and the younger generation (under forty-five) are the most positive. The elderly have pleasant childhood memories; the young still have dreams for the future. The generation in between, the lost generation of communism, is too young to remember pre-communist times and too old to adjust to a new era. For the truly old, those who remember life in a castle, coming to terms with the current state of the family home is often difficult, but they can tell their grandchildren stories that they have kept from their own children. The grandchildren usually know more about the past, both before and under communism, than their parents.

In the three cases in which castles or country estates were sold, it was the lost generation that made the decision, people who mainly remember the communist era and seem relieved to be able to free themselves from the ghosts of the past. I can understand that. I recently went with Ilona to visit Margitmajor, the estate in the south of Hungary where her grandmother grew up. After expropriation it became an old people's home. The once elegant country house has been permanently defaced by the addition of an extra storey. The director gave us a very thorough tour; she walked into all the rooms without knocking, showing us the elderly ladies lying there six to a room. I felt like a voyeur in an ossuary. The floors were covered with gleaming tiles. The house smelt of lard and was permeated by death. I couldn't get out of there quickly enough.

Zsigmond's life story and his explanation as to why he is not sure whether he wants to live in Transylvania go some way towards endorsing my theory while at the same time contradicting it. He tells me: 'As a child I watched a man flee into our block of flats. I was home alone; I could hear footfall in the stairwell. The man was in a panic. He had a pack of Kent cigarettes that he hid in the tiled stove. Two policemen appeared on the stairs and they beat the man mercilessly with sticks. I watched through a crack in the door. I was five years old. They didn't stop, just kept on thrashing the man, who was on the ground. It made me deeply fearful of the police. On the way to school I had to pass police officers. If I crossed the street at the wrong place the transgression would be noted in my school file. We lived in an atmosphere of aggression and fear.

'I often went to visit my grandmother. I loved the atmosphere in her flat. I felt accepted there, not to say loved. She was deeply religious, but not in a mindless way; she continued to think for herself. She didn't go to church, but she was convinced that her redemption would come from God. She prayed a lot. For the final ten years of her life she was blind. She was always ready to talk about her childhood, which had been fantastic. Her memory for details and for the way people behaved was extremely vivid. At the age of twelve she moved to Aranyosgerend. That house was inherited through the female line and over the years it had been owned by the Keménys, the Klebensbergs, the Wesselényis and the Bánffys. My grandmother thought it would be hers one day. Life in that house was tough; her mother made all her daughters work hard, from morning to night. They had to cook and clean. The only thing they didn't have to do was the washing up. It was the period between the two world wars. They no longer had large estates and they couldn't afford many staff.'

The house we're in now was used for sixty years as the headquarters of a state farm. It's badly in need of repair. Rain and snow come straight through the roof. The lawn has been paved over and concrete blocks of flats have been built in the grounds. Only a few of the rooms are furnished, with worn-out Eastern Bloc furniture, and just one room in the immense building is heated, by a tiled stove that dates from socialist times. Sitting in that room, I listen to stories of how Zsigmond's grandmother kept the family alive by straightening bent nails in a crate workshop and brushing the dirt off vegetable boxes.

The only thing in the enormous house that points to a past of elegance and grandeur is an oil painting in the hall, showing dozens of slender horses in a tall pine forest, jumping over fallen tree trunks or galloping with flowing manes. They are the horses bred a century ago on the Zabola estate of Ármin Mikes. The painting has a warm reddish glow. At the end of the First World War, Zsigmond's great-great-grandfather rode to Hungary with the horses, two hundred of them, along with his daughters. It was a journey of hundreds of kilometres through mountains, valleys and forests, to keep both horses and daughters out of the hands of the advancing Romanian troops.

Zsigmond: 'My grandmother was deported like everyone else on 3 March 1949. She ended up in Kolozsvár, in the Donát út, in a tiny house. My grandfather couldn't work because of a bone disease; he was confined to bed. Grandmother had to do everything. The 1950s were a time of great poverty, but she was supremely happy in that little house. It was a one-hour walk to Kolozsvár. She later worked in a crate factory with people who swore and got drunk. If anyone behaved badly she'd never forget it. She was strict. On my eighteenth birthday she told me we were going to eat at five o'clock. I arrived an hour late. My grandmother was sitting at the table with one of my aunts, both of them waiting for us in their best clothes. The meal was on the table. I sat down. For five minutes there was absolute silence. Then my grandmother said: "Can you feel it?"

'Her time was so different from mine. It doesn't matter to me whether I'm in Romania or Germany. I thought I'd find a life for myself in Romania. Now I think things are different these days and I shouldn't expect to find the country the way it was. Life in Transylvania was colourful, with the Saxons, the gypsies, the Széklers, the Romanians and Hungarians. You learnt to respect individuals, since there was no homogenous group. But I can't find the secret here now. I need to look for it in my grandmother's soul; maybe I'll find it there. All the values she clung to were imparted to her in her youth. There were high expectations. Great demands were made. You had to behave properly and acquire knowledge, as well as being punctual and having manners and a sense of humour. There was a humanist tradition too. Those expectations of people, far higher in every respect, are of no interest to today's society, especially in the sense of what it all added up to. It's as if people were more complete in those days.

'I've changed. Transylvania as an idea is no longer so important to me. Fifteen years ago I thought Transylvania was so beautiful and so special, so close to my soul, that I couldn't do anything but live here in the hope that the family property would be returned. Now we're all here because we've got something back, except for Tibor Kálnoky. He's created something; he was here before anything at all was returned to him. It's a mistake to think that possessions amount to a reason to exist. Now I can see that in my living conditions and my happiness I'm not dependent on property but on human relationships. My grandmother's Transylvania has gone. That atmosphere and tradition, the values and the multi-ethnic composition of the population have all gone. I'm afraid this place will produce the same people as Hungary, and that therefore we can't expect a better life. Here too, more and more people are allowing themselves to be driven by materialism. They have less time for each other. They increasingly devote themselves to earning money. Fortunately in the villages there are still people who aren't in a hurry. People should be at the centre of life. I want to be surrounded by people with plenty of time. If there's no time for pointless things, then life won't be any better here than in Tokyo or New York.'

A class dying out

In Centrál Kávéház in Budapest I meet Baron János Gudenus again. Centrál Kávéház is one of the few coffee houses from the era of the Dual Monarchy to have remained more or less intact. In the early years of communism, most of the large Budapest coffee houses, once the meeting places of the different peoples of the Habsburg Empire, were forced to close, as pernicious symbols of bourgeois culture. At our first meeting János Gudenus told me the communists tried to destroy the aristocracy physically, using torture, murder and labour camps. The result was mass flight to Western Europe in the late 1940s.

A major exodus of aristocrats from Transylvania had taken place earlier, after the Treaty of Trianon and the first land reform. Records show that a few decades before that, in the nineteenth century, some fifty aristocratic families lived in Transylvania. Then there was a second exodus, starting in the last year of the war. Tried and tested by life in a hostile Romanian environment, people understood what was coming. In the decades that followed, almost everyone tried to get away, but the opportunities were limited, so after the execution of Ceauşescu in December 1989, when the Romanian borders were opened, a third exodus took place.

Gudenus: 'In 1989, before the fall of communism, there were still twenty-one aristocratic families living in Transylvania, some eighty people. Now there are just twelve families left, a total of twenty-five aristocrats. I estimate the number of untitled nobles to be about ten times that.'

Almost all of the twelve families whose restitution claims were successful have relatives living in Transylvania: Apor, Bánffy, Béldi, Bethlen, Haller, Horváth-Toldy, Jósika, Kálnoky, Kemény, Kendeffy, Mikes and Teleki. Of the families I know and have spoken to, the Bánffy family is the biggest. There are still around ten Bánffys left in Transylvania, most of them now living in and around Budapest. Unlike the Bánffys, the Telekis, that other extensive Transylvanian family of aristocrats, have spread all over the world.

Castellum, founded in 1991, is an association of old Hungarian families in Transylvania. One of its committee members has recorded where the exiled Transylvanian aristocrats now live: ninety-four are in Hungary (practically all of them in Budapest), thirty-seven in Germany, thirty-two in Austria, twenty-two in the United States, ten in Switzerland, eight in Argentina, seven in Britain, seven in Australia, seven in Belgium, four in Canada, four in France, four in Italy, three in Sweden and three in Costa Rica. Partly because of the internet, the Transylvanian aristocratic diaspora is able to keep in close touch.

Béla Haller, president of Castellum, tells me that seventy families have now joined the foundation, bringing the total number of members to two hundred and twenty. Some live in Transylvania, some elsewhere, and around fifteen per cent are from families with titles while eighty-five per cent are untitled nobles. The average age of the members is well over sixty. János Gudenus estimates the current total size of the Hungarian aristocracy to be three thousand people from a hundred and forty families in thirty countries. Of those, two thousand five hundred make up the diaspora, while five hundred live in Hungary and twenty-five in Transylvania. Most of them, too, are well over sixty.

Gudenus: 'Four-fifths of the aristocracy lives abroad and will never come back. In those families the third generation no longer speaks the language. In fifty years' time the Hungarian aristocracy will have died out.'

If what he says is true, then there's a good chance that in half a century from now all that is left to remind people of a vanished class, other than Budapest street names, will be the cuisine and the drinks named after families in whose castles cooks invented the dishes and on whose estates the grapes ripened. Several of their names can be found on the menu at Centrál Kávéház: gróf Degenfeld Tokaji, gróf Károlyi rosé, Batthyány rizs (a rice dish), Károlyi saláta (salad), Rákóczi túrós lepény (a curd cheese pasty à la Rákóczi), töltött fácán Széchenyi módra (stuffed pheasant á la Széchenyi) and the Esterházy torta (cake).

In many cultures the begetting of sons is more highly valued than the bearing of daughters. Sometimes it represents a last hope of avoiding the extinction of a lineage or a tribe. Sons perpetuate the family surname, and in some cases guarantee the continued existence of both a name and a title. It is a mathematical certainty that in countries where no one is any longer ennobled, the entire noble class will become extinct. Patents of nobility are passed down only through the male line. Given that the chance of having a daughter is around fifty per cent, the nobility is bound to die out eventually. John Fante, author and the son of Italian emigrants, writes in his novels about the desperate efforts of his devoutly Catholic mother to increase her chances of begetting sons. She first turns to the

Holy Virgin Mary, but when her prayers go unanswered she listens to relatives and friends. Diets, rituals and certain positions in bed are recommended to her, but it seems strong garlic above the love nest can also do wonders.

I was told that dominant women have more sons, whereas dominant men produce more daughters. I asked a friend's opinion, a gynaecologist who specializes in helping women who are having trouble conceiving. Krysztof gave me his 'advanced-level sex education' during a poker evening. We were drinking whisky at the periphery of the gaming tables.

'What do you mean by a dominant woman?' I asked Krysztof.

'Well, dominant, strong, someone who imposes her will.'

He explained that a dominant personality helps because a woman has the best chance of conceiving shortly after ovulation. The woman who can influence her husband and impose her will on him at that particular time has a greater likelihood of becoming pregnant. One thing that increases the chance of having a son considerably is the achievement of orgasm by the woman during conception. The uterus flutters rapidly open and shut and the male sperm, which on average swim more quickly than female sperm, have a statistically greater chance of reaching the wall of the womb first than when the uterus opens and closes more slowly. Krysztof looked at me: 'It's not a matter of dominance but of achieving female orgasm.'

I wouldn't dare mention this to the mild-mannered expert on nobility János Gudenus, even if I knew how to explain it in Hungarian. The grand coffee house, with its resounding acoustics, does not invite stories about uteruses. It's cowardly of me to withhold this ray of light from him, but there's another reason why I think that János Gudenus is right, or will be proven right eventually, and that despite Krysztof's practical tip, the Hungarian aristocracy will die out. After the collapse of the European monarchies at the end of the First World War, the aristocracy in Europe became an anachronism (except in

England, where it still has a real, institutionalized influence). As a group, and as a buffer between ruler and people, aristocrats no longer have a function in society. They can hold out for a long time as an anachronism in a friendly environment such as France, Germany or Austria, where their class retains its economic, social and cultural capital, but not in a hostile environment, such as Hungary or Romania.

The more fortunate of the Hungarian and Transylvanian aristocrats still left in Hungary and Romania have professions associated with the comfortable middle classes, making their living as artists, antique dealers, teachers, professors, lawyers or doctors, but they have no access to real power. Eighty per cent of new tycoons in Hungary and Romania, the young men sharing out the spoils between them – ministers, secretaries of state, bankers, captains of industry and 'investors' – have their origins in the old communist nomenklatura.

The aristocracy's most important and most useful cultural capital – consisting of easy manners, a knowledge of languages and a broad international outlook – was lost under communism. Aside from the occasional family visit, it was cut off from all international contacts and influences in those years. In the older generation, in Ilona's Hungarian grandmother, for instance, who died a few years ago, or in Erzsébet T. and Stefánia Betegh, you see a command of that cultural capital. In the generation after them, born and brought up under communism, it has been noticeably eroded.

A few years ago, just after I came to live in Hungary, I was invited to a newly founded Rotary Club, which held weekly breakfasts in the Gellért Hotel. It was trying to be the first Rotary Club in Eastern Europe to have no members who had been communists. The grandson of the last emperor of the Dual Monarchy was a member. In total there were twenty of them, all from the old Hungarian families. I'd been invited as an exotic element. Several members had grown up abroad, but three-quarters were born and raised in Hungary. There was one half-Transylvanian among us – his mother was a Bethlen – and a young man who had grown up in Transylvania: Botond.

I felt the greatest affinity with Botond. At the weekly breakfasts I noticed a huge difference between people of the same social background who had stayed in Hungary and those who had grown up in the free West. It showed in small things like table manners and overeating, but even more so in attitude. Those raised abroad had retained the cultural and social traditions of the nobility; they seemed more naive, less cynical, more optimistic, and they set greater store by transparency. With a few exceptions, the generation that had grown up under communism was unfamiliar with the manners, the self-assurance, the disguised assertiveness and the humour that often come so naturally to that class in Western Europe. An apparent triviality such as the wearing of Eastern Bloc off-the-peg clothing is a break with tradition and an offence against something I regard as an essential element of the aristocracy: elegance. Bearing in mind what the class enemy endured, it's embarrassing to talk about the wrong shoes or an ill-chosen jacket, but in reality the sartorial impoverishment of the aristocracy in Eastern Europe is a belated triumph of communism.

Faced by the material wealth of Western Europe, Eastern Europe points to its own spiritual and moral superiority. In Hungary I've often been told I don't understand anything because I'm from Western Europe and haven't suffered like the Hungarians. The stigmatization, exclusion and suffering under communist terror bound the nobles who survived it even more strongly together. In a sense they were ennobled all over again.

In Transylvania the collective trauma of 3 March created a DO aristocracy. Domiciliu Obligatoriu swept away the differences in wealth and status between nobles, leaving only naked human beings.

In Transylvania, nobility has been internalized. The values the noble class imposed on itself are far closer to the austerity of a Father Superior in a Franciscan monastery than to the flamboyance of a dandy in a Paris salon. Today's aristocrats have modest desires; they want to do good things for the community and, most importantly of all, to avoid tarnishing the family name. There is no talk of noble rank (actually I believe this applies almost universally to the nobility) double-barrelled names are not used, titles are left off calling cards. Of the Transylvanians I asked about what it meant to be of noble birth, almost all answered: do your duty and bring honour to the family name. They come from lineages that placed themselves at the service of their country for centuries, thereby often acquiring great power. Half a century of the systemic sabotage of every ambition has left them with a distilled residue: be a good person.

That was what I liked so much about the people I got to know in Transylvania. They were clear as mountain streams. Béla Haller, Stefánia Betegh, Kati Ugron, Pál Lázár, Béla Bánffy junior, to name just a few, were all averse to pretention, possessing great strength, honesty and integrity, at least as far as I could judge. The stigmatized are by definition morally superior. If you live under a system in which you can achieve hardly anything materially and are excluded from any career, then you will do well to focus on spiritual things. The Transylvanian aristocrats bore their fate like pillar-saints.

Béla Bánffy senior implied that the aristocrats were the real communists, in the sense that they worked hard and were public spirited, whereas the communists sponged off the work of others. One of the nobles in Marosvásárhely said that communism was an attractive idea in theory, very close to the Christian concept of charity, but it had proven disastrous in practice: 'Communism is the absolution of criminality.'

The system helped criminals into leading positions in every country where it was put into practice, people who chose to be inspired by Machiavelli rather than by Erasmus. It's difficult for the people of Romania, Hungary and other former Warsaw Pact countries to stomach the fact that since 1989 it is the ex-communists who have become the biggest capitalists.

'I hate the Hungarian elites,' says Gáspár Miklós Tamás, who comes from Transylvania. He is now a professor at the Eötvös Loránd University and at the Central European University in Budapest, and one of Hungary's leading left-wing intellectuals. In the 1930s his parents belonged to the first generation of communists in Romania – cultivated, idealistic people who were elbowed out of the party by the crooks surrounding Gheorghiu-Dej. I met him in a café next to the university to hear his views on the aristocracy. 'I hate them all, but in the time of the aristocrats there were at least people with some sense of decorum, who knew how to behave. Now it's many times worse. Today we have an elite that doesn't even pretend to want to do anything good for the country. It's naked egotism now, and shameless graft.'

Pista Pálffy wrote to me: 'The worst thing about fifty years of communism isn't the sweeping away of the aristocracy, the worst thing is the wiping out of the old civil society, of all the people and classes with a long tradition of honest work, service, independence of mind: merchants, farmers, entrepreneurs, academics, professionals. In their place we have generations filled with cynicism and an attitude of "what the hell, we're just doing what we can to survive". Most are detached from any consciousness of history and tradition, and they tend towards idiotic forms of political extremism. They know nothing about the underlying concept of a civil society familiar to happier, Western countries. That is the great tragedy here.'

Back to Bonchida
and Zabola

Bonchida, July 2010

The Házsongárd cemetery in Kolozsvár is the most beautiful graveyard I know. Ilona and I are hoping to find the grave of Miklós Bánffy. I've been here once before. Házsongárd is close to the old centre of Kolozsvár, at the foot of a hill. The grave of Carola Bornemissza must be somewhere

here too, the grave that was heaped high with red roses by Miklós Bánffy.

As well as being an author, Miklós Bánffy was director of the Budapest Opera House, minister of foreign affairs, a landowner and one of the greatest champions of the Transylvanian idea – the belief that Transylvania's strength lay in its mixture of ethnic groups. In 1926, after his term as a minister ended and his father died,

he returned to the family palace of Bonchida, near Kolozs-vár. He involved himself in local politics, founded a publish-ing house, became editor-in-chief of the liberal magazine *Er-délyi Helikon*, encouraged Transylvanian writers and painters, worked on his Transylvania trilogy and in the meantime fell in love with Carola Bornemissza.

The cemetery has become a wood. Ivy grows across the ground, over the rusty Art Nouveau gates, the gravestones and the classical sculptures. Moss has coloured the sandstone steps, seats and plant troughs deep green. It's the most com-forting sight I know: nature slowly taking over what humans have made; proof that nature will win in the end, no matter how much of a mess we make of things. Decay of this kind is particularly beautiful when the wilderness grows over such loving craftsmanship.

At the end of his life Voltaire concluded that a person cannot really do much more than tend his garden, in oth-er words devotedly look after everything for which he is re-sponsible. This idea, with its long-term thinking, is deeply in-grained in the aristocratic tradition. In its place a new elite has emerged that engages only in short-term thinking: poli-ticians who can see no further than the next election; man-agers and boards of directors whose lives are governed by quarterly results. Many members of today's elite in Eastern Europe got where they are today by devious means, which ex-plains their need to enrich themselves as quickly as possible, like pashas in the time of the sultans. They don't know how long the game can last.

Naturally there are disadvantages to a semi-feudal system. For a start, the chances of improving yourself and getting on in life are unfairly distributed – in that respect it's a system that continues more or less unchanged in nepotistic Eastern Europe. But the deeply rooted sense that one must above all be a steward was part of it too, and that was lost when communism arrived. With the disappearance of the aristocracy the world became shorter of breath.

Ilona and I come upon a grave with a statue of a woman kneeling, desperately sorrowful, her hands clasped in a gesture of piety, probably the scene the deceased was hoping would follow his departure. So many dead; so many graves. There are moss-covered freemasons' pyramids and lavish temples for the nouveaux riches of a century ago. Architect Károly Kós was commemorated with a simple double column, whereas aristocratic families had classical chapels built, small palaces, large enough to serve as accommodation for a young family – although no doubt musty inside.

To our left is a wonderful grave guarded by four sleeping stone lions. An elderly woman in a black T-shirt with silver lettering that reads FASHION MODEL is sluggishly hoeing. It's a sweltering hot day. I assume the old families must be higher on the hill, so we follow the path upwards. Ilona questions the veracity of my assumption, just as she questions the point of this entire expedition. It doesn't help that it's 38 degrees Celsius.

Ilona finds my interest in the local aristocracy odd at the best of times. She never says a word about her origins, doesn't use her double-barrelled name in public, and thinks that what's important is what you yourself add to the world. Your origins are irrelevant; at best they determine the moral standard you're committed to. I see the same attitude in her sisters. Ilona hates looking back and from time to time she points out to me that I have too romantic a view of Hungarian history – which is undoubtedly true. So be it. She tolerates with mild tetchiness my interest in the matter, the way that in a marriage you eventually come to accept that your partner in life will never put the top back on the toothpaste tube.

I manage to persuade her to climb further up the hill. I can hear noise coming from the top. A stone wall is being relaid. In

the middle of a plot no larger than a tennis court stands a neo-gothic chapel that reminds me of the west wing of Bonchida. Above the door a coat of arms has been carved into the stone. It's the Bánffy family crypt.

The tall iron gate is open, as is the door to the chapel. We walk along a wheelbarrow plank, then up steps and into the darkness. We're alone in the high space. On one wall is a plaque in memory of Miklós Bánffy, with a wilted wreath below it. His huge, slightly pompous coffin, covered in building dust, lies in a niche. On the lid are some faded plastic flowers that are starting to disintegrate and on the ground next to it sacks of cement have been piled up to hip height. I look at the coffin for a while, then at the ceiling, which has exactly the same sky painted on it as the ceiling of Ilona's family chapel: blue with gold stars. It's possible that both were painted by the same craftsman a century ago. Ilona has also noticed it and she nods to me.

It's sixty years since Miklós Bánffy died, in 1950, and the restoration of Bonchida, his family's baroque palace, is almost

half complete. The work has coincided almost exactly with the translation of his Transylvania trilogy into English: *They Were Counted, They Were Found Wanting* and *They Were Divided*. The trilogy appeared in Britain between 1999 and 2001, and other languages followed. That the family grave is now being renovated would probably have made Miklós Bánffy smile, had he known.

Not long ago the diaries of Bánffy's great and secret love, Carola Bornemissza, were deposited in the archive of the Far-kas utcai templom, a Calvinist church in Kolozsvár, where they are accessible to any interested researcher. The diaries were found twenty years ago in an attic, but the finder didn't dare make the discovery public until recently. A cookery book compiled from Carola Bornemissza's notes was published back in 1998 and a selection from her diaries will no doubt follow. Gentleman that he was, Miklós Bánffy wrote not a word about his mistress in his autobiography. I'm curious to know whether she is equally discreet in her diaries.

Outside the chapel some ten men are working, amid laughter and shouting. They're Romanians and Széklers. In the

shade of a tree are countless bottles of water. I make the mistake of looking for a little too long at them and so, despite my protests in broken Hungarian, I'm unable to leave without accepting a large bottle the wall-layers are determined to give me. I fumble a few lei from my pocket but am reprimanded by the moustachioed foreman, who crossly waves away the money. 'That's not the way we are here! No money. Are you crazy?! We're in Transylvania!' I give a bow of gratitude. Ilona and I wander back down the path, the burning sun on our heads, taking turns to put the bottle to our lips in an attempt to drown our thirst.

In the Bánffy palace at Bonchida, Transylvania's Versailles, Gergely Roy Chowdhury has organized the second Transylvanian Rolling Ball, helped by others including Farkas and Béla Bánffy. In a village between Bonchida and Kolozsvár, cars and people are grouped outside a church. It's hard to see whether they've gathered for a wedding or a funeral; all the women are in black. I have relatives who regard the wearing of black dresses and skirts as denoting a lack of refinement and taste. In

Eastern Europe the length of the skirts is generally the only indication of whether someone is being married or buried – for weddings they are on average about thirty centimetres shorter.

In the evening two hundred of us dine in the half-renovated stables at Bonchida. Wooden tables and chairs have been set into the sand. On duckboards in the huge palace courtyard we dance until dawn. Candles have been placed in what were once windows and are now black holes like the eyes of a skull. Bonchida is being restored and the organizers of the Transylvanian Ball want to reinstate the tradition of festivities, gaiety and serenity that used to be characteristic of Transylvania. In contrast to almost all the balls held in present-day Eastern Europe, which are pure showing off, they want to use the simplest of devices to hold an elegant party: a local band, wooden tables, candlelight amid the ruins, and fine food by Jonas Schäfer, Transylvania's best cook.

A number of our old friends from the early 1990s are at Bonchida. They include two British adventurers married to Hungarian beauties: Old Etonian Grant, and Dominic, son of Hugh Arbuthnott, the former British ambassador to Bucharest who in 1988 advised Coen Stork on how to help Romanian dissidents. Then there is György Kégl, Ilona's second cousin, the driving force behind, and deejay at, the Piaf Bar, the haggler who traded secondhand computers for consignments of Transylvanian timber. He now lives as a married man with four gems of daughters in a suburb of Budapest. His ancestral home on Lake Balaton is still under scaffolding; the family has failed to regain ownership. Gábor Teleki is here too. Of the whole Piaf crowd with their high expectations I think he's the only one who, along with his relatives, has had a palace returned to him – in Transylvania, naturally.

The Piaf Bar itself, where out of misplaced sentiment Ilona and I still end up sometimes deep in the night after a party,

is an unaltered dark cavern, except that it's now populated by tattooed young men and by women with bleached blonde hair.

Mihály, that more distant cousin of Ilona's, still works for a large insurance company. Years ago he bought a centuries-old parsonage in a village thirty kilometres to the east of Budapest, where he lives with his family. His ancestral palaces still have children's homes in them, or have been sold to new-rich Hungarians and transformed into flashy hotels with shiny granite floors. Pál Festetics chose to end his life in 1995 and Felix Schilling left for Bulgaria in 2006. After the revolution, Coen Stork helped to set up the Institute for Contemporary History in Bucharest. Now that I've been living in Central Europe for several years, I understand how important such an institution is.

Houses and estates in Hungary have not been returned to their former owners, so only a few families there have managed to restore something of the old glory. Of the three thousand palaces and country houses in Hungary, fewer than a dozen have been bought back by the families who once owned them. There are a few aristocratic families – Batthyány, Hunyady, Pallavicini, Széchenyi, Wenckheim, Zichy – who have succeeded in building up landed estates of old-fashioned proportions once more. Without exception this has been achieved by go-getters who left communist Hungary as children or young men, and made their fortunes through hard work abroad. Ilona's father is one of them. In the 1990s he bought land bit by bit, not far from the former estate of his mother's family in the south of Hungary, where he now grows maize, sunflowers, rapeseed, and summer and winter wheat. Ilona's grandmother died several years ago, but she lived to see the glorious reinstatement of the family tradition. She toured the family's new estate in a landau driven by her son and granddaughter, and looked out across the bright yellow fields of rape in silence, beaming.

The urge to redress the injustice and humiliation inflicted on parents is a primal force in all human beings. Ilona and I bought land belonging to the Márffy and Széchenyi families when we moved to Hungary, twenty-five kilometres from Ilona's father's property. Her father's agricultural team prepared the fields for us. Several times a year, a column of tractors with raised ploughs and harrows would drive along the loose dirt roads from Széplak to Erzsébet-puszta. The drivers would stay for two or three nights in the back rooms of the overseer's house, with the couple that watch over Erzsébet-puszta. Sowing time and harvest worked like an aphrodisiac on the overseer's wife, and at night she would creep on stockinged feet to the tractor drivers' rooms. Her advances might have been something we could handle – the men who race across the fields in their John Deeres aren't as fragile as all that – but unfortunately she was as ugly as sin (with hardly any teeth left), and after two seasons the tractor drivers refused to make the trip to Erzsébet-puszta any longer. That, along with the fact that it's not particularly fertile ground and nothing, not fires, mounds of human hair, cycle patrols nor wires with flapping rags, could dissuade the wild boar from churning the poor soil at night, led us to decide to plant acacias and oaks. So it was that Ilona and I joined the noble, patient guild of forest owners. We will not live to see the day when the oaks are sawn into planks.

A week before the Transylvanian Ball, Ilona and I took the night train to Braşov for the wedding of Sándor Roy Chowdhury and Katalin Apor. Three quarters of the Transylvanian aristocrats I knew and had interviewed were there. The reception was held at the five-hundred-year-old country house of the Apor family in Torja and the party that night was at Zabola, a house almost as old. The restoration work was finished just in time. Under Sándor's artistic direction it has become a fantastic place. Sixty years after Kata Apor's grandfather and Sándor Roy Chowdhury's grandmother were taken away in trucks in the middle of the night by militia from Torja, and Katalin Mikes in Zabola was loaded onto a truck as a little girl while the furniture, library and family archives were flung out of the windows and burned, there was once again an old-fashioned party at Zabola. Sixty years after the final assault on the Transylvanian aristocracy began, it seemed for a whole weekend as if nothing had ever changed. From the terrace you could survey lawns bordered by box and yew, and gaze out beyond the old maples and oaks of the park to distant mountain meadows and the fir-covered peaks of the Háromszéki-havasok.

The party began with a dinner for the two hundred and fifty guests. The band, made up of wrinkled men with violins, cymbals and clarinets, played tirelessly. The army of staff was in local dress: men wearing tight beige trousers and boots as if about to jump onto horses; women in dirndl blouses with puffed sleeves, tightly laced bodices, ribbed aprons and laced boots. Descendants of the local aristocracy had poured in from all over Europe. The Hungarians and Transylvanians wore the traditional *bocskai*, while the foreigners were in dinner jackets, the women in long skirts.

At dinner, during an inappropriate skit by a small group of Austrians who depicted the Transylvanian Hungarians as anti-Romanian, I watched as tears ran down the face of one of the young aristocrats. The aspiration to live in harmony with all ethnic groups – Romanians, Hungarians, gypsies and those few Saxons who remain – is profound. Zoltán Kodály, who travelled through Transylvania in the early twentieth century to note down the region's folk music, concluded that the most interesting compositions were always to be heard in the ethnically mixed villages. He reviled the villages that were home to a single ethnic group, saying they rendered up a mediocre twanging.

I realize I'm an incurable romantic. Sometimes I catch myself thinking there's a parallel between Transylvania and the village of Armorica in *Asterix & Obelix* – and it's not just the bearded faces of the Hungarian Transylvanians that make me think of the Gauls, it's their stubbornness too. All of Gaul is under Roman control. All of Gaul?! No, one small village of indomitable Gauls still holds out against the Romans... All of Eastern Europe is damaged and warped, in a moral vacuum after half a century of communism. All of Eastern Europe?! No, one small band of indomitable people continues bravely to resist, refusing to be dragged into the corrupting nepotism characteristic of the region.

After dinner the partygoers spread out around Zabola. Farkas Bánffy sang and danced and stamped his feet on the wooden floor, clapped his hands and slapped his thighs at a ferocious speed. An Ugron with an imposing beard and a beautiful singing voice, wearing the *bocskai*, galvanized the band and his nephew Farkas, while four couples flung themselves wildly across the dance floor. A little later, Bence joined us, a forestry expert who took charge of the Esterházy forests and now manages those of Roy Chowdhury-Mikes. He and Farkas are magicians of the dance floor, both able to dance like dervishes to the old Transylvanian folk music. Like two boxers seeking a gap in each other's defences, they circled around one another.

It was a night with a full moon. Ilona and I drank and danced until half past five in the morning, until the mountains and forests became visible again. The diehards danced and sang for another four hours. Drunk on champagne, wine and *pálinka*, Ilona and I walked down the hill, along the avenue of old chestnuts, past the great lake, where two lovers rocked a rowing boat between the water lilies. I was drunk not just on alcohol and moonlight but on love. The aristocrats with their square bearded faces, the mysterious, beautiful women, the dionysian young men who could dance until dawn, drink like front-line troopers and sing along passionately with the wrinkled musicians for hours – I have a soft spot for this wild romantic country and its inhabitants, just as I have a soft spot for women who can whistle through their fingers.

A well-mannered bear

Dornafalva, July 2010

The mayor and deputy mayor of Dornafalva both have hands like coal shovels. We're here to consult on the restoration of Dornafalva castle, the ruin that has at last been returned to Erzsébet. The mayor's room is four metres by five and has a classic Soviet T-shaped layout: a desk with a conference table perpendicular to it. We have come as a committee: Erzsébet, Dario my new Italian banker friend, whom I've asked along because of his thorough familiarity with Romania, and Erzsébet's son. Two sweet-natured middle-aged ladies also belong to our retinue. The grandmother of one of them worked in the castle before the war as a kitchen maid; the other is here to take photographs. Erzsébet's son leans against the tiled stove holding a video camera. He's planning to film the meeting for use as evidence.

The mayor has laid two mobile phones on the desk in front of him. Every five minutes a jolly Brazilian samba rings out and he bellows into one of them in Romanian. A grey man comes in, along with his corpulent wife, an old communist with her hair dyed red. The man has a stack of ring binders under his arm. The conversation hops around all over the place, one moment focusing on the fence around the castle, the next on all the things that have been stolen. Then the man goes into detail based on one of his ring binders, which are full of modernistic sketches for the restoration of the castle. He's the village's former teacher and self-appointed castle expert. One day this village schoolmaster chiselled the centuries-old carved stone out of the façade of the castle tower, and with that stone he is holding Erzsébet and her family to ransom. If the castle is renovated, he'll tell us the name of the museum in which he deposited the stone years ago – or so he says.

Yesterday a gypsy came up to Erzsébet at the ruin to ask how much she wanted for the last two big statues still standing at Dornafalva. Erzsébet told him they were not for sale. 'Name your price,' the man said. 'They'll disappear anyhow.'

Since the 1970s, and especially over the past twenty post-communist years, the castle has virtually disappeared from the face of the earth. Whole towers, main buildings and outbuildings have gone, leaving the foundations, which proved too much work to dig out.

The former teacher with his binders full of irrelevant sketches keeps butting in. The mayor promises nothing. He claims to have no authority over the village policeman; he can't stop the stealing. Erzsébet's son stands in the corner by the sink, leaning on the crumbling plasterwork, and films every word.

The meeting makes me think of the tactic deployed by the communists sixty years ago to break the spirits of the peasant population during the expropriation of their land: as many speakers as possible, all going on endlessly about boring subjects. I'm certain the schoolmaster with his pile of sketches and his wife, who also keeps putting her oar in, have been invited purely to sabotage the meeting. From time to time there's a knock at the door and someone comes in with a question for the mayor.

After an hour I clap my hands. It's in my nature to leave my options open, to wait and see, but the ocean of idiocy we're bobbing about on has become too much even for me. The mayor and his deputy must ensure that the stealing stops; I and my Italian friend, who has many contacts in Bucharest, will try to get the money together to renovate Dornafalva. 'That will be good for everyone here.'

The mayor promises to compose a statement saying that the council will support the restoration work in every way possible. He calls for his secretary. A man appears who looks as though he's been fetched from a pigsty. There is shouting in the corridor. After forty-five minutes we're given two documents with countless stamps and the mayor's signature. Time to go. Erzsébet hands over bottles of wine, I produce Dutch cheeses. The corridors of the village hall are full of shabby young men, come to beg favours from the mayor. The Bánffys have described to me how they were sabotaged for years by the local authorities. Now I've seen for myself how it's done, if on a smaller scale. We've been here for two hours without advancing a single step. We've simply been fobbed off.

In the grounds of Dornafalva castle a football pitch has been laid out and a school built. The south-east tower, still miraculously intact, is used by footballers and passers-by as a latrine. Next to the two remaining life-sized statues in front of the gatehouse tower, a fence has been put up and someone is keeping sheep and goats. All the solid stone ornamentation, window-surrounds and cornerstones have been hacked out of the buildings. To remove what's left you'd need a hydraulic crane and a semitrailer.

We walk through the tall grass around the ruins of the castle, Erzsébet's son filming us. Erzsébet points across to the far side, to the new district built where the park and her father's zoo used to be. 'Under that yellow house are the family graves. And beside that white house was the grave of our bear Nicolai. This was my room and next to it was the corner room, where Nicolai slept. Over there, with those three windows, was my father's study.'

On the veranda where Nicolai used to wait in a chair for Erzsébet's father to come back from hunting expeditions lies a torn school photo of smiling pioneers, glowing boys and girls wearing their much-coveted red pioneer's neckties. The újkastély ('new' castle), where Erzsébet lived in her youth, is the best preserved building because it housed a school for many years. I ask where Nicolai went to the bathroom.

'That's a mystery. He was very discreet. He would disappear into the park, into the bushes, and appeared again a short time later. He never bothered other people with that sort of thing. He was a well-mannered bear.

'He usually lay on his back in the library, like a lord. We used to lie on his belly. My brother would hold his jaws open with both hands while I stuck my arm in as far as it would go, to count his teeth. One time father came into the room with a throng of visitors while we were doing that, lying on his belly. Everyone said it was disgraceful, but father told them: "The children love him and Nicolai loves them. At this age bears have forty-two teeth; is that how many he has Erzsébet?" "Yes!" my arm was in Nicolai's mouth up to the armpit. I was four at the time. All the guests photographed him, so there must still be photos of him around. He put out a paw to the visitors, gentle and affectionate. He smiled as he did it. Nicolai could smile. When he played with us he was always very careful. I never felt his claws. Father would stroke him and he'd moan with pleasure. Nicolai was much bigger than father, even though father was a big man. Nicolai used to stand up and put his front paws on father's shoulders.'

I step into the darkness of the building. Erzsébet refuses to set foot inside. It's a mess: holes in the ceiling, broken glass

in the window frames, doors hanging off their hinges, bottles, toilet paper, newspapers and porn magazines in the corner, puddles of water on the tiled floor.

She points. 'In these rooms I danced with my brother. Like father, he was good at everything he did and no one was a better dancer. We won all the competitions. We danced together from early childhood. We would turn the gramophone up to top volume, open all the doors and whirl from room to room, the two of us, all around the house.'

We set off in the direction of the older part of the castle. A thin horse on a rope, owner unknown, stands grazing in the courtyard. I know from photographs how splendid all this looked seventy years ago. Erzsébet points to a large spiraea bush and tells me it's more than two hundred years old. At our feet grow purple flowers. *'Männertrau'* they're called in German. The loyalty of men.

'If you blow on them, all the flowers are gone in an instant. *Männertrau*. If you pick them the flowers fall off. I've never yet met a man who was faithful,' says Erzsébet. 'Never.'

We walk to the main tower, the tallest, the one that functioned as a gatehouse. Erzsébet doesn't want to step into the tower and onto the bridge. I look back and ask whether she's coming, but she stands still and shakes her head. She refuses to go any further, stubborn as a horse refusing to cross flowing water. I stand in the tower, look at the bridge and suspect that a tragedy took place here that she doesn't want to tell me about.

'The last time I went to Dornafalva was on 14 September 1944. I walked home from the station with a small suitcase. There was only a very narrow path up the hill to Dornafalva. I threw my suitcase and sandals into a little copse. I knew this would be the last walk. I thought: "I've never walked this way before." I lay down. Four eagles were turning circles in the sky; it was very peaceful. I picked up my suitcase and sandals and walked on. Eventually I found father in his museum. I said: "I have to go." He answered: "I have to stay." Watch over me and I'll watch over you. In the stables I washed my hands and plunged my head into the water. I cried for a long time with my face in the water-trough in the abandoned stables.

'The Germans had taken all the horses and ponies. The Russians were perhaps twenty kilometres away. I went with father to the farm, up on the hill. The cattle were there. We had Dutch piebald cows, Simmentals, sheep, pigs and chickens. Father told the farmer to release all the animals. The cows were on chains. The farmer and his labourer freed the animals. Outside their stalls they instinctively walked over to father and stood around him. He had to shout and wave his arms about to chase them into the forests and hills. He didn't want them to fall into the hands of the Russians and be slaughtered in their stalls.

The stone bridge leads across a dry moat full of empty bottles, rubbish bags and discarded plastic pots. The two life-sized statues from Erzsébet's family coat of arms stand on either side of the bridge. The view is magnificent. Through a broad lazy valley flows the Szamos, beneath distant hills. The elderly lady to whom I've become so attached stands next to me.

'I promised father I'd make sure Dornafalva wasn't lost,' she says. She can't die until she's fulfilled that promise.

'I ran to the Szamos and threw off my sandals. There was a little bathing place there and I washed the buffalo, wiping their gleaming black backs. Then I went to the family church and stood among the gravestones. I laid flowers and lit candles. I knew I'd never see it again, never bring any more flowers for my ancestors. Then I said farewell to father. He'd arranged for a horse, I don't know how, and a small cart, food, ham and bread. The cart took me away. I don't remember anything of the journey.'

I am the last

Márianosztra, July 2010

Erzsébet has explained to me how to get there. The village is famous for its Black Madonna. No, there's no need to bring any shopping. As I drive into the village I must phone her and then she'll walk down the hill, which takes her six minutes. Erzsébet T. will be standing next to the fence. The landscape is overwhelming. These are the same hills I drove through twenty years ago with Ilona, looking for her ancestral home in Tésa. Somewhere no more than twenty kilometres to the north stands the hopeless ruin where Ilona's grandfather was born. In all these years we've never been back. Golden evening light skims the forests. The trees exude a benevolent coolness. It rained here earlier today; the world is washed clean for a time.

Ilona has told me how as a little girl, when Hungary was still communist, she once visited the former family estate at Tésa with her father. Her grandfather grew up there. When people in Tésa discovered who the visitors were, elderly women from the village knelt before Ilona's father, deeply moved, and kissed his hand.

In the autumn of 1991 I set off for Tésa one foggy day with Ilona. Tésa – even the name made it sound like a distant loved one. The estate lies near the border with Slovakia. We drove along winding roads through extensive woodland and hill country. In Ilona's grandfather's memoirs I'd read about his childhood there. We weren't sure it would still be standing. Perhaps the bricks had been used to build new stables or

a local cultural centre. We walked uphill, down dale, into dripping beech woods, ploughing our way through deep piles of shrivelled leaves with the image of a white baroque palace in the backs of our minds. We expected it to appear out of the fog at any moment, with flapping shutters hanging at an angle, like a ghost ship. As branches lashed our faces and our socks sloshed in our shoes I imagined the life of the past in that house: the glowing tiled stoves, servants placing jugs of water next to washbasins, the excitement and tumult of the kitchen as dinners were prepared for the hunting parties, the nocturnal banging of horses' hooves against the wooden stalls in the stables.

At last we found it, in a field of chest-high weeds. The roof had been demolished, the chimneys dismantled, the veranda and the pillars next to the entrance pulled down, the shutters removed, the window frames hacked away – it was like a face with the eyebrows and eyelashes scorched off and the nose cut out. Grooves had been chiselled into the façade for cables to be laid. Electrical wiring hung crisscross down the front wall and in many places the bricks showed through the stucco. The centuries-old cedar in front of the house and the giant beeches next to it had been felled. This was a venerable seventeenth-century manor house transformed into a nondescript storage barn.

Ilona and I walked around the building and returned to the car. We were as wet as dogs that had jumped into a stream; our sopping trousers and hair steamed up the windows. We were silent as we drove through the dark forests to Vác and on to Budapest. Perhaps it would be better to forget the ruin as quickly as possible. It no longer had anything to do with the house of Ilona's grandfather's youth.

There she is, a kilometre beyond the nondescript village, next to the fence, wearing blue tracksuit trousers: ninety-one-year-old Erzsébet T. I greet her. She looks strong and healthy. She's been working in the garden all day, but she insists on walking up. I follow her along a narrow forest path and after five minutes we reach the fence around her hectare of woodland. It's a steeply sloping plot. At the top stands a small wooden cabin shrouded in ivy. Here she lives half the year in complete isolation. The nearest building is an abandoned school, several hundred metres away.

Erzsébet looks at me and asks what's the matter: 'You've changed.' I shrug. She goes on staring at me.

'Now I feel it,' Erzsébet says. 'You've grown up. That's what it is. You're no longer a child; you've become a man!'

I growl: 'Maybe.'

The doors are open, the lights on. There's a guest room, a shower cubicle. She built it all herself, including the doors. I notice Transylvanian tables in the rooms and Transylvanian floral designs in the embroidery she's hung on the walls and spread on the bed as a counterpane. The hut looks out on a lawn with two large acacias. Across the valley are wooded hills. Less than fifty kilometres from Budapest, I've arrived in a little Transylvania.

'In September you can hear the stags roaring on the far side of the valley.'

We walk through the garden. She stops at plants and trees and tells me about them. Most grew at Dornafalva too, and from time to time she mentions that her father was hugely fond of a particular one. We reach a reddish boulder with a candle on top. In front is a lemonade glass of wildflowers and behind it rises a spruce tree she planted herself, ten metres tall now, overgrown with ivy. She leaves it that way; her father liked to see a jungle grow up.

She looks at the red rock. 'It's father's birthday. He'd have been a hundred and twenty today.'

We stand side by side, facing the boulder. Her father isn't buried here, nor in the family grave at Dornafalva, on which houses have been built; he's in a cemetery in a small town in Transylvania, in a modest grave surrounded by Romanians, Hungarians and Saxons. Erzsébet has a small black-and-white photograph clasped in her fist. We don't look at each other. It's easier to speak as we would in a car, staring at the asphalt.

'After he got out of prison he lived in a hovel in the town, without heating, without water, electricity, without anything. They'd taken his revolver away; his last three dogs were dead. He had nothing left. Through a man he used to know, he found work at a power station. In 1955 a committee came from Bucharest and said: "Why do you have this man working here, a Hungarian? A count!" At four in the afternoon that same day he was sacked. His boss hated doing it, because he was a very good worker. Two hours later father had a heart attack and was taken to hospital. In Vác I received a telegram saying I should come at once.'

For the first time in all the hours I've spent talking to Erzsébet I have the feeling she's about to crack – not something that would come easily to this tough ninety-one-year-old, certainly not in company.

'I rushed to the Vörösmarty út in Budapest to get an exit visa for Romania, but they wouldn't give me one. Whatever I said or did, none of the officials would give me an exit visa. I cried and shouted: "Why not? He's my father!" They answered: "We don't need to explain ourselves here." I shouted at them: "There will come a day when you'll have to explain yourselves!"'

Erzsébet stops for a moment. She holds the photograph close to my face. It's a small square snapshot with a scalloped edge. I'm looking at a handsome man of about thirty-five, holding a gigantic set of antlers in the air in front of him. She lowers her arm and shakes her head.

'Father died a few days later. Poor and lonely. I never saw him again. It's such a burden to me, the fact that I didn't manage to be with him. That I couldn't be with him in his final hours. After 1944 we never saw each other again. All those years he went to the station every day to see whether the train from Szeged would bring his daughter. And she never came. At a certain point a new law made it possible for people to see each other at the border between Hungary and Romania, from a distance. Father and I decided not to do that. Waving to one another... It would be too painful. You weren't allowed to talk, to touch. He warned me he'd lost twenty-six kilos in jail; his face was no longer the face I knew.'

She falls silent. We're still standing in front of the boulder. In the distance, in the valley, a dog howls.

'Neither my brother nor I could go to the funeral. Even that was forbidden. More than five hundred people were there, with many, many flowers. Father was loved.

'Look,' says Erzsébet. She brings the photograph up close to my nose again. 'He's holding those antlers as if they're two apples. Everything he did he did well. The violin, saxophone, cimbalom – he played better than the gypsies. And he had a wonderful singing voice, a dark-brown baritone. That's what they called it. The Vienna opera wanted him, but my grandfather forbade him to join, saying: "My son isn't going to stand on stage and bow a hundred times every evening." He painted beautifully, too. He painted all the birds, their nests, the eggs. He always won prizes with his hunting trophies, including the medal for the largest bear in Europe. One day a bird made a nest under the roof of Dornafalva and dislodged a roof tile. It threatened to come down. Our housekeeper wanted to fetch the fire brigade to remove the tile. Father heard that, looked up and said: "Forget the fire brigade." He drew his revolver, took aim and blew the loose tile to smithereens with his first shot. That's what he was like. He had a solution to every problem.'

It's beginning to get dark.

'After mother died, he was father and mother in one. He was a giant; he was everything to me. That's why I found it so hard to get married. Father towered above everyone. All men paled into insignificance beside him.'

We turn away from the boulder and walk in silence across the plot, then slowly down the hill.

'My brother had served in the Hungarian army, so he was an enemy of Romania. After 1945 there was a sentence hanging over him, we don't know what it was, maybe the death penalty. In the 1970s he managed to flee to the West via Yugoslavia. He was always prepared to tackle anything. That's what we Transylvanians are like. No work is beneath us. We're far stronger than the Hungarians, we always were, it's been that way for centuries. He died ten years ago. He never went back to Dornafalva.'

We stand at the bottom of the lawn and look up. Twenty metres above us is the little wooden cabin. Warm yellow light shines out from it. It looks like a cottage in a fairytale.

Erzsébet: 'You know, before the war the term "class enemy" didn't exist. In the beginning, when I was refused work,

I couldn't understand what people meant by it. Everywhere I applied I was turned down, so I had no choice but to become a charlady. I've worked all my life and at ninety-one I still have to. In winter I do editorial work and proofreading for publishers. My monthly pension is 70,000 forint (about 230 euro). It's not enough, because apart from myself I also have a couple of vagrants to maintain in Vác.

'I worked hard as a cleaner. I always saved money. I never wore make-up in those days and the money I saved I put away in a drawer. I've never been to the hairdresser's, I gave up cigarettes, and when the right moment came I even gave up coffee. Everything I saved went into that drawer. That was the money I used to buy this bit of land. I bought silverware for my granddaughters, too. I never had any silverware after Dornafalva was taken, but my grandchildren do. You have to have possessions, things to love, to care for, to project your love onto. You can't live without love. The highest achievement possible for anyone is to care for others, for animals, for the earth. That's the only thing you can do, and must do.'

Step by step we walk uphill. Erzsébet leans on my arm.

'Look at this yew tree. The seeds were smuggled out of Transylvania through a crossing point on the border with Romania, in the north, near Máramaros, and I carefully planted them. I wanted to grow all the hundred and forty species of shrubs and trees that used to grow in the park at Dornafalva. One by one I planted them and cared for them. Now they're all around me here, all the trees of my youth.'

We're standing near the acacias on the sloping grass, Erzsébet in her old tracksuit trousers. It's a clear starry evening. Swarms of mosquitoes fly at me with suicidal greed. We climb up to the covered veranda behind the cabin. There's an old oil lamp with a bulb mounted in it that's attracting mosquitoes from far and wide. Rubbing my right arm, then my left, I ask if she isn't afraid, alone here in the woods.

'No, I'm not. I never learnt fear as a child. I don't know what it is. Fear is something you learn from your parents, from your nannies. Father let me sleep on top of Nicolai when I was a toddler. Everyone said it was terribly dangerous to leave a small child alone with a bear. Father knew no fear and he didn't pass any fear on to me during my upbringing. I simply don't have any conception of it.'

Erzsébet is right; fear is something you learn. The dictatorships in Hungary and Romania did a good job of teaching it to the people, in fact it was all the state wished to impart. That legacy is inside them still. You see it in the way mothers hold their children's hands, you see it in the submissiveness of schoolchildren, and in people's eyes. You often see it in the churlish behaviour of counter staff, the endless, deadly dull, platitudinous speeches that result when people have to address an audience, and the horror and harangues with which parents react when I let my obedient dogs loose in the park. The effect of the terror didn't stop when the torture chambers and labour camps closed. The culture of blackmail and betrayal is deeply ingrained. A Hungarian I know says that a tiny Stalin is still lodged in everyone's head.

Erzsébet notices that I'm trying to fend off the mosquitoes and she turns out the light. It takes a while for my eyes to adjust.

'I'm the last of the T.s. My brother's daughters are all married. They have different names and they don't speak Hungarian or Romanian. None of them will come back. I've collected everything about the family. That was my task in life – I didn't know it, but that's what I did. I have three thousand pages of documentation: patents of nobility, property deeds, photographs. I regained possession of the ruins of the castle at Dornafalva without paying a cent. I wrote letters for twenty years. I think the Romanian government gave it back to me so that I'd stop bothering them. One tower is still standing, but apart from that the castle loses height every year. The whole village is using the bricks to build houses.'

'The good memories become more and more vivid, the bad ones grow darker, gloomy and drab, faded. I have only good memories of my childhood. We lived in paradise. When you get old you have far fewer impressions; you see less of life. If you have beautiful memories then you can think back. I took everything with me. My footprints were all I left behind in Dornafalva. My first steps in my little red boots – the tracks are still there, in the place where my ancestors left their footprints for 400 years, on that stretch of earth. Many millions of footprints. That's what remains.'

Erzsébet's voice sounds soft in the night.

'I've never been poor. To be poor you have to have a certain talent and it's a talent I don't possess. With the last of the money I saved I was able to buy a grave in the front row at the Farkasrét cemetery in Budapest. I've transplanted evergreens and shrubs to it from here. They originally came from Dornafalva. My grave will be beautiful. Even when I'm dead it will be green. The power of human beings is not eternal. Come and visit me there. Promise me you'll come and look some time in spring and say hello to me.'

Appendix

Acknowledgements

Numerous people and institutions have helped in the writing of this book. My heartfelt thanks go to all of them.

Botond Bilibók, Lidis Gârbovan and Judit Hajós, who helped me find my way around Transylvania and introduced me to many people there.

Kata Apor, Hugh Arbuthnott, Béla Bánffy Jr., Béla Bánffy Sr., Farkas Bánffy, Miklós Bánffy, Neil Barnett, Anikó Bethlen, Miklós Bethlen, Cosmin Budeancă, Stefánia Betegh, Dezső Bustya, John Chrissoveloni, Ágnes Csíky-Szabó, Boldizsár Csíky, Borka Boglárka Csíky, Dennis Deletant, Géza Entz, András Gerő, Dénes Ghyczy, János Gudenus, Béla Haller, Bas Hoekstra, Tibor Kálnoky, György Kégl, Endre Kemény, Krystyna Larkham, Pál Lázár, Zsigmond Mikes, Peter Oostveen, Marius Oprea, István Pálffy, László Péchy, Zsófia Peres, Bence von Puttkamer, Gergely Roy Chowdhury, Katalin Roy Chowdhury-Mikes, Sándor Roy Chowdhury, Zsolna

Roy Chowdhury-Ugron, Harm Scholten, Coen Stork, Péter Szalántzy, Kinga Széchenyi, Gáspár Miklós Tamás, Toni Tartar, Virgiliu Târău, Gábor Teleki, Ádám Ugron, Gábor Ugron, György Ugron, Kati Ugron-Lázár, László Ugron, László Varga, Larry Watts, László Zichy and many others who do not wish to be named but who gave me their time, their stories and their help.

The following organizations were helpful to me: the Institute for Investigating the Crimes of Communism in Romania, the National Council for the Study of Securitate Archives; and the Central European University, whose founder George Soros did not look at me once as I was presented with my degree certificate but instead at the pretty student behind me.

Ayse Caglar and Vlad Naumescu, my professors at the Central European University who supervised my thesis *From Ballroom to Basement. The Internal Exile of the Hungarian Aristocracy in Transylvania*, assisted me at the start of this project. Also of help were Victor Karády, Ildikó Nagy Moran and Zsuzsanna Szunyogh of the Central European University.

Tibor Bérczes, Countess Lily Blanckenstein, Countess Gabriella Kornis, Zoltán Piri and Alexandra Jankovich, née Baroness van Voërst van Lynden, read the manuscript to check for omissions.

Bibliography

On page 270 I quote from Viktor Sebestyén's *Revolution 1989. The Fall of The Soviet Empire*. I have also made use of the following books and articles:

Books

Archer Wasson, Ellis. 2006. *Aristocracy in the Modern World*. London. Palgrave MacMillan.

Archer Wasson, Ellis. 1999. 'Teaching about Elites in the Era of Equality'. In *The History Teacher*, 32.

Bánffy, Miklós. 2003. *The Phoenix Land*. Translated from the Hungarian by Patrick Thursfield and Katalin Bánffy-Jelen. London. Arcadia Books.

Bánffy, Miklós. 2005. *They Were Counted*. Translated from the Hungarian by Patrick Thursfield and Katalin Bánffy-Jelen. London. Arcadia Books.

Bánffy, Miklós. 2000. *They Were Found Wanting*. Translated from the Hungarian by Patrick Thursfield and Katalin Bánffy-Jelen. London. Arcadia Books.

Bánffy, Miklós. 2007. *They Were Divided*. Translated from the Hungarian by Patrick Thursfield and Katalin Bánffy-Jelen. London. Arcadia Books.

Bourdieu, Pierre. 1986 [1992]. *Distinction: A Social Critique of The Judgement of Taste*. London. Routledge.

Bitoleanu, I. and A. Radulescu. *Istoria românilor dintre Dunăre şi Mare: Dobrogea*. Editura Ştiinţifică şi Enciclopedică. Bucharest.

Carp, Matatias. 2000. *Holocaust in Romania. Facts and Documents on the Annihilation of Romania's Jews*. Translated by Sean Murphy. Simon Publications.

Cartledge, Bryan. 2006. *The Will to Survive. A History of Hungary*. London. Timewell Press.

Chirot, Daniel. 1978. 'Social Change in Communist Romania'. In *Social Forces*.

Cipăianu, George and Virgiliu Târău (eds.). 2000. *Romanian and British Historians on the Contemporary History of Romania*. Cluj-Napoca. Cluj University Press.

Connerton, Paul. 1989. 'Social Memory'. In *How Societies Remember*. Cambridge / New York. Cambridge University Press.

Courtois, Stéphane, Nicolas Wert et al. *The Black Book of Communism. Crimes, Terror, Repression*. Cambridge, Mass. Harvard University Press.

Csősz, Irma. 2000. *A disznajói Rhédeyek és Fráterek nyomában*. Kolozsvár. Tinivár.

Damokos Csabáné Gálfalvy, Ilona. 2009. 'Domiciliu Obligatoriu (Kényszerlakhely)'. In *Háromszék*.

Deletant, Dennis. 1995. *Ceauşescu and the Securitate. Coercion and Dissent in Romania, 1965-1989*. London. Hurst & Company.

Deletant, Dennis. 1999. *Communist Terror in Romania. Gheorghiu-Dej and the Police State, 1948-1965*. New York. St. Martin's Press.

Deletant, Dennis. 1998. *Romania Under Communist Rule*. Iași, Romania / Portland OR., Civic Academy Foundation.

Elias, Norbert. 1939 [1969]. *The Civilizing Process. The History of Manners and State Formation and Civilization*. Oxford UK & Cambridge US. Blackwell.

Farkas, Zoltán and Judit Sós. 2007. *Transylvania*. Budapest. Kelet-Nyugat.

Fischer-Galați, Stephen. 1991. *Twentieth Century Rumania*. New York. Columbia University Press.

Gál, Mária. 1996. *DO*. Kolozsvár. Minerva könyvek.

Gârbovan, Mariana. 2008. Lucrare de disertație, Universitatea de Vest din Timișoara, Facultatea de Litere, Istorie și Teologie Regimul Comunist din România: 1945-1989. Timișoara.

Gudenus, János and László Szentirmay. 1989. *Összetört címerek*. Budapest. Mozaik.

Halbwachs, Maurice. 1992. *On Collective Memory*. Chicago / London. The University of Chicago Press.

Igloo (publisher). 2008. *Kastello, Roma Palaces in Romania*. Bucharest. Igloo.

Iordachi, Constantin and Dorin Dobrincu. 2009. *Transforming Peasants, Property and Power. The Collectivization of Agriculture in Romania. 1949-1962*. Budapest / New York. Central European University Press.

Kirmayer, Laurence. 1996. 'Landscapes of Memory: Trauma, Narrative and Dissociation'. In *Tense Past: Cultural Essays in Trauma and Memory* by P. Antze and M. Lambek. New York / London. Routledge.

Kornis, Gabriella. 2002. *Elődök és utódok. Erdélyi főnemesek a XX. században*. Budapest. Unikornis Kiadó.

Kovács, András. 2005. *The History of the Wass de Czege Family*. Translated from the Hungarian by Ágnes Baricz. Hamburg. Edmund Siemers-Stiftung.

Lázár, István. 1997. *Transylvania. A Short History*. Hungary. Corvina.

Leigh Fermor, Patrick. 1986. *Between the Woods and the Water*. London. John Murray.

Lendvai, Paul. 2003. *The Hungarians. A Thousand Years of Victory in Defeat*. London. Hurst & Company.

Lieven, Dominic. 1992. *The Aristocracy in Europe 1915-1914*. London. The Macmillan Press.

Lukács, John. 1988. *Budapest 1900. A Historical Portrait of a City and its Culture*. New York. Grove Press.

Lütgenau, Stefan August (publisher). 2005. *Paul Esterházy 1901-1989. Ein Leben im Zeitalter der Extreme*. Innsbruck. StudienVerlag.

Magocsi, Paul Robert. 2002. *Historical Atlas of Central Europe*. Seattle. University of Washington Press.

Mikó, István. 1996. *Vár állott, most kőhalom*. Misztótfalu. Erdélyi Református Egyházkerület.

Nagy, Iván. 1987. *Magyarország családai czímerekkel és nemzedékrendi táblákkal*. A-B. Budapest. Helikon.

Ormos, Mária. 2007. *Hungary in the Age of the Two World Wars 1914-1945*. Translated from the Hungarian by Brian McLean. New York. Columbia University Press.

Orwell, George. 1949. *1984*. London. Secker & Warburg.

Paget, John. 1850. *Hungary and Transylvania; with remarks on their condition, social, political and economical*. Philadelphia. Lea & Blanchard.

Pál, Judit. 2008. 'The Transylvanian Lord-Lieutenants after the Austro-Hungarian Compromise'. In *Cultural Dimensions of Elite Formation in Transylvania (1770-1950)*, edited by Victor Karády and Borbála Zsuzsanna Török. Cluj-Napoca. EDRC Foundation.

Pálffy, Stephen. 2008. *The First Thousand Years*. Budapest. Balassi.

Polcz, Alaine. 1998. *A Wartime Memoir. Hungary 1944-1945*. Translated from the Hungarian by Albert Tezla. Budapest. Corvina.

Rosetti, Radu. *Povestiri amare. Bitter Essays*. Cavallioti.

Rusan, Romulus. 2008. *Romania During the Cold War*. Bucharest. Civic Academy Foundation.

Rusan, Romulus. 2007. *The Chronology and the Geography of the Repression in Communist Romania*. Translated from the Romanian by Alistair Ian Blyth. Bucharest. Civic Academy Foundation.

Scholten, Jaap. 2008. *Heer & Meester. Berichten uit de voormalige Dubbelmonarchie*. Amsterdam-Antwerp. Uitgeverij Contact.

Scholten, Jaap. 2009. *From Ballroom to Basement. The Internal Exile of the Hungarian Aristocracy in Transylvania*. Budapest. Central European University Thesis Collection.

Scholten, Jaap. 2002. *Van Tanger tot Horizon City*. Amsterdam-Antwerp. Uitgeverij Contact.

Sugar, Peter (general editor). 1994. *A History of Hungary*. Bloomington, IN., Indiana University Press.

Széchenyi, Kinga. 2008. *Megbélyegzettek, a kitelepítések tragédiája*. Pomáz. Kráter.

Székely, László. 2009. *Emlékezés gróf Mikes János szombathelyi megyéspüspökre*. Vasszilvágy. Magyar Nyugat Könyvkiadó.

Szerecz, Thomas. 2006. *The Role of the Hungarian Aristocracy in the Life of the Hungarian Minority of Transylvania*. Budapest. Central European University Thesis Collection.

Sztáray Kézdy, Éva. 2001. *Descendants of Former Aristocrats' Families in Today's Hungary*. Budapest. Budapest University of Economics and Administration Thesis Collection.

Tamás, Gáspár Miklós. 2008. *Telling the Truth about Class*. Budapest. Central European University reader 'Class on Class'.

Țărău, Virgiliu. 2009. 'Strategies in Collectivization Policy in the Cluj Region: The Aiud and Turda Districts'. In Constanti Iordachi and Dorin Dobrincu (eds.), *Transforming Peasants, Property and Power. The Process of Land Collectivization in Romania, 1949-1962*. Budapest / New York. Central European University Press.

Thorpe, Nick. 2009. *'89: The Unfinished Revolution. Power and Powerlessness in Eastern Europe*. London. Reportage Press.

Thursfield, Patrick. 2003. Introduction to *The Phoenix Land. The Memoirs of Count Miklós Bánffy*. London. Arcadia Books.

Tomasi di Lampedusa, Guiseppe. 1996. *The Leopard*. Translated from the Italian by Archibald Colquhoun. London. The Harvill Press.

Varga, László. 1998. *A fegyencélet fintorai, Románia 1956 után*. Budapest. Püski.

Articles

Bächer, Iván. 1998. 'The Taste of Old Transylvania'. In *Hungarian Quarterly*, Vol. XXXIX. No. 152. Winter 1998.

Baleanu, V.G. 1996. 'A Clear And Present Danger To Democracy: The New Romanian Security Services Are Still Watching'. Conflict Studies Research Centre, Sandhurst.

Bjel, Peter E. 2004. 'Trenchant Legacies, Trapping Pitfalls. The Case of Post-Communist Romania and EU Enlargement'. Written for 'Theories of European Integration', University of Toronto.

Blackshell, Mark and Karl Martin Born. 2002. 'Private Property Restitution: The Geographical Consequences of Official Government Policies in Central and Eastern Europe'. In *The Geographical Journal*, Vol. 168. No. 2.

Bogdan, Catalin. 2004. 'Monuments in Ruin'. In *Family History*.

Breslau, Karen. 1990. 'Overplanned Parenthood: Ceaușescu's cruel law'. In *Newsweek*, 22 Jan. 1990.

Bucur, Maria. 2004. 'Communist Terror in Romania: Gheorghiu-Dej and the Police State. 1948-1965'. In *The Slavonic and East European Review*, Vol. 82. No. 1.

Burawoy, Michael. 2001. 'Neoclassical Sociology: From the End of Communism to the End of Classes'. In *The American Journal of Sociology*. Vol. 106. No. 4.

Burchett, Wilfred G. 1951. 'The New Hungary'. In *Peoples' Democracies*.

Deletant, Dennis. 1995. 'New Light on Gheorghiu-Dej's Struggle for Dominance in the Romanian Communist Party'. In *The Slavonic and East European Review*. Vol. 73. No. 4.

Domnisoru, Ciprian. 2006. 'Was not the Iraqi sovereign debt to be part of the Property Fund?' In *Restitution Romania*.

Fejtő, François. 'The Development of Social Structures'. In François Fejtő. *A History of the People's Democracies*. New York, Washington, London. Praeger Publishers.

Hall, Richard Andrew. 2000. Review of Dennis Deletant, *Communist Terror in Romania: Gheorghiu-Dej and the Police State, 1948-1965*. In *Europe-Asia Studies*. Vol. 52. No. 7.

Hihn, Monalise. 2006. 'Retrocedare de milioane – Mostenirea familiei Kendeffy' In *Jurnalul National*.

Kálnoky, Boris. 1996. 'Ceaușescus Reichtum hatte einen Namen: Raffgier'. In *Die Welt*, 16 Feb. 1996

Kanterian, Edward. 2002. 'Knowing Where the Graves Are'. *Neue Zürcher Zeitung*. 24 June 2002.

Kiss, George. 1942. 'Landed Estates and Peasant Farmers in Hungary'. In *The Scientific Monthly*. Vol. 54. No. 5.

Kunszabó, Ferenc. 1979. 'Modern Genocide and its Remedy'. In *Witnesses to Cultural Genocide. First-Hand Reports on Rumania's Minority Policies Today*. New York.

Linden, Ronald H. 1997. Review of Dennis Deletant, *Ceaușescu and the Securitate: Coercion and Dissent in Romania, 1965-1989*. In *Europe-Asia Studies*. Vol. 49. No. 8.

Mosse, Werner. 1993. 'Nobility and Bourgeoisie in Nineteenth-Century Europe: A Comparative View'. In Jürgen Kocka and Allen Mitchell (eds.) *Bourgeois Society in Nineteenth-Century Europe*, Oxford, Providence, Berg.

Nelson, Daniel N. 1976. 'Organs of the State in Romania'. In *The International and Comparative Law Quarterly*. Vol. 25. No. 3.

Nelson, Daniel N. 1978. 'Background Characteristics of Local Communist Elites: Change vs. Continuity in the Romanian Case'. In *Polity*. Vol. 10. No. 3.

Pálffy, István. 2010. 'Soha nem lesz arisztokráciánk'.

Paul, Dragos Aligica and Adina Dabu. 2003. 'Land Reform and Agricultural Reform Policies in Romania's Transition to the Market Economy: Overview and Assessment'. In *Eastern European Economics*. Vol. 41. No. 5.

Pop, Ioan-Aurel. 'Nations and Denominations in Transylvania (13th-16th Century)'. Universitatea Babeș-Bolyai din Cluj-Napoca.

Rompres. 2005. '2005.10.17'. In *Family History*.

Saunders, Robert Alexander. 2006. 'Romania: Transylvania Rising'. In *Translations Online*.

Schmitt, Günther H. 1993. 'Agrarian Reform in Eastern Europe after World War II'. In *American Journal of Agricultural Economics*.

Scholten, Jaap. 2009. 'Hongaarse aristocratie'. In *Hollands Diep*. Nov./Dec. 2009. No. 14.

Stan, Lavinia. 'Inside the Securitate Archives'. In *Cold War International History Project*.

Vatulescu, Cristina. 2004. 'The Secret Police File in the Soviet Union and Romania'. In *Comparative Literature*. Vol. 56. No. 3.

Verdery, Katherine. 'Inequality as temporal process. Property and time in Transylvania's land restitution'. In *Anthropological Theory*. London / Thousand Oaks, CA / New Delhi. Vol. 1. No. 3.

Vergouwe, Suzanna. 'Dynamics of the Holy and the Powerful: Stately Regimes and Development of the Greek Catholic Church in Transylvania'. In *Student World*. 2003 / 1.

Watts, Larry L. 2003. 'Control and Oversight of Security Intelligence in Romania'. In *Geneva Centre for the Democratic Control of Armed Forces (DCAF) Working Papers*. No. 111.

Photographs and illustrations

All photographs and illustrations are the property of the author unless otherwise stated.

Page 16–17: Szent Benedek (from family collection).

Frontispiece page 6 and page 98: Carola Bornemissza dressed for a Transylvanian Ball, 1910 (from *Wass-Kor* by Ilona Siemers)

Frontispiece page 10: The ruins of Bonchida, 2010.

Frontispiece page 12 and page 90: Count Olivér Wass (from *The History of the Wass de Czege Family*, Edmund Siemers-Stiftung)

Frontispiece page 22 and page 330: Dániel Bánffy, grandfather of Farkas Bánffy (photo courtesy of Miklós Bánffy collection)

Page 39: From a private family collection

Page 40: Nicolai, the Carpathian pet bear, with Erzsébet's father (photo courtesy of Erzsébet T.)

Page 41: The car belonging to László Lázár that István (Globus) and Patrick Leigh Fermor borrowed to sneak off to Kolozsvár for the weekend with Angéla (courtesy of Kati Ugron).

Page 44: Ilona at the wheel of the Peugeot, 1991

Page 45: Dirt road in the Harghita mountains, seen from the Peugeot, 1991

Page 46: Ilona's great-grandfather, who from 1913 to 1917 was minister of education in Count Tisza's government. He was an old-fashioned renaissance man. After the Theresianum in Vienna he gained a degree in law and political science at Budapest before going on to study philosophy at the Sorbonne in Paris, economics in London and medicine in Freiburg. Then between 1889 and 1891 he travelled the world, including Japan, China, Indonesia, India and Egypt. He wrote a dissertation about his travels that gained him membership of the Hungarian Academy of Sciences. While he was in office, Islam was recognized as an official religion in Hungary. He is flanked by four of his five sons – the other son had died on the Italian front in June 1918, near the end of the First World War. All five men are wearing their *díszmagyar*. On the far right is Miklós bácsi, the man who wanted to hear the geese fly over from where he lay in his grave. He was married to a Countess Nádasdy. The photograph was taken in 1933 at the wedding of Ilona's grandparents on the Margitmajor estate, not far from Pécs.

Page 49: Panorama close to Zabola (courtesy of Sándor Roy Chowdhury)

Page 50: With Ilona and the Franciscan monks in Szárhegy, 1991

Page 51: The monks in Szárhegy with our car, 1991

Page 55: Cover of Securitate dossier on Coen Stork. His code name was 'Stan'. It's about 2,000 pages long, built up during the last two years of the Ceausescu dictatorship. Coen was the Dutch ambassador in Bucharest and the 'dean' of the diplomatic corps in that city. He was active in helping dissidents and for that reason cherished by many Romanians. Reading his securitate dossier he was most indignant about the stealing of towels by Anna, his charlady.

Page 57: Nicolae Ceauşescu as a celebrated leader

Page 59: With Ilona on a mountaintop in the Harghita range, 1991

Page 65: György Kégl, Mihály and Pál Festetics in Slovakia, early 1990s

Page 69: Stamps showing the Széchenyi, Dőry, Batthyány, Esterházy and Festetics palaces

Page 75: The car belonging to László Lázár that István (Globus) and Patrick Leigh Fermor borrowed to sneak off to Kolozsvár for the weekend with Angéla (courtesy of Kati Ugron)

Page 76: Gaucho László Lázár with his wife at Laposnyak (courtesy of Kati Ugron)

Page 78: Coach at the Lázár house at Laposnyak (courtesy of Kati Ugron)

Page 79: László Lázár with his sons and daughter, Pál Lázár on the left (courtesy of Kati Ugron)

Page 89: The mother of Stefánia Betegh with her five children, János, Stefánia, Margit, László, Imre and the two Szalantzys. Mária Betegh married Teleki. (from the collection of Stefánia Betegh)

Page 91: Countess Katherine Bánffy, Bonchida 1900. From the collection of Tamas Barcsay, grandson of the sister to writer Miklós Bánffy

Page 92: Group photograph of Transylvanian aristocrats at the wedding of Carla Blomberg and Dénes Bánffy in 1928. From left to right in the back row: Baron János Bánffy, Baron István Jósika, Baron Gyula Blomberg, Baron Dénes Bánffy (the bridegroom), Count Miklós Wesselényi, Baron Lajos Blomberg, Count Károly Kornis, Count Ernő Teleki, György Hye. In the front row from left to right: Baron Lajos Jósika, István Ugron, Baron Albert Bánffy, Baron Frigyes Blomberg, Baron Gábor Jósika, Baron János Jósika, Baron Dániel Bánffy (from *Elődök és utódok* by Gabriella Kornis)

Page 95: After a Transylvanian bear hunt, in the courtyard of the Kemény castle at Marosvécs, which now houses an institution for the mentally handicapped. The photograph was taken in 1919. It is very likely this was the last big hunting party held in Transylvania before the Treaty of Trianon. Sixth from the left is Carola Bornemissza. The numbers after the names refer to the number of bears shot. From left to right: Count Géza Teleki (4), Goodwin (2), Count György Béldi, Baroness Berry Kemény, Count Arthur Teleki, Baroness Carola Bornemissza, Baroness Gizella Kemény, Baron Dani Bánffy (1), John Patton, husband of Countess György Béldi (3), Baron Ákos Kemény (1), Baron László Huszár, Count István Haller (1), Count Ádám Bethlen (1), Béla Fráter (1), József Hajós (1) (courtesy of Judit Hajós)

Page 99: Bonchida, winter 1900. It was known as the Versailles of Transylvania before its destruction by both Nazis and communists. (from the collection of Tamas Barcsay)

Page 101: Carola Bornemissza, as a nurse during World War I.

Page 102: The inner courtyard of the house of Carola Bornemissza in Koloszvár, as it looks now, the blue house at Strada Memorandumului 4. The house is now owned by the Reformed Church. When I was there I was able to walk through the empty rooms where once, on opposite walls, the oil paintings of her two lifelong admirers hung: Béla Bethlen and Miklós Bánffy.

Page 105: Group photograph of Transylvanian aristocrats at the wedding of Carla Blomberg and Dénes Bánffy in 1928 in Kolozsvár: Baroness Erzsébet Blomberg, Helena Zeyk, Countess Mária Wesselényi, Baroness Carla Blomberg (the bride), Countess Hanna Mikes, Countess Margit Teleki, Mári Zeyk. The little girl sitting in front is Countess Gabriella Kornis (from *Elődök és utódok* by Gabriella Kornis)

Page 118 and page 167: The house at Aranyosgerend, 2009

Page 135: A Transylvanian count with his daughter before the war (from private collection)

Page 144: Mass grave at the paupers' graveyard in Sighet, showing the remains of executed prisoners (courtesy of IICCMER)

Page 146: Memorial room in the prison at Sighet, commemorating the victims of communist dictatorship

Page 147: Map showing concentration camps, prisons, places of interrogation and mass graves, on display in the prison at Sighet

Page 151: The stables at Bonchida in the early twentieth century

Page 152–153: Bonchida in the 1930s and now (from the collection of Tamas Barcsay)

Page 154: Interiors of Bonchida before it was destroyed; below is the dining room. (from the collection of Tamas Barcsay)

Page 157: The Bánffy palace in Kolozsvár

Page 161: Photograph album belonging to Béla Bánffy sr., with a picture of Aranyosgerend in its old glory

Page 166: Béla Bánffy jr. in Kolozsvár, 2006

Page 170: The militia courtyard in Marosvásárhely, 2010; the steps at the centre led to the offices of the militia

Page 175: Count Béla Haller in a corner of the inner courtyard of the militia headquarters in Marosvásárhely, where his parents met weekly on the afternoons when they had to appear before the militia as people with DO and fell in love, a love that would have been unthinkable before.

Page 176: The Haller castle in Kukullovar, now owned by an oligarch from Constanza

Page 179: Judit Hajós with two gypsies who had come to sell tablecloths at Anikó Bethlen's house, 2006

Page 186: Bethlen castle in Keresd

Page 204: The entrance to the prison in Gherla and a watchtower. There are several watchtowers around the walls.

Page 212: Lidis in the water cell at Gherla (courtesy of Lidis Gârbovan)

Page 213: Glass case in the memorial room at Gherla (courtesy of Lidis Gârbovan)

Page 218: Cartoon in *Lúdas Matyi*: This is not a joke. 'Why the hard work, old chap? This land will be mine again!' 'You're wrong my lord, the cemetery is over there.'

Page 226: Cartoon in *Lúdas Matyi*: The new constitution of the Hungarian Republic: Repression, slavery, that was the system for years, but now work is giving new meaning to our existence. Long live the Republic!

Page 228: Cartoon in *Lúdas Matyi*: April 1940: 'Come on! Work my land!'; April 1950: 'Come on! Work our land!'

Page 235: The Mikes mansion in Zabola (from Roy Chowdhury-Mikes family collection)

Page 256: Mass grave, showing the remains of those executed (courtesy of IICCMER)

Page 259: The Danube – Black Sea Canal near Poarta Albă, 2010

Page 263: Boundary of former labour camp Peninsula, 2010

Page 267: Women working in the Baragan, the low-lying land near the Danube delta to which tens of thousands of 'enemies of the people', including many kulaks and nobles, were deported. They lived in miserable conditions. I took this picture in the tiny but superb Memorial of the Victims of Communism at Strada Jean Luis Calderon no. 66, Bucharest, a museum which has as its main motto 'do justice through memory'. 'The greatest victory of communism, a victory dramatically revealed only after 1989, was to create people without a memory – a brainwashed new man unable to remember what he was, what he had, or what he did before communism.'

Page 270 and page 292: Kemény castle at Marosvécs

Page 278: Nicolae Ceauşescu as the first chants are heard during his speech on 21 December 1989

Page 279: Nicolae Ceauşescu on a tour of inspection, Louis de Funès style

Page 285: Count Kalman Tisza, a nurse and the young Mihaly Teleki in the parc of Gerneszeg (from the Teleki family collection)

Page 286: Mihály Teleki with his wife and his son, also called Mihály, before the war. (from the Teleki family collection)

Page 287: The Teleki palace in Gernyeszeg

Page 290: Apor house in Torja

Page 291: Design sketch and photograph of Zabola, 2010

Page 293: Bonchida 1900 (from collection of Tamas Barcsay)

Page 294–295: Szent Benedek, before the war and now (from private collection)

Page 296: The Teleki palace in Gerneszeg (from the Teleki family collection)

Page 308: Jidvei wine folder, with at the top what was once the Bethlen-Haller castle, 2009

Page 327: Gypsy palace in Bánffyhunyad, 2010

Page 331: Farkas Bánffy in front of the Bánffy house in Fugad, 2010

Page 334–335: A bear hunt on 19 November 1977 in Homoródszentmárton, during which Ceauşescu shot sixteen bears in four hours. He is standing at the centre, with the dead bears, wearing an Astrakhan hat. To his right, wearing a chequered jacket and holding a shopping bag, is Elena Ceauşescu. They are surrounded by senior party functionaries who were forced to come along to watch. The fifth man to Elena's right is Dénes Pintyó, chief gamekeeper that day and the man who gave me this photograph (courtesy of Dénes Pintyó)

Page 343: Kálnoky hunting lodge in Miklósvár, 2006

Page 363: Writer Miklós Bánffy

Page 364: Carola and Elemér Bornemissza. Remarkably, he shows some resemblance in this picture to Miklós Bánffy in his later years.

Page 367: József Barcsay, Tamas Barcsay (married to Katherine Bánffy, older sister to Miklós Bánffy), Count Miklós Bánffy and Count George Bánffy in front of the west wing of Bonchida, 1909. (from the collection of Tamas Barcsay)

Page 368: Dinner in the stables at Bonchida at the second Transylvanian Rolling Ball

Page 369: The second Transylvanian Rolling Ball, nine o'clock in the morning (courtesy of Sándor Roy Chowdhury)

Page 371: The 2nd Transylvanian Rolling Ball, early morning, at Bonchida, 2010

Page 380–381: Szent Benedek before the war and now (from private collection)

Page 384: Tésa, birthplace of Ilona's grandfather, in its old glory

Chronological overview

896 – The Hungarians occupy the Carpathian basin, including present-day Transylvania.

1222 – The Golden Bull gives the Hungarian nobility the right to depose a king in the case of misrule or any erosion of their privileges.

29 August 1526 – The Battle of Mohács. Sultan Suleiman I defeats the forces of the king of Hungary and Bohemia.

1527 – Ferdinand I of Austria becomes the first Habsburg emperor to be crowned king of Hungary.

29 December 1540 – Treaty of Gyula, whereby Hungary is divided in three. The treaty was put together by bishop and diplomat George Martinuzzi, Brother György (György Fráter in Hungarian). Ferdinand von Habsburg ruled over the Kingdom of Hungary in the northwest, Suleiman II ruled over central Hungary, including Buda and Zápolya, while Transylvania became an independent principality under Turkish suzerainty. Martinuzzi's policy was to preserve Transylvania's neutrality by cultivating amicable relations with Austria without offending the Ottomans. During Transylvania's century and a half as a semi-independent principality, the prince of Transylvania was chosen by the Transylvanian noblemen.

1568 – The Edict of Torda. Freedom of worship is guaranteed to Protestants, Catholics, Unitarians and Calvinists.

1613-1629 – Gábor Bethlen, a devout and proselytizing Calvinist, is prince of Transylvania.

1683 – The Holy Alliance is established by Pope Innocent XI. In 1683, along with the king of Poland and the Republic of Venice, he deploys an army of volunteers and mercenaries from all over Europe to prevent the Ottoman Turks from taking Vienna. The Ottomans are roundly defeated, largely thanks to the Polish cavalry.

2 September 1686 – Liberation of Buda by Charles V of Lotharingen, with the aid of troops of the Holy Alliance.

1711 – The Peace of Szatmár marks the end of a rebellion against the Habsburgs led by Ferenc Rákóczi II. The Hungarian nobles are allowed to keep their privileges as long as they swear loyalty to the Habsburgs.

1740-1780 – During the reign of Maria Theresa, reforms are implemented in Hungary and closer cooperation develops between the court in Vienna and the Hungarian nobles.

1839 – Non-nobles gain the right to own land and to fill administrative posts.

15 March 1848 – A popular uprising in Pest under the leadership of Lajos Kossuth develops into a Hungarian war of independence against imperial Austria.

August 1849 – The emperor of Austria defeats the Hungarian armed revolt in Transylvania with the help of Tsar Nicholas I of Russia. After the revolt is crushed, an Austrian reign of terror begins that will last for many years. The Hungarian nobles are stripped of their privileges and their exemption from taxation. Serfdom is abolished.

1867 – After Austria loses the war against Prussia, it reaches a compromise with the Hungarian nobles, known as the *Ausgleich*, whereby a new constitutional alliance is created between Austria and Hungary in the form of a Dual Monarchy.

1914-1918 – First World War, in which the Dual Monarchy fights on the German side and more than a million of its soldiers die. Defeat leads to the Treaty of Trianon.

1917 – Revolution in Russia. The communists under Lenin's leadership take power. The House of Romanov falls and the Russian aristocracy flees or is persecuted.

1 December 1918 – The new Romania is established, uniting Wallachia, Moldavia and Transylvania.

4 June 1920 – The Treaty of Trianon imposed by the Allies robs Hungary of two thirds of its historical territory. Some 350,000 Hungarians leave Transylvania, including half the Hungarian aristocracy.

1921 – First Romanian land reform. Around 300,000 poor peasants are each given a hectare of land, mainly taken from large Hungarian landowners, who are allowed to retain no more than 200 hectares of agricultural land. Forested areas are exempt. Most aristocrats do not have sufficient land left to maintain their estates and houses adequately.

1931 – The stock market crash of 1928 does not impact upon Hungary and Transylvania fully until 1931. Along with the banks, agricultural prices collapse. The end of the Dual Monarchy in 1919 has already led to the fragmentation of a large internal market of fifty million inhabitants paying steady prices. In Transylvania the large landowners with their reduced estates are forced to look for other sources of income.

2 November 1938 – First Treaty of Vienna. Slovakia is returned to Hungary.

30 August 1940 – Second Treaty of Vienna. Romania is forced to cede the northern part of Transylvania (including Székelyföld, or the Széklerland) to Hungary. Hundreds of thousands of Romanians leave Northern Transylvania, where everything becomes Hungarian once again: the language, the schools, the police force, the institutions. Hundreds of thousands of Hungarians move north from Southern Transylvania.

27 June 1941 – Hungary declares war on the Soviet Union.

1943 – Secret contacts between Hungarian admiral Horthy and the Allies about withdrawing from the war.

19 March 1944 – Hungary is occupied by the Germans.

23 August 1944 – Romania sides with the Allies.

1945 – Land reform legislation in Romania. Large landowners are permitted to keep a maximum of fifty hectares.

4 April 1945 – The Soviet Union occupies Hungary. From 1950 to 1989, 4 April is a public holiday in Hungary.

26 December 1945 – Moscow Agreement. The United States and Great Britain accept the Soviet occupation of Romania.

1946–1947 – Romania hovers on the verge of severe famine. The war has caused mass destruction of livestock and the Communist Party needs to tread carefully in its dealings with the peasants. Nevertheless, the leaders of the Peasants Party are arrested and thousands of its supporters 'disappear'.

1946-1953 – The Cold War reaches its peak.

November 1946 – Elections in Romania are 'won' by the communists.

1947 – The titled and untitled nobility are outlawed in Hungary and Romania.

10 February 1947 – Hungary officially gives up any claim to Transylvania.

20 March 1947 – The first nocturnal arrests. In the dead of night, 315 members of opposition parties are dragged from their beds.

4 May 1947 – Another 600 members of opposition parties are arrested. These arrests have no legal basis but are made under the provisions of a top secret order by the ministry of the interior. Those detained are sent to prisons in Gherla, Pitești, Craiova and Miercurea Ciuc.

August 1947 – Revaluation of the Romanian currency (20,000 old lei = 1 new lei). No citizen may exchange more than a certain sum, so all savings are lost.

30 December 1947 – Establishment of the People's Republic. The foundations of a totalitarian state can now be put in place.

13-21 February 1948 – Gheorghe Gheorghiu-Dej becomes General Secretary of the Romanian Workers' Party.

14 February 1948 – Signature of the Treaty of Friendship, Cooperation and Mutual Assistance with the Soviet Union. This cements Romania into the Soviet Bloc's military alliance.

27 February 1948 – Romanian criminal law is adjusted to fit the Soviet model, introducing onto the statute book new concepts such as 'counter-revolutionary sabotage and propaganda'.

June 1948 – Nationalisation of industry, mining, transport, insurance and banks.

August 1948 – Educational reform. All foreign schools as well as schools run by religious orders are closed. A purge of teachers, professors and students takes place. New textbooks are introduced, characterized by a Marxist-Leninist approach.

August 1948 – The destruction of the opposition parties is followed by the elimination of the free press, with all media being brought under total state control. Libraries and bookshops are purged of politically incorrect titles, and the activities of journalists, writers, artists and musicians are henceforth controlled by the Agitprop section of the Central Committee of the Romanian Communist Party.

18 August 1948 – A decree supplementing the Law on the Prosecution and Punishment of Those Guilty of Crimes Against Peace and Security reinforces the legal basis for repression. One thousand officers of the SSI, the Siguranța and the Jandarmeria are arrested and replaced by Communist Party appointees.

12 January 1949 – The death penalty is introduced for high treason and sabotage. Refusal to cooperate with expropriation can lead to a sentence of fifteen years' hard labour.

23 January 1949 – The militia (Direcția Generală a Miliției) is set up to take the place of the police, under the control of the ministry of the interior.

7 February 1949 – The Securitate (Trupele de Securitate), the secret police, is set up to replace the military police and placed under the control of the ministry of the interior.

2 March 1949 – Introduction of the law on land reform. Ownership of land is completely removed from private hands, permitting the elimination of the remnants of the old landowning class and of the *chiaburi* (the Romanian kulaks). The Securitate and the militia are brought in, in the middle of the night, to deport the large landowners.

3 March 1949 – The Securitate and the militia round up all the families of large landowners who live on their land. 7,804 people are deported.

May 1949 – Work starts on the building of the Danube – Black Sea Canal.

6 December 1949 – The 're-education' programme is introduced in the prison at Pitești. Prisoners are tortured over a long period in four steps (external unmasking; internal unmasking; public moral unmasking; re-education). Each prisoner has to renounce everything he holds dear before finally being made to torture his best friend. The 're-education' programme is later expanded to include the prison at Gherla and the Danube – Black Sea Canal labour camps.

13 January 1950 – Construction of labour camps begins, for the 're-education' of hostile elements in the Romanian People's Republic.

Autumn 1951 – Introduction of the 're-education' programme in the prisons at Gherla and Aiud, and at Camp Peninsula on the Danube – Black Sea Canal.

22 August 1952 – Ten new categories of persons liable for internment are added to those listed in the order of April 1950. The same resolution introduces the penalty of fixed domicile, known as 'Domiciliu Obligatoriu', aimed at those who have not been 're-educated' in prisons or labour camps and are deemed a threat to state security.

5 March 1953 – Stalin dies. After his death, Khrushchev's critique of 'past excesses' heralds significant changes to the Soviet secret police. The Romanian secret services will undergo a similar process of de-Stalinization, but not until almost a decade later. These changes are reflected in the secret police archives. As repression becomes less overt, the number of arrests dwindles and with them the number of files dealing with investigations. At the same time, the number of surveillance files soars.

Spring 1953 – The Danube – Black Sea Canal project is halted and most of the political prisoners held in the nearby labour camps are freed.

23 October to 4 November 1956 – Revolt in Hungary. During the uprising, demands are heard for free elections, the withdrawal of Soviet troops and press freedom.

1956–1957 – Show trials in Romania, mostly against members of the Hungarian minority. They include the 'Steel Fist' trial.

1958 – Withdrawal of Soviet troops from Romania.

27 April 1962 – Gheorghiu-Dej announces at a plenary session of the Central Committee that collectivization in Romania is now complete.

1963 – Gheorghiu-Dej's anti-Russian measures include the closing the Russian Institute in Bucharest, the removal of Russian as a compulsory school subject and the replacement of Russian names for streets and public buildings.

1964 – Rift with Moscow. An amnesty for political prisoners is announced

16 February 1964 – A start is made on the release of 17,000 political prisoners who are in labour camps or under house arrest. Those with the designation 'Domiciliu Obligatoriu' are in theory granted greater freedom and equal treatment.

19 February 1964 – Romania becomes a member of a special commission of the United Nations tasked with developing guidelines for international law and cooperation between states.

19 March 1965 – Death of Gheorghe Gheorghiu-Dej.

22 March 1965 – Nicolae Ceaușescu is 'elected' as General Secretary of the Romanian Communist Party.

1 October 1966 – Decree no. 770 makes abortion punishable by law, and contraceptives are forbidden in Romania. Women are obliged to have four children (the number was raised to five in December 1988).

December 1967 – Speech by Nicolae Ceaușescu in which he announces that the class war in Romania has been won: 'Liquidation of the exploiting classes, assuring the unity of fundamental interests of the leading members of society, in agreement between individual aspirations and collective interests, have created optimum conditions for the cementing and blossoming of a socialist nation...'

1970s – Huge advances in surveillance technologies lead to their wide adoption by police and other security agencies. From 1972 onwards, files on Romanian dissidents will begin to overflow with detailed descriptions of daily activities and conversations, including the brushing of teeth and nocturnal trips to the bathroom.

June 1971 – Nicolae and Elena Ceaușescu visit China, North Korea, Vietnam and Mongolia. They are inspired to initiate a 'mini cultural revolution' at home, which marks the start of the delirious cult of personality around the Ceaușescus.

1972 – Romania becomes a member of the IMF and the World Bank.

April 1982 – Nicolae Ceaușescu decides to pay off Romania's national debt of eleven billion dollars. He introduces a tough austerity regime.

28 March 1983 – Decree no. 98 requires that all photocopiers and typewriters in Romania must be registered.

26 May 1984 – The first arm of the Danube – Black Sea Canal comes into use (the second will follow in 1987).

20 August 1986 – Nicolae Ceaușescu announces the best harvest in Romanian history and the introduction of the title of honour 'Hero of the new agricultural revolution', of which he is the first recipient.

1987 – Many babies die in maternity wards as a result of power cuts. To disguise high child mortality, birth certificates are issued only when babies are two weeks old.

23-24 June 1987 – The Romanian state adopts a norm for the minimum size of villages. The implementation of the law necessitates the disappearance of a great many villages and even small towns.

27 April 1988 – In a speech in London, the Prince of Wales denounces the systematization of Romanian villages and sets up an organization to protect them.

2 August 1988 – The former King Michael of Romania appears on Hungarian television to address the Romanian people and condemns the Ceauşescu regime for its destruction of villages.

Autumn 1988 – Ceauşescu's systemization plans are further extended. A total of 13,129 villages must go, including many Hungarian and German villages in Transylvania. Fierce protests abroad result.

23 October 1989 – The Socialist People's Republic becomes once again the Republic of Hungary.

11 November 1989 – The fall of the Berlin Wall heralds the break-up of the Soviet Bloc.

20-24 November 1989 – Under the motto 'Ceauşescu re-elected at the fourteenth congress', the last meeting of the Romanian Communist Party takes place.

15 December 1989 – Uprising in Timişoara. Ceauşescu demands strong measures and dozens of demonstrators are shot dead.

21 December 1989 – In front of the television cameras, Ceauşescu is jeered by thousands of workers brought together in the main square in Bucharest. He flees the city by helicopter. More than 1,100 people are killed in the chaotic days that follow, either in hand-to-hand fighting or by gunfire.

25 December 1989 – After a hasty trial, Nicolae and Elena Ceauşescu are executed.

1995 – Romania adopts restitution law no. 112.

July 2005 – The last in a series of restitution laws, no. 247, is adopted.

1 January 2007 – Romania joins the European Union.

Glossary

Aristocracy

In the history of Hungary and Transylvania there is an important distinction between untitled and titled nobility, the latter referring to barons, counts, dukes and princes. Not until the coming of the Habsburgs in the sixteenth century were aristocratic titles introduced in Hungary, and they arrived in Transylvania even later, in the seventeenth century. Until that time the entire noble class had been *una eademque nobilitas*; in other words, in an official or legal sense they all had the same status.

Ausgleich

The compromise between Austria and Hungary in 1867 that created the Austro-Hungarian Dual Monarchy. Hungary, Croatia and Transylvania together formed a single autonomous nation with its own government. The Dual Monarchy had one army, and its foreign policy was determined by the Austrian emperor.

ÁVO/ÁVH

Államvédelmi Osztály / Államvédelmi Hatóság: the Hungarian state security service and state police between 1945 and 1957, first called the ÁVO, later the ÁVH. Its headquarters were at Andrássy út 60 (which now houses the Terror Háza Museum), but the service had a number of buildings in Budapest where interrogations and torture took place, including villas on the Rózsadomb.

Bărăgan

A steppe between Bucharest and the Black Sea. From 1951 onwards, tens of thousands of people were deported there. Its isolation and inhospitable landscape and climate made it the perfect location for labour camps.

Class enemy

A term from Marxist class theory. People who did not belong to the proletariat and had once owned land and capital were usually referred to as 'parasites' and 'exploiters', and were persecuted.

Danube – Black Sea Canal

A Romanian canal with a length of sixty-four kilometres, it reduced the distance by water between the Danube and the Black Sea by 400 kilometres. It is said to have been built on the initiative of Stalin, who advocated making opponents of the regime work themselves to death. The canal would enable the Soviet Union to send troops more quickly to Tito's troublesome Yugoslavia. Work began in 1949, with around 60,000 prisoners, thousands of whom died. It was known as the grave of the

Romanian bourgeoisie. It was completed in 1987 under Ceauşescu by conscripted soldiers, workers and ordinary (not political) prisoners.

Dictatorship of the proletariat

Originating from the teachings of Karl Marx, this concept was reintroduced by Stalin when he set up the Cominform in Szklarska Poręba in September 1947. It was used as a justification for the ruthless persecution of the class enemy, which included aristocrats, the bourgeoisie, entrepreneurs, anarchists, kulaks, monarchists, Trotskyites, emigrants, saboteurs and 'social parasites'. The leaders of the satellite states competed to show Stalin how loyal they were by trying to outdo each other in terrorizing the class enemy.

Dobrogea

A marshy area to the north of Bărăgan, between the Danube and the Black Sea. Another place ideally suited for labour camps.

Domiciliu Obligatoriu

Literally: compulsory place of residence. The living space allotted was usually a cellar or attic, or some kind of work premises. People regarded as a potential threat to the state, who would have to be 're-educated', were given the status 'Domiciliu Obligatoriu'. Their identity papers were stamped DO, a stigma with far-reaching consequences. DO meant an official pariah status and therefore an absence of any protection. They were not allowed to leave the towns where they had been sent. They were excluded from all employment except manual labour, and both they and their children were barred from attending high school or university. They had to report to the militia weekly and were closely watched by the Securitate. DO was in full force, with all its restrictions, from 1949-1964. It was supposedly abolished after the 1964 amnesty, but the letters DO remained in identity papers until 1989. Although no longer an official designation, in practice it still meant people suffered discrimination.

Dual Monarchy

The alliance between Austria and Hungary that resulted from the *Ausgleich* of 1867. After Russia, the Dual Monarchy was the largest country in Europe, stretching from Tyrol to Galicia and from Bohemia to Bosnia. It included thirteen of the countries of present-day Europe, either entirely or in part, and had fifty-three million inhabitants, who spoke twelve different languages. In principle Austrians and Hungarians had equal status within the Dual Monarchy. Foreign policy, defence and a great deal of financial policy was outlined by Vienna, but beyond that the Kingdom of Hungary had internal autonomy. The emperor of Austria was also the king of Hungary.

Gadjos

The name used by the Sinti (a gypsy people) for everyone who is not a gypsy. Its literal meaning is 'citizen'.

Golden Bull

Drawn up in 1222 by King András II and remaining valid until 1848, this is the basic document that conferred privileges on the Hungarian nobility. It stated among other things that the nobles could depose the king, by violent means if necessary, should he rule the country badly.

Gotha, Almanach de

The genealogical handbook of the European nobility, published annually since 1763. It has three sections: the *Hofkalender*, which deals with the sovereign houses, the *Taschenbuch der Gräflichen Häuser* for counts and the *Taschenbuch der Freiherrlichen Häuser* for those with lesser titles. It is still in print today, under the title *Genealogisches Handbuch des Adels*.

Gulag

A Russian acronym for Chief Administration of Corrective Labour Camps and Colonies, also used to refer to the camps themselves. Stalin believed you must destroy your opponents while they work for you.

Hereditary titles

Aristocratic titles were inherited by the legitimate offspring. The titles baron and count were introduced in Hungary in the sixteenth century and in Transylvania in the seventeenth century. Foreign aristocrats who married into the Hungarian aristocracy could have their titles converted. In its period of independence (1526-1687) Transylvania was ruled by the prince of Transylvania, but his title was not hereditary. Hereditary titles were conferred for the last time in 1917, by the Hungarian king Charles IV.

Kulak

Rich and independent farmer. The term comes from the Soviet Union; its Romanian equivalent was *chiabura*. It was a term used in the communist system to condemn anyone the regime had chosen to persecute.

Mămăligă

Maize polenta

Militia (Direcţia Generală a Miliţiei)

Set up on 23 January 1949 to replace the police, the Romanian militia fell under the authority of the ministry of internal affairs. It was recruited from among loyal communists.

Nobility

A term used from the fourteenth century onwards to refer to free men. Transylvania and Hungary had a centuries-old feudal tradition, in which all power lay with the king and the nobles. In the thirteenth century the king acquired the right to confer patents of nobility, which were hereditary. Nobles were exempt from taxation and could own land. Until 1693 all nobles were equal, without titles, *una eademque nobilitas*, whether rich or poor. The Transylvanian nobility is predominantly Hungarian in origin, descended from those ennobled before 1526 by the Hungarian kings and from 1693 onwards by the Habsburg emperors. For more than nine centuries, until 1918, it played a leading role in Transylvania. In both Hungary and Romania, the nobility was abolished in 1947.

Primogeniture

The right of the firstborn to inherit the entire estate. It applied in Hungary but was not in fact implemented by all families, although in many cases the eldest son would inherit the most important landed property, whereas the younger children would receive lesser properties or an allowance, which in some cases was barely enough for an adequate supply of cigarettes. In Transylvania, by contrast, primogeniture was not the common tradition. As a result, aristocrats often married relatives in order to combine their estates, or to keep them together.

Re-education

A form of forced labour that was imposed without a trial. This might happen to anyone with the wrong social background. The term was also used to refer to a particularly cruel programme of torture used in Romania in 1949-1951.

Restitution

In this context, the return of property expropriated by the communists to its original owners, or to their heirs.

Restitution legislation

In Romania a number of laws were adopted between 1991 and July 2005 that relate to the restitution of property expropriated by the communists. In theory the Romanian government is obliged to return all property and land seized between 6 March 1945 and 25 December 1989, or to pay appropriate compensation. Such payments take the form of shares in a Property Fund (Fondul Proprietatea) set up by the government.

Romanian Workers Party

In 1948 the Romanian Communist Party and the Social Democratic Party merged to become the Romanian Workers Party (Partidul Muncitoresc Român). Its first general secretary was Gheorghe Gheorghiu-Dej. In 1965 it changed its name to become the Romanian Communist Party and from 1965 to 1989 Nicolae Ceauşescu was its general secretary.

Saxons

German people who settled in Transylvania from the twelfth century onwards. In the middle ages the Saxons, Széklers and Hungarian nobles were the three population groups that had a voice in government.

Securitate

The security troops (Trupele de Securitate) established on 7 February 1949 to replace the military police. Many of its earliest officers were recruited from among the Romanian fascists, members of the since banned Iron Guard. The Securitate was the Romanian Communist Party's most important instrument of terror, modelled after the Soviet NKVD (the forerunner of the KGB). According to its own records, more than 70,000 people were arrested between 1948 and 1958. After Ceaușescu's death in 1989 the Securitate was officially abolished and a multiplicity of organizations took its place, using various names.

Systematization

A programme implemented by Ceaușescu, aimed at reorganizing villages and towns. He planned to demolish 13,129 villages by 2000. Farmhouses were to be replaced by concrete blocks of flats.

Széklers

Hungarian ethnic group in Transylvania with its own distinctive culture. From 896 they were the border guards of the Hungarian Empire. The part of the country where the Széklers live is known as the Széklerland (Székelyföld).

Transylvania

A geographical region in the northwest of Romania called 'beyond the forests' by the Hungarians and hence, in Latin, Transylvania. The Saxons used the name Siebenbürgen, after the seven fortified towns they built there. Since the Treaty of Trianon, the name Transylvania has been used to refer to an area of 103,000 square kilometres that includes Máramaros and the southern Bánát as well as historical Transylvania.

Trianon

The Treaty of Trianon was signed on 4 June 1920 in Versailles in the aftermath of the First World War. The conditions imposed on Germany by the victors the previous year in the Treaty of Versailles are generally seen as one of the main causes of the Second World War. Hungary lost more than two thirds of its territory and half its population, with Transylvania and the Bánát becoming part of Romania, Slovakia (Upper Hungary) becoming one half of the First Czechoslovak Republic, Croatia and Slovenia joining Yugoslavia, and Burgenland being absorbed into Austria. From one day to the next, some five million Hungarians found themselves living outside their own borders.

Voivode

In Transylvania the voivode, *voievod* (Romanian) or *vajda* (Hungarian) was one of the earliest state functionaries. He was governor of the territory. Saint Stephen I (Szent István in Hungarian), king of Hungary, appointed the first voivode in 1008 to rule Transylvania, which was rich in minerals and salt and a strategically important territory until the Ottomans conquered Central Hungary.

Important geographical names

Hungarian	Romanian	German
Altorja	Turia de Jos	
Aranyosgerend	Luncani	Neusatz
Békás	Bicaz	Bicaz
Bonchida	Bonţida	Bonisbruck
Brassó	Braşov	Kronstadt
Bucsecs-hegység	Munţii Bucegi	Bucegi-Gebirge
Déva	Deva	Diemrich
Fiatfalva	Filiaş	
Fugad	Ciuguzel	
Gernyeszeg	Gorneşti	Kertzing
Gyulafehérvár	Alba Iulia	Karlsberg
Hadad	Hodod	Kriegsdorf
Hargita	Munţii Harghita	Hargitha
Hídvég	Hăghig	Fürstenberg
Keresd	Criş	Kreisch
Kolozsvár	Cluj-Napoca / Cluj	Klausenberg
Kőrösmező	Frasin	Jassinja
Kőröspatak	Crişeni	
Kund	Cund	Reussdorf
Küküllővár	Cetatea de Baltă	Kokelburg
Laposnyak	Lăpusnic	
Magaré	Pelişor	Magarey
Malomvíz	Râu de Mori	Mühldorf
Maros (river and district)	Mureş	Mieresch
Marosvásárhely	Târgu Mureş	Neumarkt am Mieresch
Marosvécs	Brâncoveneşti	Wetsch
Máramarossziget	Sighetu Marmaţiei	Maramuresch
Medgyes	Mediaş	Mediasch
Miklósvár	Micloşoara	

Hungarian	Romanian	German
Nagybánya	Baia Mare	Frauenbach / Neustadt
Nagyenyed	Aiud	Straßburg am Mieresch
Péterfalva	Petreşti	Petersdorf
Pusztakamarás	Cămăraşu	
Segesvár	Sighişoara	Schäßburg
Szamosújvár	Gherla	Neuschloss / Armenierstadt
Szárhegy	Lăzarea	Grünberg
Szatmár	Satu Mare	Sathmar
Temesvár	Timişoara	Temeswa

Main figures and interviewees

Béla Bánffy jr. (b. Kolozsvár, 1967)
Full name: Baron Béla Bánffy de Losoncz. He runs a travel agency and produces hand-made paper at home for the production of bibliophile editions. He also runs a small traditional printing works. Béla junior belongs to the branch of the Bánffys that has had 10,000 hectares of expropriated forest returned to them on paper and has claimed another 20,000. His family also recovered two ruined castles, one of them in Aranyosgerend. In the communist period Béla worked as a labourer in a metal works.

Béla Bánffy sr. (b. Hadad, 1936)
Full name: Baron Béla Bánffy de Losoncz, father of Béla Bánffy jr. The first written mention of the Bánffys dates from 1166, and in 1674 they were given the title of baron. Béla's grandparents are Baroness Ágnes Jósika and Count István Wesselényi on his mother's side and Countess Zichy and Baron Endre Bánffy on his father's side. The baron branch of the Bánffys was repeatedly offered the title of count by the Habsburg emperors but consistently declined. For thirty years Béla sr. worked as a manual labourer and as a truck driver.

Farkas Bánffy (b. Budapest, 1981)
Full name: Baron Farkas Bánffy de Losoncz. He is of the same branch of the Bánffys as the two Bélas, who are his cousin and uncle respectively. Two days after graduating from university in Hungary he returned to Fugad, to his grandfather's country house. He now works 400 hectares of Bánffy forests and supervises forests returned to other families. He is a second cousin to Anikó Bethlen. Gergely and Sándor Roy Chowdhury and Zsigmond Mikes are his third cousins.

Miklós Bánffy (b. Kolozsvár, 1873; d. Budapest, 1950)
Full name: Count Miklós Bánffy de Losoncz. As well as being the greatest major landowner in Transylvania and heir to Bonchida, he was director of the Budapest opera, organizer of the coronation of the last king of Hungary, Hungarian minister of foreign affairs, and most importantly the author of the Transylvania trilogy. It seems he waited most of his life for a chance to marry Carola Bornemissza, eventually wedding the actress Aranka Váradi-Weber in 1939, at the age of sixty-six.

Stefánia Betegh (b. Aranyosgyéres, 1938)
Scion of a noble Transylvanian family, Betegh de Csíktusnád. She escaped from a band of robbers from Bessarabia (present-day Moldavia) at the end of the war by hiding with her mother and sisters behind the vats in the wine cellar of the family house in Fugad. For much of her life she worked in a factory that made tin plates and cutlery. She is godmother to Gábor Teleki and lives in Marosvásárhely.

Anikó Bethlen (b. Kolozsvár, 1938)
Full name: Countess Anikó Bethlen de Bethlen. Paralysed by meningitis as a child, she is the social centrepoint of Marosvásárhely, as well as single-handedly keeping legions of potters and embroiderers in work. Her mother was a paediatrician, her father an agricultural engineer. Her paternal grandmother was Baroness Marianne Bánffy. The Bethlens have recovered ownership of the Renaissance castle at Keresd.

Carola Bornemissza (b. 1879; d. Kolozsvár, 1948)
Born Carola Szilvássy. Her father belonged to a family of lesser nobles and her mother was Countess Antónia Wass. In 1896 Carola married Baron Elemér Bornemissza, eleven years her senior, who was born at Zabola to Countess Etelka Mikes. He died in 1938. In 1908 Carola travelled extensively in South Africa to ensure that a relative who had been killed in the Boer War was given an appropriate grave. She was a muse to many writers. Miklós Bánffy immortalized her as Adrienne Miloth in his Transylvania trilogy.

Dezső Bustya (b. Kolozsvár, 1935)
As a child he joined an anti-communist group and distributed pamphlets. The police arrested the schoolchildren, aged between fourteen and eighteen, and interrogated them for six weeks in the Securitate cellars in Kolozsvár. Dezső was sentenced to a term in a labour camp on the Danube – Black Sea Canal and is now a retired clergyman living in Marosvásárhely.

Pál Festetics (b. Vienna, 1968; d. Vienna, 1995)
Full name: Count Pál Festetics de Tolna. The family was given its title in 1766. Pál studied law for a short time, then in the early 1990s he attended the art academy in Vienna and became a painter. He showed talent and was offered various student grants abroad. In the early summer of 1995 he ended his own life.

János Gudenus (b. Budapest, 1947)
Full name: Baron János Gudenus. János is the most authoritative specialist on the Hungarian and Transylvanian nobility and the author of works including *Összetört címerek* (Broken Blazons), which records in great detail the recent history of the Hungarian noble families.

Judit Hajós (b. Budapest, 1978)
Full name: Judit Hajós de Dömsöd et Hajós. The family was ennobled in 1527. Judit was given her mother's surname, since the family name had otherwise died out. Her father's family is Jóos de Kisborosnyó, whose title dates from 1776. That family has Dutch origins, as well as traces of Armenian, Italian and Székler blood. Judit's grandfather is currently fighting for restitution of the family castle in Gödörhat in Transylvania. Judit lives in Budapest, where she works as executive director of the innovation and entrepreneurship project and director of external relations at the Central European University's Business School.

Béla Haller (b. Marosvásárhely, 1953)
Full name: Count Béla Haller de Hallerkő. The Haller family was ennobled in 1553 and given its title in 1713. Béla's paternal grandparents were Count Jenő Haller and Countess Rosalie Béldi. His maternal grandparents, Kálmán Korek and Erzsébet Kováts, were members of the wealthy bourgeoisie. Béla teaches

Italian and French. The Hallers' family castle in Küküllővár has fallen into the hands of a businessman from Constanța.

Tibor Kálnoky (b. Munich, 1966)

Full name: Count Tibor Kálnoky de Kőröspatak. He has lived in the United States, Germany, The Hague, Juan-les-Pins, Paris, Budapest and Bucharest. The first mention of the family dates from 1182 and in 1575 they received their patents of nobility. In Miklósvár Tibor runs a number of guesthouses in old farm buildings, works on the restoration of the family property and assists Prince Charles in restoring Saxon farmhouses. The main focus of his efforts now are the Kálnoky family castle in Sepsikőröspatak and the hunting lodge in Miklósvár.

Pál Lázár (b. Laposnyak, 1939)

Full name: Pál Lázár de Csíktaploca. From a noble Transylvanian family that owned an estate close to Déva – not to be confused with the Lázár counts, a family that has died out. His father, imprisoned by the communists, was an adventurer who worked as a gaucho in Argentina and is described at length in Patrick Leigh Fermor's *Between the Woods and the Water*. His mother was Baroness Judit Kemény. Pál worked as a carpenter. He and his family (including his niece Kati Ugron) have recovered ownership of the house and estate at Laposnyak.

Zsigmond Mikes (b. Oradea, 1977)

Full name: Count Zsigmond Mikes de Zabola. The Mikes family can be traced back to 1289 and received its title in 1696. Zsigmond is a second cousin to Katalin, Gergely and Sándor Roy Chowdhury. He and his family have recovered possession of a castle in Uzon, badly run down after years of use by the local kolkhoz. It is icy cold in winter, but he lives there for part of the year and plans to turn it into a hotel.

Emma P. (b. Kolozsvár, 1925)

Pseudonym. Scion of an ancient noble Transylvanian family that appears in records as early as 1390 and was allied to the Keménys by marriage repeatedly between the early fifteenth century and the late eighteenth. Emma studied chemistry in Kolozsvár. She and her husband lived for sixteen years in damp cellars, where she experienced what she says were the happiest years of her life. She now lives in a flat in Marosvásárhely.

Pista Pálffy (b. Budapest, 1933)

Full name: Count István Pálffy de Erdőd. István was born in Hungary, imprisoned as a class enemy and freed during the popular uprising of 1956. When the revolt was crushed by the Russians he fled on foot to Austria and secured a grant to study at Cambridge. He lived in England and returned to Hungary after the fall of communism in 1989. His grandfather, Count Albert Apponyi, became a Hungarian hero by refusing to sign the Treaty of Trianon and was given a state funeral in 1933 to rival that of Winston Churchill.

Gergely Roy Chowdhury (b. Graz, 1977)

Full name: Gergely Basu Roy Chowdhury de Ulpur. Gergely is the product of a marriage between an exiled Transylvanian aristocrat, Countess Katalin Mikes, and an exiled Bengali aristocrat. After graduating from the London School of Economics, he worked as a banker for five years. Deciding that was not the life of his dreams, he travelled to Romania to attempt to recover and restore the family property, Zabola. He succeeded. With his brother Sándor and his mother, he now manages several thousand hectares of forest, the country house, the park and a guesthouse.

Katalin Roy Chowdhury (b. Szombathely, 1944)
Born Countess Katalin Mikes de Zabola, she was able to leave Romania at the age of sixteen with the help of a German relative. The names of her grandparents – Count Kelemen Mikes, Countess Emma Béldi, Count Armin Mikes and Countess Klementina Bethlen – demonstrate how endogamous the Transylvanian aristocracy was until a century ago. She has recovered ownership of the family estate, Zabola, where she now lives.

Coen Stork (b. Bussum, 1928)
Dutch ambassador to Romania during the last two years of the regime of Nicolae Ceauşescu. In just those two years he managed to build up a Securitate dossier two thousand pages long by his headstrong behaviour, mainly involving efforts on behalf of Romanian dissidents. Hugh Arbuthnott, British ambassador in Bucharest at the time, showed him how to organize creative gatherings to which Romanian dissidents could be invited.

Erzsébet T. (b. Dornafalva, 1919; d. Budapest 2004)
Pseudonym. Born at the family castle in Dornafalva as Countess Erzsébet T. Her family can be traced back to the thirteenth century. Since 1951 she has lived in Vác and during the communist period she worked as a charlady and maid of all work. For half the year she lives in a cabin in the hills near Márianosztra. On paper, the ruined castle of Dornafalva in Transylvania has been returned to her in its entirety. Since the whole village uses the bricks to build houses, not much is left of the ruin.

Gábor Teleki (b. Marosvásárhely, 1968)
Full name: Count Gábor Teleki de Szék. The family received its title in 1696. Gábor was born in Transylvania but has spent a great deal of his working life in Hungary and Germany. He has now returned to Romania and works in Bucharest. He and his family were recently successful in reclaiming ownership of the immense baroque Teleki palace in Gernyeszeg. It has functioned for years as a children's home.

György Ugron (b. Marosludas, 1942)
Full name: György Ugron de Ábránfalva. He comes from an old Transylvanian family of nobles who were once *primors* (leaders) of the Székler people. Written records of the family go back to the early twelfth century and from the seventeenth century onwards they regularly intermarried with the Keménys, the Bánffys and the Apors. The family has always stubbornly resisted all titles offered to it. Under communism György worked as, among other things, a stable hand in a circus.

Kati Ugron (b. Déva, 1965)
Born Katalin Lázár de Csíktapolcai. Pál Lázár is her uncle. She is married to Ádám Ugron, a distant relative of György and Zsolna Ugron. The marriage between Kati and Ádám was a source of great joy to the older generation of

nobles during the difficult Ceauşescu years. Kati worked for most of her life as an infant school teacher and lived in Marosvásárhely, 200 kilometres from the Lázár estate of Laposnyak, which the family now owns once again.

Zsolna Ugron (b. Kolozsvár, 1978)

Full name: Zsolna Ugron de Ábránfalva. The daughter of György Ugron and wife of Gergely Roy Chowdhury, she is a journalist and author of several books. The Ugron family never accepted a title from the Habsburgs. Their family house in Pusztakamarás, which functioned as a school, has been donated to the local authorities.

Jaap Scholten on his first trip in Transylvania in 1991

Jaap Scholten is a Dutch author living and working in Budapest. He was born in 1963 in Twente, an outlying region of the Netherlands close to the German border. He studied industrial design at the University of Technology in Delft, graphic design at the Willem de Kooning Academy in Rotterdam and social anthropology at the Central European University in Budapest.

In 2011 Scholten created and presented a six-part television series for the VPRO about hidden worlds in Central and Eastern Europe. He has written widely praised short stories and novels, including *Eighty*, *Morning Star* and *Spengler's Law*, which was chosen as the booksellers' 'novel of the year'. *Comrade Baron* is his first non-fiction book.